Challenges to the Nation-State in Africa

Edited by

Adebayo O. Olukoshi and Liisa Laakso

Nordiska Afrikainstitutet, Uppsala
in cooperation with
The Institute of Development Studies, University of Helsinki

Indexing terms

Conflicts
Ethnicity
Political development
Religion
State
Nation-building

Africa

Language checking: Elaine Almén

ISSB 91-7106-381-1
© the authors and Nordiska Afrikainstitutet 1996
Printed in Sweden by
Motala Grafiska, Motala, 1996

Contents

DEDICATION

To the eternal memory of Ken Saro Wiwa, indefatigable fighter for the rights of the Ogoni people of the Nigerian oil Delta, executed on Friday, 10 November 1995 by the military junta of General Sani Abacha over his non-violent but persistent struggle for the recognition of the rights of his people and those of other minority groups.

Preface and Acknowledgements

This book is the product of a seminar jointly organised by the Nordiska Afrikainstitutet, Uppsala, Sweden and the Institute of Development Studies, University of Helsinki, Finland under the auspices of the former's programme on *The Political and Social Context of Structural Adjustment in Sub-Saharan Africa*. The seminar was held in Helsinki at the end of January 1995 and the theme on which it focused, namely, the challenges facing the nation-state in contemporary Africa, was one which enabled researchers from several African and Nordic countries to delve into aspects of the decomposition and recomposition of popular political identities in Africa and their implications for the post-colonial (secular) unitary nation-state project. As the studies presented in this volume show, the challenges to the post-colonial nation-state project in Africa have mainly taken ethno-regionalist, religious, and separatist forms. These challenges have been shaped and exacerbated by the environment of steep, long-drawn out economic crisis, zero-sum, market-led structural adjustment, and the legacy of decades of political authoritarianism and exclusion that dates from the colonial period.

The wave of political liberalisation which swept through most parts of Africa during the late 1980s and early 1990s has given vent to the re-assertion of ethnic and religious identities whose single-minded suppression was central to the earlier efforts at promoting nation-building in much of the continent. It is argued in this volume that the tendency to regard ethnic/religious pluralism as essentially incompatible with the goal of nation-building is grossly mistaken and ought to be jettisoned in the quest for a more solid basis on which to build national unity in African countries. Rather than suppress the expression of ethnic/religious forms of consciousness, the post-colonial state itself should be re-structured simultaneously to embody and transcend the socio-cultural pluralism that is so characteristic of many African countries. Democratisation is, of course, absolutely essential to any effort at re-structuring the state. The contributors to this book however point to the limitations of the recent experience of political reform in Africa insofar as the re-establishment of the nation-state project on a democratic foundation is concerned. They argue the position that, among other things, more representative forms of government, power sharing, electoral pluralism, the re-invention of the post-colonial "social contract" (and with it public institutions), cultural autonomy for minority groups, and the devolution of power are central ingredients in any efforts at promoting national unity and a supporting civic identity in Africa.

In organising the Helsinki seminar in January 1995 and preparing the revised papers from the meeting for publication, several debts were incurred which we would like to acknowledge here. We start by thanking the Finnish Academy, especially Professor Jukka Siikala, for the generous support which they offered to facilitate the hosting of the meeting in Helsinki. Thanks also go to Ms Ulrica Risso and Ms Lena Klossner, respectively of the Nordiska Afrika-institutet and the Institute of Development Studies, who very meticulously handled all of the administrative details connected with the meeting. The contributions of Björn Beckman, Karuti Kanyinga, Andrew Kiondo, Ann Schlyter, Pekka Seppälä, Jarle Simensen, and Ulla Vuorela who served as the main discussants at the seminar went a long way to enrich the debates that took place. Colleagues at the Nordiska Afrikainstitutet, including Kajsa Övergaard, Karl Eric Ericson, Anne-Marie Kempe, Louise Simann, Sonja Johansson, and Susanne Ljung Adriansson played various crucial roles in the preparation of the manuscript for publication; we thank them for their support. Finally, our thanks also go to those colleagues at the Institute of Development Studies, particularly Pertti Multanen, who joined in our debates and helped to make our stay in Finland enjoyable.

Just as we were about to go press, news came in of the decision of the Nigerian military junta, headed by General Sani Abacha, to hang the minority rights activist, environmentalist, and author, Ken Saro Wiwa and eight of his associates over their campaign for a more decent livelihood for the Ogoni people of Nigeria in particular and the communities of the oil Delta in general. This callous act of murder underlines the role which the exercise of unaccountable power and the imposition of state terror has played in discrediting the post-colonial African state and its unitary project. Saro Wiwa was one of the people in the front-line of the on-going debate about the ways in which the Nigerian federation might be re-configured (see Chapter 4 of this volume). He was an ideas person, who followed the path of non-violence, preferring to allow the compelling force of his arguments and the widespread evidence of Shell's (the Anglo-Dutch oil major) dirty war against the Ogoni and the environment to speak for him. His murderers, the soldiers who have hijacked the Nigerian state, not being people given to sobriety or ideas, have tried to silence him by their dastardly act. But we are sure that Saro Wiwa's cause will live forever and that victory ultimately belongs to the down-trodden Ogoni and all oppressed Nigerians. It is to the memory of Saro Wiwa that we dedicate this book.

Adebayo Olukoshi, Uppsala,
Liisa Laakso, Helsinki.

Chapter 1

The Crisis of the Post-Colonial Nation-State Project in Africa

Liisa Laakso and Adebayo O. Olukoshi

INTRODUCTION

The period since the late 1980s has witnessed many incidences of violence and conflict, some with clearly genocidal dimensions, in various parts of Africa, Asia, Europe, and the Middle East. With a greater frequency and on an increasing scale than ever before, these occurrences of violence and conflict derive from racial, religious, and ethnic sources and a vast majority of them are intra-, as opposed to inter-state in nature. Also, a growing number of recent inter-state conflicts have roots in cross-border ethnic and religious tensions as state authorities, often bowing to chauvinistic domestic pressure, attempt to "protect" the interests of their citizens who constitute ethnic or religious minorities under other jurisdictions. More than ever before, progressively larger numbers of civilians, as opposed to only professional armies, have become involved in the outbreaks of violence—and often for no apparent, or for ill-defined, political reasons. Ethnic and racial cleansing have combined with acute religious extremism, intolerance or pure criminality to suggest a growing social crisis in the international system (UNRISD, 1995).

At the heart of this turmoil is the crisis of individual and group identity which, in the context of deepening social inequality/fragmentation, the weakened administrative and policy apparatuses of the state, the decline of the ideologies of communism and anti-communism that dominated the Cold War years, and an accelerating process of globalisation, has called into question some of the basic premises of the contemporary nation-state project. The accelerating pace of globalisation, coinciding as it does with the spread and deepening, world-wide, of market forces and relations on a scale never before witnessed, has had direct implications not only for state capacity and legitimacy but also for social processes as various groups and individuals seek to re-define themselves in a rapidly changing domestic and international environment (Bangura, 1994a; UNRISD, 1995). The changing requirements and environment of globalised capital accumulation have, together with the pressures of an increasingly international consumption culture and a globalising mass media, influenced identity formation and diversification in a most complicated manner all over the world.

The multiplicity of problems thrown up by or associated with the on-going transition in international affairs has been brought out in sharp relief by the collapse of the bipolar structure of the Cold War years which, all things consid-ered, endowed international relations with a certain sense of predictability. Taking stock of that transition, which is popularly captured by the notion of the New World Order, *Africa Confidential* was to argue that "There are signs every-where that the era of the nation-state is fading... The awkward marriage of the 'nation' in the sense of an ethnic coalition and the state as the principal source of political authority is coming under pressure from above and below" (*Africa Confidential*, 6 January 1995). While the conclusion which *Africa Confidential* draws from the pervasive evidence of the deepening crisis of the nation-state system may be over-stated, there is now little disagreement in the scholarly community that the entire nation-state project is, to varying degrees, in different forms, and with differing manifestations and consequences, in a state of some disarray. The inability of international and national institutions to cope ade-quately with the new challenges they are confronted with, deep-seated signs of social fragmentation and dislocation, a massive internal and cross-border flow of people (both legal and illegal, enforced and voluntary), and the search by people of different social backgrounds for a set of anchoring values through which they might cope with or make sense of change are in evidence all over the world (Bangura, 1994a, 1994b, 1994c; Ake, 1994; UNRISD, 1995).

It is perhaps in Africa, more than in other parts of the world, that the crisis of the nation-state project has been most obvious and overwhelming (Davidson, 1992; Zartman, 1995). The dramatic collapse of the nation-state in Somalia and Liberia, the state of paralysis in Zaire, Cameroon, and Togo, the genocidal violence in Rwanda and Burundi, the organised killings carried out by govern-ment forces and Muslim fundamentalists in Algeria and Egypt, the ethnic cleansing episodes in Kenya's Rift Valley, the gradual slide of Sierra Leone into a civil war and the worsening crisis in the Sudan, the continuing political tensions in Angola and Ethiopia, the uneasy state of affairs in Nigeria following the annulment of the 1993 presidential election by the ruling military junta, the numerous low-intensity, mostly ethnically-based confrontations in various parts of Africa as diverse as Ghana (Nanumbas vs. Konkonbas), Nigeria (Kuteb vs. Hausa, Jukun vs. Tiv, Ogoni vs. Andoni), South Africa (Zulu vs. Xhosa), Zimbabwe (Shona vs. Ndebele), and Niger and Mali (where sections of the local populations have been pitched against the Tuaregs), and the increasing salience of popular religious identities, often mixed with competing ethnicities, in the political processes of most countries have combined to create a sense of profound disorder on the continent.

Reflecting on the enormity of the problems confronting African countries today and the apparent failure of some thirty years of independence to make a decisive difference for the better in the lives of most Africans, Basil Davidson was to conclude his life time of committed scholarship to the continent by contending that the African crisis is little more than a crisis of institutions borne out of what he describes as the particular *nation-statism* of the post-colonial years. This *nation-statism*, built around the problematic frontiers associated with Africa's partition by European imperialist powers, not only reproduced the subjection of Africa and African history to Europe and European history, it also produced a system of alienation (as opposed to liberation) which reinforced a mentality of dependence on irrelevant European models and thrived on a "...Tammany Hall-style patronage, dependent on personal, family, and similar networks of local interest" (Davidson, 1992:12). For Davidson, the crisis of the post-colonial nation-state project derived essentially from the construction of the project on the basis of European models rather than on the basis of Africa's own rich and varied history and experience. We would add that the problems of this nation-statism were compounded by the absence of enduring structures of democratic governance and popular political participation, with the consequence that efforts at tackling the National Question were not organically tied to the question of democratisation in much of post-independence Africa.

The nation-state project, as we know it in European history, has, over a period of time, been both a cause and a consequence of some kind of "homogenising" culture within the borders of the state, providing an economic environment where all citizens can share some commonality of interests and are able to develop a political will to maintain national unity. Despite the many internal divisions and differences that characterised the post-colonial African nation-state, there were clear processes at work which tended to produce such a "homogenising" culture to which most groups could relate in one way or another. However, because the contemporary economic and social crisis in Africa is eroding precisely the cultural, economic and political "glues" that were acting to integrate the different elements of the nation-state, the very future of the nation-state project itself is being called directly into question. These "glues" were part and parcel of the post-colonial "social contract" on the basis of which most African countries were ushered into independent statehood. As we shall argue later in this chapter, structural adjustment, in feeding into the dynamics of crisis on the continent, has contributed to the erosion not only of the "glues" that bind the different elements in the post-colonial nation-state in Africa together, but also of the basis of the "social contract" of which they were an integral part. The potential for the survival of the nation-state project in Africa has, therefore, come to depend substantially on its capacity to re-create itself to respond effectively to the new challenges confronting it, the economy, and society.

Our concern in this chapter is to present in a critical, overview fashion, some of the sources and dimensions of the challenges to the nation-state project in

Africa today. We do this on the basic assumption that the nation-state world-wide, not solely in Africa, is faced with enormous challenges that have severely taxed existing capacities and structures. If Africa has been the theatre of some of the most tragic manifestations of the crisis of the nation-state project in the con-temporary international system, this should not be completely surprising. As a continent with a traumatic colonial inheritance, where democratic forms of gov-ernance have been lacking for a long time, where the modern nation-state project has its most recent history, and where, therefore, the roots of the nation-state are shallowest, Africa has been more susceptible to and is more directly and visibly affected by all the sources of internal and external pressure that have called existing political frameworks into question and stretched existing institutional capacities to their limits.

We argue that the deep-seated economic crises on the continent, dating back in the cases of some countries to the early 1970s, combined with the neo-liberal structural adjustment programmes for the reform of African economies popu-larised in the late 1970s and during the course of the 1980s served, in many important respects, to further undermine state capacity and legitimacy in Africa whilst, simultaneously, reinforcing the structures of authoritarianism. As we noted earlier, both the economic crisis and the adjustment programmes ate deep into the post-colonial "social contract" that was an important part of the foun-dation on which the legitimacy of the independent nation-state was built. They also contributed to the growing informalisation of the economy (thereby making it, *inter alia*, no longer properly taxable), the erosion and/or diminution of state resources in the administrative and policy domains, and a deepening of dependency on foreign financial aid and donor personnel on a scale which some countries had not experienced even during colonialism (Olukoshi, 1995; Himbara and Sultan, 1995). In the most extreme cases, the state has, more or less, been reduced to its coercive apparatuses (army, police and prisons), which are then employed, crudely, to safeguard the authoritarian political framework within which governments, faced with a host of donor conditionalities, attempt to abide by the neo-liberal agenda for the reform of the economies—and poli-tics—of African countries (Bangura, 1994c; Beckman, 1993b; Gibbon *et al.*, 1992; Simon *et al.*, 1995).

Partly in response to the growing authoritarianism associated with or exac-erbated by economic crisis management and structural adjustment implemen-tation, and partly drawing inspiration from a rapidly changing international geo-political environment at the centre of which were the events that unfolded in the former Soviet bloc in the late 1980s, local pressures built up in various African countries for an expansion of the national democratic space (Gibbon, 1992; Olukoshi and Wohlgemuth, 1995). The fact that the opening of the politi-cal space occurred in a context where spirited attempts had earlier been made to stifle or suppress the diversity of ethnic and religious identities that were thought to be detrimental to the "national unity" project of the 1960s and 1970s, led to the re-birth and flowering of latent ethnic, religious, and other popular forms of identity (see Chapter 5 of this volume for an elaboration). The social decay associated with the economic stagnation of the 1980s and 1990s, coupled with the dislocation brought about by structural adjustment and globalisation as well as the gradual reversal of aspects of the modernisation process in many countries, tended to reinforce the process by which these forms of identity reasserted and/or consolidated themselves (Adekanye, 1995; UNRISD, 1995). The responses of governments to this reassertion of popular identities has been mostly negative with the consequence that the terrain for national dialogue has, in most places, been shrinking in spite of the simultaneous introduction of liberal political reforms—like electoral multi-party competition. We argue that the path to the re-invention of a viable nation-state project in Africa must involve the negotiation of a new social and national bargain, which takes full cognisance of ethnic, linguistic, cultural and religious diversity, the require-ments of social equity, and the importance of effective and efficient public insti-tutions in a democratic framework that is fully representative.

THE MODERN NATION-STATE PROJECT IN AFRICA: BACKGROUND ISSUES

The modern nation-state project arose out of the social and political crises in Europe associated with the rapid national territorial spread of capitalist social relations and productive forces during the industrial revolution of the 18th and 19th centuries. In pre-industrial agrarian societies, the creation/consolidation of a political community extending beyond the immediate environment within which people made their livelihood made very little sense from the point of view of the majority of the populace. This is because for predominantly peasant communities leading self-contained, inward-looking lives and tied to their localities by the need for food production, the state was mainly an agency for taxation and warfare. But the nation-state in its modern form was always going to be a necessity for the proper functioning of a mobile industrial society. The industrial society required a dynamic diversification and division of labour, social mobility and, above all, universal education. The creation of a national "high culture" contributed to the emergence of a nation which, guided by the "progressive" political, economic and academic elites of those societies, opened up real promises of a better life for the masses of the people (Gellner, 1983). At a more mental level, capitalism and the development of print technology made it possible for large numbers of people to think of themselves and relate with others in a manner that created a profoundly new form of "imagined commu-nity" (Anderson, 1991). The connections between the industrial revolution and the requirements of industrial society and the modern nation-state project are, therefore, unmistakable.

However, at the heart of the modern nation-state project was the idea, flawed from the outset, of a tight correspondence between the nation and the state whereby each sovereign state was seen as a nation-state of people who shared a common language or culture (Bangura, 1994a; UNRISD, 1995). This notion of the nation-state stood in direct contradiction to the reality that most states were, in fact, multi-cultural, multi-lingual and multi-religious and that not all ethnic groups (however defined) were sufficiently large or powerful or even willing to achieve a state of their own. Given that the different communities that were constituted into one state during the 18th and 19th centuries in Europe did not all "imagine" themselves as being one nation, the result, partly at least, of the inherently uneven development of capitalism, and since not all were, in any case, willing to surrender their distinct cultural or linguistic identity to an overarching project of "one nation", it is not surprising that there was a lot of repression, especially directed at local cultures and minority groups, associated with the nation-building project in Europe as spirited attempts were made to eliminate linguistic or cultural differences and create one "official" national identity.

This "official", essentially European notion of a culturally homogenous and modernising nation-state was carried over to Africa during the course of the late 19th and early 20th centuries when the forces of European colonialism changed the political map of the continent. Driven by an overwhelming economic logic, European colonialism resulted in the creation of nation-states which were largely multi-ethnic from the outset, with many ethnic groups finding themselves divided among the different jurisdictions which the principal powers of the colonial conquest (Britain, France, Germany, and Portugal) carved out for themselves during their scramble for territory on the continent. In several cases, ethnic groups which, prior to the arrival of the forces of colonialism had been in conflict with one another as part of the autonomous state formation process that was underway on the continent, were welded together under one new state. These pre-colonial conflicts, exploited by the forces of European colonialism to ease their military-political conquest of the continent, fed into a pattern of "collaboration" and "resistance" to colonialism that kept ethnic consciousness alive and made the task of nation-building that much more difficult.

The principle and practice of the colonial policy of divide and rule, together with thriving academic interests developed within colonial anthropology resulted in the invention of new ethnic identities and characteristics which helped to consolidate colonial rule whilst simultaneously reinforcing conflicts between groups that were, for example, denigrated as "cowards", "laggards", or "simpletons" and those that were designated as "brave", "courageous", or "honest". (For an elaboration of this in the context of Zaire, see Chapter 7 of this volume). Because the narrow correlation between ethnicity and some professions served as a new cultural coding for the division of labour and socio-economic stratification, the increasing mobility of the people in the colonial economy paradoxically reinforced ethnic identities and consciousness at some levels. In many parts of Africa, soldiers, domestic servants, messengers, or clerks were recruited from particular ethnic groups with severe consequences for the management of power after the departure of the colonialists. Furthermore, settlers originating from other colonial territories outside Africa—Lebanon or India, for instance—were introduced into many parts of Africa and encouraged to take on a compradorial/merchant role necessary for the deepening commercial relations between the metropolitan countries and the colonies. Because the Indians and Lebanese were deliberately groomed as an intermediate social category between Europeans and the "natives" over whom they ruled, they were, not surprisingly, to be the targets of post-colonial policies of "Africanisation" which defined them as essentially foreign. Without doubt then, the task of modern nation-building was, from the outset, going to be a difficult one.

At independence, most African governments set themselves the task of undertaking a vigorous process of nation-building with the aim of welding their multi-ethnic, multi-lingual, multi-cultural, and multi-religious countries into "one nation". A central element of this official project of nation-building was the assumption that only the state could constitute it (UNRISD, 1995). The nation-building project was, therefore, state-driven from the outset, often relying on a top-down approach that carried far-reaching centralising implications. In time, the unity project increasingly took on the form of a unitary project which sometimes rested on a narrow ethnic base around which a system of patronage networks was then built linking other groups and their elites. Another key element of the nation-building project was the assumption that the diversity of ethnic identities was inherently negative and obstructive and that it was a requirement of successful nation-building that the different identities be eradicated, submerged under or subordinated to the identity of the group(s) that dominated state power.

In pursuit of their goal of top-down nation-building, post-colonial African governments embarked on programmes of vigorous economic and social modernisation which, it was hoped, would weaken ethnic consciousness and ties, "secularise" the society, and promote a new sense of nationhood just as the experience of industrialisation had supposedly done in Europe. However, replication of the European model was not going to be very easy due to the constraining specificities of the post-colonial economy, particularly as they related to its general internal economic disarticulation, its monocultural character, its reliance on an export sector dominated by raw materials, and its disadvantaged position in the world division of labour (all extensively analysed in the dependency literature). Although the immediate post-colonial economic boom experienced by many of Africa's newly independent states initially favoured the state-led socio-economic modernisation programmes undertaken by the post-colonial governments, achieving sustainable, self-generating economic development turned out to be extremely difficult, perhaps more so than was anticipated. Soon after independence, most African governments, one after the other, abandoned the multi-party political framework on the basis of which freedom from direct colonial rule was attained and adopted single party rule or slid into military rule.

Both the single party and military regimes that dominated the political land-scape of the continent made spirited efforts to push a unitary state project of one kind or the other. At the ideological level, a variety of unifying ideologies was invented, among them Mobutu's *authenticité*, Nyerere's *Ujamaa* socialism, Sekou Touré's and Nkrumah's variants of African socialism, Kaunda's African humanism, and Kenyatta's *Harambee*. There were also attempts to project incumbent heads of state as national father figures who embodied wisdom and the national interest. A variety of titles was invented or re-invented by which such leaders came increasingly to be addressed by the citizenry: *Osagyefo* for Ghana's Nkrumah, *Mwalimu* for Tanzania's Nyerere, *Mzee* for Kenya's Kenyatta, *Le Vieux* for Côte d'Ivoire's Houphouët-Boigny, and *Le Grand Syli* for Guinea's Sekou Touré, to cite a few examples. These ideologies and symbolisms were deliberately fed into the nation-state project but, in time, they became difficult to disentangle from the power monoplolization and consolidation projects of some of the life presidencies that were being foisted on the'peoples of Africa by increasingly unpopular rulers alienated from the bulk of the popu-lace.

Almost without exception, a major reason given by incumbent African leaders for the abandonment of political pluralism was the urgent necessity to rid Africa of the cultural divisiveness which Western-style multi-party politics seemed to be keeping alive and which appeared to sap political and develop-mental energies in a multiethnic environment. By eliminating political institu-tions which appeared to keep ethnic divisions alive, the hope was that the task of achieving national unity and economic development would be made easier, as if ethnic consciousness and diversity were inherently inimical to or incom-patible with national unity, democracy and economic development. The domestic ethnic, linguistic, cultural and religious diversity of the countries of the continent was therefore seen by the post-independence governments as a source of weaknesses, the representation of which had to be suppressed in the political arena. Yet, in spite of the efforts at enforcing homogeneity and elimi-nating diversity, African societies did not seem to develop rapidly enough towards modern industrialised societies. From the perspective of Africa's largely rural populace, a unitary national culture such as was promoted by many post-colonial governments did not make any real sense nor did it have a content that they could meaningfully relate with. Without an economic and social push towards the kind of national "high culture" experienced in Europe, the idea of national unity came, paradoxically, to be reduced to an almost perfect negation of a common culture.

Armed with the rhetoric of unity, the post-colonial African state, instead of enhancing its capacity to provide new economic and professional opportunities to all segments of the society, increasingly resorted to protecting itself against the populace. The idea of unity which leaders sought to impose on Africans and the almost worshipful notions of the national father figure that they developed together with the ideologies that underpinned them served increasingly to distinguish the state culturally from society and to prevent any meaningful confrontation between the ruling elites and the masses. The character of the bureaucracy inherited by post-colonial state agencies and the persistence of the language of colonial governance exacerbated this cultural distance between the governors and the governed and further strengthened the position of those in power at the expense of the populace over whom they ruled and to whom, increasingly, they failed to account.

Many African one party and military regimes, in spite of their supposed aversion to ethnicity and in spite of their apparently secular character, rested on distinctly ethnic political foundations and reproduced themselves on the basis of definable, and in most cases, narrow ethnic alliances. By the same token, the moderate leadership of the orthodox religions, both Christian and Muslim, interacted with the political elite in a manner which produced mutually beneficial patrimonial and clientelist relationships for them (Haynes, 1995). For example, in the case of Tanzania, the Roman Catholic Church played an important role in training the political leadership and, thus, contributed to what can be called "secularised religiosity" (see Chapter 8 in this book). Thus, post-colonial Africa increasingly witnessed a situation in which single party and military rule represented thinly disguised monopoly of power by an elite drawn from one or a combination of ethnic and religious groups even as the masses were marginalised or felt themselves excluded from the mainstream of political power and patronage.

In retrospect, when measured against the levels and costs of conflicts that have been witnessed in Africa since the 1980s, the post-colonial unitary project did achieve some degree of relative stability, although it is also clear that the unity that was achieved was more apparent than real and carried increasingly unacceptable authoritarian political costs. During the 1960s and the 1970s, the memories of the humiliations associated with colonial rule were still close enough in the minds of many political actors/actresses to permit people to maintain some confidence in their governments and to have some patience in awaiting the promised fruits of independence. Furthermore, the post-colonial economic boom experienced in the early post-independence years facilitated the steady expansion of social services and bureaucracies in a manner that enabled governments to accommodate the emerging elites—political, religious, economic, bureaucratic, and social—of various ethnic groups and cater for the basic welfare and social needs of the populace as part of the post-colonial "social contract".

The international environment for this state-driven expansionism in the economy, social services, and the bureaucracy was, by and large, favourable as the period up to the late 1970s was dominated by a system of "nationalist welfarism" underpinned by a Keynesian ideology of development in the West and communism in the East (UNRISD, 1995; Simon *et al.*, 1995; Olukoshi, 1995).

Furthermore, the Cold War competition for politico-military allies boosted state expenditure on military-security matters, including expenditure on the expansion of national armouries and the extension of the size and education of the military elite. The international financial environment was also accommodating of state interventionism in the development process. This was a product of several factors, including the existence of large petro-dollar deposits in Western banks that needed to be re-cycled to developing countries and the Cold War competition between the East and the West in which loans and aid were seen as instruments for constructing political alliances with the countries of the South (Gibbon, 1993:36). In general, the international environment during the 1960s and most of the 1970s had little difficulty with the expansion of the public sector in Africa.

ECONOMIC CRISIS, STRUCTURAL ADJUSTMENT AND THE CRISIS OF THE POST-COLONIAL NATION-STATE PROJECT

For all the relative stability of the 1960s and 1970s in Africa, the approach to nation-building which was favoured by the post-colonial authorities was one which, by its increasingly centralising, top-down logic, was also authoritarian especially as the legitimacy of the state and of the post-colonial nationalist project started to weaken. The weaknesses that were built into the nation-state project began to be brought out in sharp relief when the model of state expansionism and patronage that underpinnned it was called into question by the economic collapse experienced during the late 1970s and early 1980s. This collapse was triggered off by a host of factors, among them the growing problems of dependency facing most post-colonial African economies, sharp price fluctuations, mostly of a downward nature, on the raw materials markets, downward fluctuations that fed into diminishing terms of trade for most African primary commodity exporters, the introduction of substitutes for certain minerals exported by Africa which resulted in market loss for some countries, and the oil shocks of the 1970s that threw the payments position of many African countries into disarray and laid the basis for the debt crisis of the 1980s.

Deep-seated domestic economic problems in the context of a recessionary international economic environment meant that the post-colonial "social contract" and the various alliances and networks built around it to create relative political stability became increasingly unsustainable. As the economic crisis worsened in various African countries, so too did the capacity of the state to provide welfare services to the populace and patronage to the political and economic elite diminish. Battered by the economic crisis, the legitimacy of the state, and of the model of nation-building which it pursued, was called into question as various groups began to devise strategies and mechanisms for coping with the deteriorating domestic economic environment and the social costs which both the crisis and governmental austerity measures were exacting (Beckman, 1988).

The sources, nature and dimensions of the African economic crisis have been extensively discussed in the many lively debates that dominated analyses of the problems and future of the continent during the 1980s and so we need not detain ourselves here with repeating those issues (Sandbrook, 1985; Havnevik, 1987; Onimode, 1989; World Bank, 1989; Ghai, 1991). What is really important for us to point out at this stage is the changing international context within which the crisis and the attempts at managing it unfolded. In this regard, it is worth pointing to two important developments in the international system. The first centred around the shift that began to occur in the leading Western countries from welfarist principles underpinned by Keynesianism to neo-liberal principles that placed greater weight on market forces and the struggle against inflation whilst simultaneously downgrading the Keynesian goal of full employment and the role of the state in the economy. Neo-liberalism and its anti-statism rapidly gained in ascendancy in the 1970s as the key Western economies went into a prolonged recession that cost a lot in jobs and inflation.

Second, and occurring side by side with the shift to neo-liberal ideas in economic policy making, was the acceleration of the process of economic globalisation which had enormous implications for the management of national economic policies all over the world. Particularly important in this respect was the deregulation of financial markets from the late 1970s onwards in the leading Organisation for Economic Co-operation and Development (OECD) countries. As a direct result of this deregulation, the volume of financial capital outside the control of national and international monetary authorities increased to such a level that even the governments of the leading Western countries gradually started to lose sovereign control over their own national economic policies, while individual economic actors speculating in stock exchanges and currency markets became important forces driving the global economy (Oman, 1993; UNRISD, 1995).

Neo-liberalism eventually fed into the outlook and practice of the leading international financial institutions, especially the International Monetary Fund (IMF) and the World Bank which the Group of Seven (G7) Western powers dominates. This development had direct implications for the developing countries that had become the main clients of the Bretton Woods institutions. The ideology of neo-liberalism also fed into the process of globalisation that was strengthened by the collapse, in the late 1980s, of the Soviet bloc, the eventual disintegration of the Soviet Union itself in the early 1990s, and the rapid adoption by the erstwhile socialist states of Eastern Europe of market-based economic reforms. Ironically, the collapse of the bipolar structure also meant the withering away of the "third pole" in world affairs represented by the Non-Aligned Movement (NAM) which, in spite of its fragmentation, was able during the Cold War years to create a real political space in the international system for the countries of the South by proclaiming autonomy from the Cold War rivals

(Simon *et al.*, *1995*; Colclough and Manor, 1991; Beckman, 1992, 1993a; Gibbon, 1993).

The immediate framework for the penetration of the neo-liberal free market agenda into Africa was the debt crisis of the 1980s. This crisis provided the leverage by which the IMF/World Bank support to declining African economies faced with severe payments, budgetary, inflationary, and debt-servicing problems was made conditional on the adoption of a prescribed pro-gramme of structural adjustment. Almost without exception, the programme entailed massive and repeated currency devaluations, exchange and interest rate liberalisation, public enterprise privatisation, liquidation and commerciali-sation, the withdrawal of all subsidies and the introduction of user charges on a variety of social, welfare and other services, the liberalisation of trade, including the abolition of state marketing boards and trading agencies, the retrenchment of large numbers of public sector employees and the imposition of a freeze on public sector employment, the quest for the elimination of budgetary deficits, attempts at the reform of the civil service of African countries, and a generalised curb on state intervention in economic processes. Increasing donor co-ordina-tion and cross-conditionality meant that most African governments had little or no option than to accept the adjustment package whether or not they agreed with its policy thrust (Havnevik, 1987; Olukoshi, 1995).

A lot has been written in support of and against the neo-liberal adjustment model for the stabilisation of African economies and their recovery. There is no doubt that given the rapid decline in the economic fortunes of most African states and the enormity of the problems facing the countries, serious and urgent reform measures needed to be undertaken to stem the march towards economic collapse. The issue that was, however, in dispute was the kind of reform that would be appropriate for the economic recovery of the countries: one which strived to reform the economies without undermining the socio-economic achievements of the post-colonial years or one that saw the entire post-colonial developmental model as totally discredited and lacking in any merit and which, therefore, aimed for its root and branch destruction. In our view, an appropriate reform package would have been one which balanced the requirements of eco-nomic rationality with a sensitivity to the social and welfare gains of the post-colonial years in Africa with a view to enhancing them. Certainly, for all the weaknesses of the post-colonial model of accumulation, and these were legion, the evidence on the actual performance of African economies during the 1960s and 1970s suggests that it was not the unmitigated, unidimensional disaster which its partisan critics in the World Bank were to caricature it as being (Mkandawire, 1995a; Olukoshi, 1995).

Unfortunately, as part of the broader anti-statist philosophy that under-pinned the neo-liberal structural adjustment model and which was reinforced by a peculiar, but thoroughly misleading interpretation of African socio-politi-cal processes on the basis of a one-sided theory of rent-seeking/-generation and urban bias, the social sector in most African countries came under severe attack and gains made in the social arena in post-colonial Africa were deliberately rolled back as the new neo-liberal donor regime of economic truth gained ground (Cornia *et al.*, 1987; Olukoshi, 1995). The astonishing zeal with which the neo-liberal agenda was pushed by the IMF and the World Bank assumed the inherent correctness of their model which, in reality, corresponded to no known experience on earth: both institutions promoted the simplistic picture of an ideal country in which the economy would be fully self-regulating through open, if not perfect competition and in which the public sector will only act to provide the "enabling environment" necessary for the conduct of private business (UNRISD, 1995). It is an ideal-type notion of the state and economy which corresponds to no known reality in history but against which the actual experiences of African countries were judged.

Not surprisingly, in most cases, structural adjustment became an integral part of the dynamic of crisis in Africa, serving in important respects to complicate the economic problems of the continent. Hitting the poor and the middle classes as hard as it did, structural adjustment also complicated the deepening social crisis on the continent, crisis which led to social unrest, the adoption by various groups of multiple livelihood strategies, accelerated informalisation, and deepening social fragmentation and inequality which, in turn, frustrated the realisation of the economic objectives of the programme. In the course of this development, the international financial institutions gradually became important political actors not only in the adjusting countries but also in the emerging post-Cold War world order. In trying to capture (and co-opt) all serious criticism against neo-liberalism, they intervened in international debates on poverty, gender, the environment, governance and even human rights—including debates initiated by the increasingly important community of non-governmental organisations (Gibbon, 1993:45).

As far as the nation-state project is concerned, we have noted earlier that the deflationary thrust of the IMF/World Bank adjustment model fed into the overall zero-sum approach of the market to produce massive cutbacks in social and welfare services and thus further weaken the basis of the post-colonial social bargain that imbued the post-colonial state with some legitimacy and underpinned the quest for post-independence nation-building. So serious were the cutbacks in many cases that there emerged a clear trend in several countries towards the reversal of the entire "modernisation" process itself as people moved massively from the formal to the informal sector and as school enrolment dropped sharply and attendance at increasingly poorly provisioned health facilities rapidly declined in the face of rising user charges. The nutritional status of many a household also declined as subsidies on basic staples were removed and the agricultural sector's performance remained lacklustre. Reeling under massive budgetary cuts and with staff morale destroyed by the salary freezes and collapsing purchasing power associated with massive and repeated currency devaluations, most public institutions became considerably weakened. This situation was not helped by the departure of some of the best qualified staff for greener pastures at home and abroad (Olukoshi, 1995).

As a consequence of the adjustment measures of the IMF and the World Bank for the reform of the African political economy, the post-colonial state was gradually exposed to a growing legitimacy crisis which the authoritarianism called for by the implementation of the unpopular market reform policies tended to exacerbate—not least by constraining possibilities for the conduct of any national dialogue about the reform package itself. While the design and implementation of the market reforms were planned in guarded secrecy without any mechanisms for giving relevant information to the media or consulting any organisations of the civil society (with the exception of some representatives of business, especially those in the exporting sector with some potential for earning foreign currency which, supposedly, would be to the benefit of the adjusting economy), the final outcome was justified by resort to such a highly abstract and remote professional/technocratic language centring around narrow economic rationalities that even a potential discussion involving different segments of the society about alternatives was effectively frustrated.

With years of economic crisis and structural adjustment having undermined the capacity of African states to meet the social and economic needs of their citizens, people had increasingly to fend for themselves. In doing this, some resorted to tapping "traditional" social and spiritual resources, including witchcraft (Schlyter, 1993). Others sought solace in new or resuscitated/reinvigorated ethnic or religious associations (Osaghae, 1995). In all, in spite of the boom in associational life witnessed in most parts of Africa, the scope for social solidarity (especially of the cross-ethnic type) was generally narrowed even as the possibility for people to turn on each other in the increasingly fierce competition for access to resources and what was left of the state increased. The crisis of the nation-state in Africa is, therefore, as much a crisis of politics and institutions as it is a crisis of the economy and society itself.

There were several consequences of the socio-political crisis which structural adjustment either triggered or deepened which also had implications for the nation-state project in Africa. At one level, the conscious curbing of the developmentalist orientation of the post-colonial state undermined the delicate process of the construction of a hegemonic multi-ethnic alliance involving a coalition with moderate religious leaders that had sustained the political process in most African countries, without replacing it with a viable alternative hegemony. In several countries, ethnic and religious leaders previously bound up with the state in the nation-building project suddenly found themselves in the forefront of struggles expressing popular discontent against that very state. They were therefore forced to choose sides in a profoundly new way (Haynes, 1995). While many of them became vocal opponents of state power in their demands for democratisation, accountability, and the taming of corruption, the "winners" from the structural adjustment process were generally too few, narrowly based, and politically fragmented to constitute a credible alternative national power alliance. In this situation, the diminishing ability of the state to accommodate competing demands for development exposed the fragile basis of national unity by increasing the sense of alienation of groups that either saw the state as becoming increasingly remote or felt increasingly marginalised from the distribution of the fruits of "modernisation".

At another level, the severe contraction of the state's social expenditure created a gap which, among others, was increasingly filled by popular religious associations that were challenging the orthodox religions both intellectually and materially. They offered hope for material improvement through the application of spiritual remedies but they also nourished a counter-culture to the discredited "modernisation" rhetoric of the unitary state, involving communal sharing of fears, ills, hopes and successes (Haynes, 1995). In several cases, these associations constituted a major source of pressure on the state from below. With many feeling themselves alienated from the "modernisation" project of the state and in the face of the social fragmentation brought about or intensified by economic crisis and structural adjustment, the new religious associations provided the forums through which they sought a set of anchoring values and a sense of individual empowerment.

Furthermore, the adjustment programme not only deepened divisions along class lines, it also heightened the process of uneven development, which corresponds, in a lot of cases, to clear regional and ethnic divisions thereby heightening political tensions. Nowhere has this latter dimension been more evident than in the consequences which public enterprise privatisation has had in some cases. An intensive competition for the assets that are to be privatised together with an unequal capacity to pay for shares often takes on clear regional and ethnic patterns thus deepening the feeling of exclusion among some groups with adverse consequences for the task of nation-building. Added to this is the feeling of anger generated by the sale of common assets, some of which are either important symbols of independence or feed into the construction of national consciousness/identity. The feeling among many that their country has been put up for sale to the highest bidder (usually non-nationals) has deepened the sense of alienation felt in many of the adjusting countries. Besides, more often than not, it is precisely those people whose personal aspirations to accumulate capital "primitively" had undermined the profitability of some of the public enterprises who now appear among the minority of people who are able to buy them at give away prices.

The adjustment process has not only reinforced a sharp polarisation between a rich minority and a largely impoverished majority, it has also decimated the old middle class of African professionals mostly employed in the public sector. Many people have spoken about the "disappearance" of the old middle class, and with it the middle ground in African politics at a time when, more than ever before, compromise is absolutely essential to the political process. Yet, those groups that have borne some of the worst effects of the adjustment programme, including the civil servants, doctors, nurses, university teachers and students, whom the neo-liberals castigated as "rent-seeking" or "parasitic", are also the very ones whose class, occupational, gender, and/or generational identities had endowed them with a national outlook that was central to the construction of a post-colonial national-territorial political space. This was due not only to the fact they tended to organise on a nation-wide, cross-ethnic/linguistic/religious basis but also to their constant effort at upholding a secular definition of the national interest.

In playing this role, the groups showed themselves to be ready to contest state policies and other interest group actions that were designed or tended to undermine the secular definition of the post-colonial developmental and nation-building project. The "disappearance" of the middle class is little helped by the attempts of foreign donors to employ some of them outside the state system since what it means is that they mostly become dependent on distant political institutions and decision-making processes and lose an important part of their organic relation to their own society. Although their ranks grew with the rapid expansion of the post-colonial bureaucracy and economy, their organisations were in the front-line of public criticism of growing corruption and inefficiency in the public sector. Their decimation and decline during the structural adjustment years in Africa has contributed to the acceleration of the decline of national dialogue and the increasing saliency of popular forms of identity that have potentially adverse consequences for the promotion of national unity (Bangura and Beckman, 1991; Beckman, 1993b).

The dismantling of the "developmentalist" state and the aggressive competitiveness/naked materialism associated with structural adjustment have created a fertile environment for the flowering of religious and ethnic extremism in the political processes of several African countries. The daily hardship to which people have been exposed in the context of collapsing living standards, the decline of national solidarity, and the enthronement of a market logic without a credible social safety net system have created various layers of social dislocation at the household and community levels. The rabid individualism of globalised capitalism, where identities are increasingly formed via consumption (you are how/what you consume), and the increasing feeling of marginalisation among those who cannot enjoy the growing variety of imported goods available since the liberalisation of trade have created feelings of emptiness and anxiety for many people. It is no wonder that people of different backgrounds have sought dignity, meaning, and empowerment in a variety of popular religious sects or fanatical ethnic movements that are now enjoying a revival across the board.

In the most extreme cases, religious sects reject both the secular state and all temporal authority in favour of a spiritual authority that promises a better tomorrow. Similarly fanatical ethnicity represents something perpetual, going beyond the fate of the contemporary generations. Thus, as the struggle for scarce resources and for access to and control of the state intensifies, Africa is facing a politicisation of belief systems that does not necessarily acknowledge obligations imposed by secular, multi-ethnic state authorities. Nor does it accept compromising with people who appear different or think differently. Furthermore, politicised religion has not hesitated to use strategies that run counter to all expectations of "rational" behaviour deriving from much of existing political theory, including the "rational choice" framework.

Buffeted on all sides by the domestic social, economic, and political consequences of structural adjustment, the African nation-state has been exposed to a dynamic of economic and social decline/disintegration which is both a product of and factor in the increasing disconnection and/or recomposition, at certain levels, of the links between the state and society. The diffused nature of African economies, more evident today than ever before, is such that it has become increasingly difficult analytically to use the concept of the national economy in any meaningful manner. This is because what is left of the formal sectors of most African economies is tightly connected to the global market (this, partly, is what structural adjustment has been about) while the informal and non-formal sectors, though expanding rapidly, appear marginal from the perspective of formal national economic decision-making. While economic actors in the formal sector are being forced to be globally competitive, the informal/non-formal sectors are mainly constituted by the ordinary people's intensifying and localised struggles for subsistence and survival.

The diminishing ability of the state to regulate this kind of economy is striking. Firstly, economic activities of the informal/non-formal sectors, ranging from subsistence farming and hawking to illegal cross-border trade are, by definition, taking place outside of a system of proper state control. The informalisation of the economy has meant declining tax revenues directly affecting the capacity of the state in administrative and policy matters and eroding the inter-linkages between the state and the citizens (Himbara and Sultan, 1995). Secondly, the more the formal sector is globalised, the less the state can consciously mould it according to any national priorities.

At another level, the pressure exerted on state officials by the donor community has meant the effective loss of control over economic—and increasingly political—policy making to the IMF and the World Bank. This loss of control over policy has manifested itself directly not only in terms of the imposition of policy packages that are inspired and designed outside the countries but also in terms of the capture of key economic institutions like the central banks and finance ministries of many adjusting states by the personnel of the Bretton Woods institutions. Thus, increasingly, the life chances of many Africans are being determined in faraway places by international multilateral agencies which are "profoundly unrepresentative and unaccountable and that permit global markets to wreak havoc with the livelihoods of ... the poor" (UNRISD, 1995). This loss of control over economic policy making by African states has been reinforced by the market liberalising logic of globalisation and has resulted in the almost complete loss of a long-term perspective in the formulation of developmental policy in favour of short-term considerations.

POLITICAL LIBERALISATION, POPULAR PARTICIPATION AND THE CRISIS OF THE NATION-STATE PROJECT

One argument which was made in favour of structural adjustment in the early 1980s centred around the view that in retrenching the state, it would enable the emergence of a "proper" national bourgeoisie that would be disciplined to the ways of the market and which would lead the struggle for the "genuine" democratisation of African countries on the basis of a non-clientelist, pluralistic political framework (Diamond, 1988; Herbst, 1990). In the event, this turned out to be a forlorn hope as the deflationary thrust of the adjustment programme undermined the growth prospects of most African economies and those that profited from the environment of economic crisis and adjustment were no more "national" and no less tied to state patronage than the elites they were supposed to replace. In fact, those who were best positioned to "win" from the adjustment process were precisely those who were economically advantaged and politically connected under the pre-adjustment political model, making the notions of "winners" and "losers" that had been devised to estimate the political outcome of the implementation of market reforms completely absurd.

Also, the expectation, arrived at on the basis of a simplistic deduction from the adjustment model, that politics in Africa would be rationalised and structurally adjusted (Herbst, 1990) in a manner that would be beneficial for "democratic" governance turned out to be completely baseless. Furthermore, the fact that the adjustment programmes undermined productive activities generally whilst promoting speculative, non-productive activities served to further weaken the prospects for the emergence of any "proper" national bourgeoisie. In fact, structural adjustment, while it may have been beneficial for international capital accumulation, turned out to be detrimental to the development of national capitalism and the national bourgeoisie (Mkandawire, 1995a).

But beyond their failure to create a "proper" national bourgeoisie that would act as a midwife to "genuine" democracy, the widely unpopular adjustment programmes—often not the result of domestic consultation, always shrouded in secrecy, and having to be rammed through under the weight of conditionality—hardly elicited democratic accountability to those who bore the brunt of austerity and deflation and whose sacrifices were central to its success. Since African governments were more dependent on the donor community than on their own citizens, they became increasingly accountable to the former and were able to continue to afford not to give account at home to their own people. Local opposition to the adjustment programme was often brutally repressed or stifled. Opponents of adjustment were not left with opportunities to organise particularly at the grass roots level or in the rural areas, still less to openly discuss and canvass alternatives to the content of the structural adjustment package and the way it was implemented. The donor demand for "consistency" and "commitment" in the implementation of the reform package reinforced the tendency for governments to prevent open discussion of the economic direction of the countries. It was the popular rejection of this authoritarian and repressive disposition by most African governments which structural adjustment exacerbated that resulted in the onset or crystallisation of struggles for political liberalisation in various parts of the continent (Beckman, 1992).

We noted earlier, in passing, that there was a confluence of external factors which combined to make the popular domestic quest for the opening up of the political space in Africa possible. The first factor centred around the events in Eastern Europe and the former Soviet Union that resulted in the collapse of the monopoly on power of the ruling communist parties under the weight of sustained popular pressure. Second was the end of the sharp ideological conflict between the East and the West that in the 1960s and 1970s resulted in many unpopular and unrepresentative African governments being propped up as the Cold War rivals sought to maximise their geo-political advantages/interests. The end of the Cold War meant that support for many of the African client regimes of rival ideological blocs ebbed, exposing them to the full force and fury of local opposition.

Furthermore, the widespread movement towards liberal, multi-party politics in many of the former Eastern bloc countries conferred a new international legitimacy on local struggles within Africa for the opening up of the political space. Popular domestic opinion in many of the leading Western countries at least apparently ensured that their governments either did not obstruct or even encouraged pressures within Africa for political pluralism (Gibbon, 1992; Olukoshi and Wohlgemuth, 1995). Finally, the transition in South Africa from an apartheid to a non-racial political system influenced political developments in other parts of Africa, especially in Southern Africa. The demonstration effects of political reforms in some African countries had a direct, beneficial impact on the struggles for democratisation in others. In this regard, it is possible to speak of a wave of political liberalisation in much of the continent, a wave which was so strong that it affected the political ethos of even the most authoritarian governments to a point where they were forced to include the issue of reform at least in their rhetoric.

The political reforms which were implemented in most African countries included the abandonment by several one-party or military regimes of their *de jure* monopoly on power, the embrace of multi-partyism, and the holding of free elections (often under the watchful eyes of international observers) in what some commentators have described as the "second liberation" for the peoples of the continent, the first having been from colonial rule. These reforms were mostly praised as positive by the international donor community and in many cases they were sufficient to guarantee the flow of new (concessional) funds. However, there are important respects in which the changes that took place may have been more apparent than real. The popular discontent that resulted in efforts at political reform had, in the first place, emerged out of the economic and social crisis afflicting most African countries. What was called for was a political reform programme that would extend and guarantee economic and social democracy to the masses with the aim of empowering them and enabling them to redress their exclusion from decision-making processes that affect their lives.

However, what the political elites, moderate religious leaders, and international donor agencies offered essentially resulted in the narrowing of the objectives of the popular yearnings of the peoples of Africa to electoral competition in the framework of liberal democracy and multi-partyism. For some of the international donor agencies, even this was going a bit too far. A case in point is the World Bank which declared itself willing to coordinate all decision-making concerning aid pledges to individual countries, including the management of political conditionality while simultaneously defining political conditionality as being outside its own area of competence (i.e. "economic governance") and beyond its legal mandate (Gibbon, 1993). Even more contradictory is the French policy which has displayed a widening gap between rhetoric and actual action on the issue of the linkage between French aid and political reforms in Africa. In fact, even in official pronouncements, the French government has recently downplayed the whole aid-political conditionality linkage in favour of economic conditionality (Martin, 1995). The example of Swaziland (Neo-Cosmos, 1995) is also indicative: elections which, besides being characterised by obvious evidence of intimidation and serious voter apathy and which were also non-multi-party elections as political parties had been banned, were declared "free and fair" by the United States and other Western powers.

Clearly, the constitution of an autonomous domestic opposition in every African country was going to be far more important for the sustenance of the pressure for democratisation than the international discourse on "political conditionality". Yet, although the opposition played an important role in voicing popular discontent with the prevailing political status quo in Africa, its way of mobilising populace was doomed to be largely populistic and its momentum short-lived. Due, among other factors, to the monopolistic character of power in much of post-colonial Africa, years of repression suffered by the opposition, the domination of the opposition parties by a small group of individuals, and an acute lack of resources, the opposition was often, both ideologically and organisationally, too weak and too elitist to become a momentous force for sustained and sustainable political change in many African countries. The ideological and organisational weaknesses of the opposition were often exacerbated by the electoral system that was adopted in most countries as part of their reform process: the first past the post Westminster electoral model suitable only for countries with two dominant parties that are relatively equal in strength but which was hardly useful or relevant in multi-ethnic and multi-religious Africa.

From the outset, in many African countries, the ruling elites strove to claim significant powers to manipulate or postpone the entire political transition process in order to maximise their advantages: in Côte d'Ivoire, the multi-party elections were held before the opposition could mount an effective challenge; in

Gabon and Ghana, a tightly monitored reform process was implemented pre-empting the opposition; in Cameroon, the elections were literally stolen by the government; in Kenya, the ruling party resolutely resisted all calls for a constitutional conference and far-reaching constitutional reforms; in Guinea and Zimbabwe, calls for an independent electoral commission were ignored by ruling parties which dictated in every detail, the pace and content of reform. In a few extreme cases like the two giants of sub-Saharan Africa, Zaire and Nigeria, the governments effectively impeded the process of reforming and sharing political power in spite of apparently advocating national conferences (Zaire) and organising a transition programme (Nigeria) towards liberal democracy (Schraeder, 1995). Of all the national conferences that have been convened, particularly in the Francophone African countries, only a handful have led to real political transitions in the short-term: Benin, Congo, Mali and Niger where new political leaders and governments emerged. But only in Benin do they seem to have consolidated their legitimacy peacefully without serious political disputes. In Togo and Gabon, the incumbent presidents were able to manipulate the electoral process and retain effective power; Chad still has a military government.

Obstacles erected by incumbent regimes to prevent the emergence of a viable opposition have been exacerbated by the deepening economic problems which African countries gripped by popular pressures for political reform have to deal with. Most of the elected African governments have been compelled to stick to locally unpopular structural adjustment programmes in what Mkandawire has described as examples of "choiceless democracies" (Mkandawire, 1995b). The case of Zambia, which made a successful transition to multi-party politics amply illustrates this: the newly elected government of Frederick Chiluba, backed in its bid for power by the labour unions, among other civil society organisations, has not been able to bring about a significant change in the living conditions of most Zambians but has vigorously sought to implement IMF/World Bank structural adjustment policies in order to win the support of the donor and investor communities. The failure of the adjustment measures to produce tangible results and growing incidences of corruption among the elites of the ruling Movement for Multiparty Democracy (MMD) have resulted in public disenchantment and criticism, which the government has tackled by using the very same methods (in some cases, worse) which its authoritarian predecessor employed in dealing with the opposition (Schraeder, 1995).

At the centre of the Chiluba government's strategy is a determination to employ all means, fair and foul (mostly foul and undemocratic), to prevent the previous ruling party, the United National Independence Party (UNIP) from ever having a fair chance of gaining political power in Zambia. Clearly, the scope for meaningful opposition politics is highly limited, a situation which has had the effect of sapping the appetite among many for life as opposition politicians. More recent examples of the general frustration and confusion among opposition groups in Africa were presented by the general elections held during 1995 in Zimbabwe and Ethiopia, where important opposition coalitions boy-cotted the whole exercise because they did not regard the system as giving them a fair chance. The disaffection associated with the weakening of the opposition and the narrowing of the framework for democratic participation would seem to suggest that the experience of political liberalisation which most African countries have had is not very helpful to the task of resolving the crisis of the nation-state project.

Our view that the experience of political reform which Africa has undergone since the late 1980s is still too limited to be effective in responding to some of the challenges posed to the nation-state is reinforced by a host of other factors. True, elections are now more than ever before the major means to legitimate governments internationally and many African countries have experienced multi-party elections at one time or the other since the late 1980s. However, cases of bribery, intimidation and even rigging have not been absent, and even where the elections have been declared "free and fair" by (international) observers, personalities rather than policy issues have dominated the election campaigns and the leading contenders have not hesitated to appeal to regional, religious, and ethnic sentiments which, in the context of the economic crisis and socio-political flux in most countries, strike a chord with many people. Not sur-prisingly, cynicism and apathy on the part of the voters has become a major dilemma confronting the political elite. For example in the Swaziland elections, the turnout figures were never released by the authorities but were estimated to be as low as 13–15 per cent of the registered voters suggesting that people "voted to stay away" (Neo-Cosmos, 1995). While some aspects of apathy might be tackled by voters' education especially in the rural areas where people apparently do not always know what voting is all about, increasing cynicism poses a real challenge to the elites as it suggests a deepening of the alienation of a growing number of people from the political processes in their countries. At the heart of this alienation is the question of whether it is possible to get people to the ballot boxes without giving them much of a choice.

ETHNIC AND RELIGIOUS IDENTITIES RE-VISITED

One clear lesson thrown up by the quest for economic and political liberalisa-tion in Africa is that popular ethnic and religious identities need to be more carefully analysed as much for their trajectory as for their implications for the nation-state. This is because virtually all of those political parties and organisa-tions in Africa that seem to be viable have been formed along discernible ethnic, regional or religious lines. A host of ethnic or cultural revivalist and social agencies has also emerged as part of the opening up of the African political space. No doubt mobilisation on the basis of these identities has provided an attractive means for many (parochial) leaders aspiring to state power to realise their ambitions without making any serious efforts at empowering the ordinary citizen in any substantial way. At worst, the mobilisation of ethnic and religious identities in the course of political competition has increased intolerance among the generality of the people and led to clashes in which political opinion, dialogue, and debate count for little or nothing. In a lot of cases, the re-birth of ethnic and religious identities and the mobilisation of these identities to serve political ends has caused consternation in policy and scholarly circles and, on the face of it, would appear to justify the view that was opportunistically taken by many incumbent governments presiding over one party or military regimes that multi-partyism will undermine national unity by fanning the embers of "tribalism". What many of these incumbents forgot was that their partisan authoritarianism played a key part in keeping ethnic and religious conscious-ness, including of the parochial type, alive, waiting for an opportunity to re-assert itself.

The instinctive response of many commentators to the resurgence of ethnic and religious identities in Africa has been adverse, partly because ethnic and religious identities are seen as inherently negative in political terms and dys-functional in the task of nation-building. Although we take the view that ethnic-ity and religion should not be celebrated uncritically as inherently positive at all times in all places and in all situations regardless of the historical context, the point ought also to be underlined that the politicisation of ethnic and religious identities could, in many senses, represent a genuine mode of participation for many Africans. For, ethnic identities and religious consciousness can, and do many times, carry important mental and aesthetic loads which give dignity to people and communities and that need a public space in which to be expressed in a context where such space was previously denied.

In other words, since the expression of ethnic consciousness was deliberately stifled as part of the post-colonial, unitary nation-building project, the opening up of the political space naturally offered a platform for these identities to be asserted and to flower. In this regard, it can be argued that in suppressing these identities, the state had, in fact, already politicised them. More importantly, the lop-sided ethnicity and systematic discrimination against some groups that underpinned many single party or military regimes gave an explicit social and economic content to ethnic and religious identities. Therefore, the politicisation of these identities can at least potentially bring issues of economic and social development connected to them to the national agenda where negotiation is then possible. Ethnic and religious identities are certainly not necessarily detri-mental to national unity and this is a message which needs to be repeated at this crucial stage in Africa's political development. The path to a sustainable project of national unity is not to seek once again to suppress these identities; rather, the state itself will have to be re-constituted to embody the various iden-tities of the groups that exist within its boundaries (UNRISD, 1995).

If the notion that ethnic identities are, in all situations, inherently divisive informed much of the nation-building efforts in post-independence Africa, it is ironic that the one party or military-led unitary projects that became the norm in most African countries soon after independence did not succeed in eradicating identities; in the worst cases, ethnic wars even broke out as in Nigeria, the Sudan, Uganda, Ethiopia, Zimbabwe, Rwanda and Burundi, among others. Thus, while it is true that the assertion of ethnic identities could, depending on the context, have unsettling political implications, it should be equally recognised that their elimination as a political project is not possible under the unitary project the type of which was experienced in post-independence Africa. Similarly, by establishing relationships with one or a few (usually orthodox) religious groups and founding its hegemony on a limited religious base, the unitary state did not succeed in rooting out the large number of religious faiths and sects which operated at the grassroots and which were often a mixture of Islam, Christianity and indigenous religions (Haynes, 1995). By neglecting these important popular modes of social organisation, the unitary state, in fact, exacerbated its alienation from the people.

Looking beyond Africa to the historical example of Europe, we have tried to emphasise how the nationalism that unfolded as the promotion of one "high" culture within the boundaries of a given state was connected to a very specific historical development, namely the industrial revolution, which integrated national economies in a profoundly new way. Still, even those European nation-states that were born out of the industrial revolution were not really culturally homogeneous, for their members could be distinguished along class, gender, generational, regional, and occupational lines that carried their own particular cultural values. The reality with which we are confronted and must live with is that it is always difficult to talk about a nation having a common culture "...when such things as food habits, speech and mannerisms may differ considerably between the upper, middle, and working classes as well as regionally" (UNRISD, 1995).

Besides, all over Europe, the "post-industrial" era has witnessed a revival of minority identities, some of which were assumed to have disappeared during the last two or three generations. In the former East bloc countries, including the former Soviet Union, some of the most vigorous re-assertion of ethnic identities in contemporary world history has been witnessed, in many cases with tragic consequences, in spite of several decades of secular "socialist" socio-political engineering and a drive for rapid industrialisation. The changing economic environment in many European countries which has involved a rapid growth in the service sector, an increase in the importance of research, design, and advertising in production, the increasing tendency to produce small quantities for special consumers as opposed to mass production for a mass market, and the development of information technology is providing a totally new space for the expression of a variety of identities. In one form or another, this "post-industrial" eclecticism is also impacting on Africa as the process of globalisation gathers pace.

In this regard, it is necessary to recognise that ethnic, religious or, indeed, any other identities are not immutable or eternal and that as social constructions, they are closely connected to social and economic processes that, today, are becoming increasingly globalised even as they are constantly re-invented. Clearly then, ethnic and religious identities are not abstractions that can be wished away. They are real and they are rooted in the fabric of material social relations in the framework of which individuals and groups reproduce themselves. All too often, in the discussion of the dynamics of ethnic politics in Africa, the impression is created that ethnicity is a problem only because ethnic identities are "politicised" by ruthless politicians to serve their political and economic ends. While there is no doubt that identities in general and emotionally charged ones, like those that are rooted in ethnicity, can indeed be manipulated to serve specific ends, it is important to underline the fact that the basis for that manipulation lies, in the first place, in the popularity and credibility of the identities. Ethnic identities become seriously amenable to political manipulation either when suppressed groups feel marginalised from the political and economic processes affecting their lives or when privileged groups feel that their rights are threatened. Thus, that which is manipulated often has a popular basis in group grievances that have to do with the distribution of resources and power.

Apart from the fact that an objective, material or mental basis must exist in the first place for the "politicisation" of ethnicity to occur, it is often forgotten that ethnic identities are themselves not apolitical but are rather socially constructed and, *ab initio*, carry a specific, inherent political load in the process of their invention and re-invention. The construction of the identity of one group only makes sense in relation to the way the identities of others are constructed and not in isolation. It is this relational dimension of the definition of identities that imbues them with an inherent political load. For, ethnicity does not exist or make sense outside inter- and intra-ethnic relations. The potency of the political content of ethnic identities lies mainly in the fact that it has the potential to transcend or totalise other types of group identity—family, class, gender, age, occupational. In this regard, ethnic identities are matched by religious identities which have a similar potential for over-riding other kinds of identity. It is precisely for this reason that ethnic and religious conflicts can have a tendency to become a zero-sum game, affecting the very definition of citizenship by tying it organically to the endowment of the state with an exclusive ethnic or religious character.

Yet, properly handled in a democratic setting, ethnic and religious identities can be useful ingredients in the promotion of the nation-state project. These identities represent a domain of human dignity, honour, morality, and care. An ethnic community in the 20th century and in the era of modern media is an imagined community, just like a nation, combining together peoples a majority of whom will never know or even meet each other. It is a community where loyalties and solidarity generate from ties which are not usually chosen on the basis of opportunistic considerations but described by a language of love, kinship and home. As a group, an ethnic community might have interests vis-à-vis other groups but internally its cohesion is based on its representation as being *interestless*. From this point of view, it is possible to understand why ethnic consciousness can conjure up the ultimate sacrifice of dying for one's own community or for something that is not chosen (Anderson, 1991:143, 144). Not so differently from that, religion is founded on transcendental values giving order to human relations and fate. Most importantly, popular religion is not about official theology but it is a lived religion, because it "offers solidarity at a time of social upheaval and crisis which helps to fulfil people's spiritual and material needs" (Haynes, 1995:106). From the point of view of the nation-state project, it is imperative to note that ethnicity and religion conceal elements which make human society and which cannot be crushed without crushing a whole civilisation.

The tendency to dismiss ethnic and religious movements out of hand as obstructive of the nation-state project has only recently begun to be remedied in the literature on Africa with the resuscitation of interest in the political potential of social movements on the continent (Mamdani and Wamba-dia-Wamba, 1995). Ethnic movements can extend the framework for national dialogue both in terms of their programmes and demands (as well as the responses which they may elicit) and in terms of their form of organisation. The experience of Niger Republic presented in this book brings out aspects of this point clearly. For although the agenda of particularistic groups may, at one level, conflict or appear to conflict with the nation-state project, at another level it could advance and deepen the nation-state project by compelling the state, as is happening in Niger, to work out rules that are acceptable to and accommodating of all competing particularist interests and that provide a basis for the mediation of inter- and intra-particularist concerns as part of a broader negotiation of the "ethno-national" contract. This process could, in turn, force open and broaden particularist groups in a democratic direction. Given that particularist pressures often result from the reality or feeling of exclusion and discrimination on the part of certain groups, the potential of ethnic movements to compel states to devise political frameworks and socio-economic and cultural mechanisms for accommodating them in the nation-state project suggests that ethnicity is not inherently incompatible with democratisation and the nation-state project. Ethnic and religious divisions only begin to pose problems "...when particular groups are discriminated against: when ethnic identities also align with patterns of repression or inequality" (UNRISD, 1995).

TOWARDS A RE-CONSTITUTION OF THE NATION-STATE PROJECT IN AFRICA

A viable path towards the re-constitution of the nation-state project in Africa must begin with a recognition of the plural, multi-cultural character of its societies and of the severe difficulties posed by economic decline/disintegration as manifested by the complicated dynamics of informalisation and globalisation and exacerbated by the structural adjustment programmes of the IMF and the World Bank. This means that in the context of the new international environment, the challenges facing the nation-state in Africa, whilst universal in character in several respects, are also unique in other respects. It seems evident that in the contemporary African context, the crisis of the nation-state cannot be solved simply or solely by resort to Western forms of liberal democracy. In any case, the experience of recent efforts at political reform in Africa and the problems associated with them have shown the limits of a liberalisation process that has been mostly limited to multi-party electoral competition and little else. The need to promote social equity, a minimum standard of human welfare, a viable economy, and a clear charter of citizens' rights which aims to promote civil liberties and human rights, political and electoral pluralism, and effective public institutions (especially in the areas of education, health, and the administration of justice) ought to be more fully recognised as urgent and brought closer to the centre stage of national political and policy discourses. These are issues which are too crucial to be left to a small, largely unrepresentative political elite, foreign agencies/donors, or market forces. A relatively strong and democratic state apparatus is a necessity in Africa, if the current social crisis is to be tackled (Mkandawire, 1995a).

The task of the reconstitution of the nation-state project in Africa is one which, if it is to succeed, must not be done in any top-down, authoritarian/totalitarian manner, as, in any case, the resources and capacities of African states are simply not sufficient, and the societies are too pluralistic for this kind of enterprise. The state has to be re-invented to reflect the pluralism of society in an open, democratic process which permits the participation of popular social movements and limits the influence of the forces of statism. In our view, a first step will be to ensure that the political/electoral framework in each African state is designed in a way that is sensitive to the social and cultural diversity of the countries of the continent. This, inevitably, will mean creating a framework to enable people to participate in public decision-making; it also implies that social movements should be prepared to seriously address issues like federalism, the promotion of local administration, cultural autonomy, and proportional representation (which usually leads to coalition cabinets and to the inevitability of consensus building).

This is not to say that ethnic and religious divisions should become institutionally frozen (as in the Lebanese and Ethiopian constitutions, for instance), making the state a "theatre" reflecting a conflict or harmony between different ethnic or religious groups rather than a political actor in itself that embodies the diversity of society. As argued by Ernest Wamba-dia-Wamba in his chapter on Zaire in this volume, the state must simultaneously rest on and transcend the multiplicity and diversity of the people. Precisely by protecting a peaceful expression and recognition of cultural diversity, the state can facilitate its transcendence: "...when people feel free to express their own culture and beliefs, they are more likely to develop a civic identity and a sense that they share common goals with the rest of society" (Bangura, 1994a; UNRISD, 1995).

The development of a civic identity that is organically favourable to the nation-building project in Africa will profit considerably from a drastic revision of the terms in which citizenship and citizenship rights are presently defined in Africa. Much has been written recently about the necessity for citizenship rights to be extended beyond the narrow terrain of political rights to include socio-economic rights, the so-called notion of social citizenship (Roche, 1992). This is, of course, an aspect of the citizenship question which is extremely important in Africa's current conjuncture, especially as it relates to the prospects for the re-negotiation of a viable new social bargain. But beyond this is the issue of the persistence of most African governments in defining citizenship rights on the basis of ancestry/birth in a continent where the present national boundaries are recent creations of colonial expedience, where many ethnic groups are to be found distributed among several of the states created by the forces of colonial-ism, and where the population is very mobile (intra- and inter-state migrations remain very strong in Africa). In several countries, ancestry is defined in patri-archal terms which work to the detriment of women who marry outside their communities.

Among the most recent dramatic expressions of this continuing attempt to tie citizenship rights to very difficult and nuanced questions of ancestral origin are the bizarre cases of Alasane Ouattara in Cote D'Ivoire and Kenneth Kaunda in Zambia whose right to contest presidential elections in their countries was officially questioned because their parents were born elsewhere. This problem has also featured in the experiences of long-term Rwandan refugees in Uganda, many of whom were fighters/commanders in Yoweri Museveni's National Resistance Army but who were to find themselves practically disowned and disenfranchised once the National Resistance Movement captured power in Kampala and embraced notions of citizenship right tied to ancestry. One way out of the political problems created by the narrow coupling of citizenship with ancestry is for the social movements on the African continent to push for the re-definition of citizenship rights on the basis of people's *place of residence* and *site of labour.*

The linkage of citizenship and citizenship rights to people's place of resi-dence/site of labour should also go some way to addressing some of the politi-cal problems thrown up by the national borders created by the forces of colo-nialism, inherited by the post-independence nation-states, and frozen by the Organisation of African Unity's charter. Quite apart from the boundary disputes that have been witnessed in many parts of Africa and which have resulted, in several cases, in the outbreak of armed conflicts, the view is now being canvassed in scholarly circles that an increasing number of Africans, in their daily livelihood/survival quests, do not feel themselves as owing much allegiance to or having much faith in the unrepresentative and remote political entities arbitrarily created by the forces of European colonialism to determine their destinies. This development is reinforced, according to this analysis, by the fact that the colonially-created boundaries did not adequately take cognisance of the histories of the various ethnic groups that were involuntarily lumped together under one, mostly undemocratic, political authority. On the basis of this, some commentators have taken the radical line that the time has come to let the nation-states created by colonialism collapse as they must, thus giving way to new political entities that are less artificial and in which various ethnic groups are free to choose who they live with under what kind of political roof.

The proposition that the existing nation-states in Africa and the colonially-created boundaries on which they rest should be allowed to collapse into more "natural" political units is, on the face of things, attractive but is, in reality, extremely problematic at several levels. At one level, it is very faulty to assume that, several decades after their inception, the nation-states of Africa are all completely artificial constructions in which nobody has a vested interest. On the contrary, years of living together have produced a community of shared experiences that cannot easily be wished away in spite of the many cleavages that continue to permeate the African political landscape. At another level, it is inconceivable that the cost of dismantling existing national boundaries and drawing up new ones will not be so high in human and other terms as to undermine the rationale for the pursuit of that option in the first place.

We only need to look at the experience of the former Yugoslavia to see that the process of dismantling and re-drawing boundaries can easily degenerate into ethnic wars (complete with ethnic cleansing) that will simply worsen the plight of the majority of ordinary Africans. Furthermore, it is not certain that the current widespread dissatisfaction in Africa with the existing nation-state projects is tantamount to a call for the embracing of ethnically homogenous nation-states. It is probably a mark of the commitment which people still have to the existing multi-ethnic political frameworks that amidst all of the chaos and crisis of the last few years, they have found it possible to articulate popular demands for national self-renewal, political accountability, and democratic governance. Although these demands may not have been fully met with all of the resultant frustrations, it is necessary not to underestimate the political will among Africans to improve themselves and their societies within existing boundaries. This is all the more so as dissolution into ethnic nation-states will not necessarily guarantee democratic governance the lack of which is central to the current crisis of the multi-ethnic nation-state.

In our view, some of the problems associated with the inherited colonial boundaries would be redressed where a more democratic approach is taken to the definition of citizenship rights. Apart from the proposal which we have made for a coupling of citizenship rights to place of residence/site of labour (as opposed to ancestry/birth), a conscious programme of political and economic decentralisation and cultural autonomy in a framework of shared and account-able power should strengthen confidence in the political institutions of the multi-ethnic nation-state. Furthermore, African social movements should pay closer attention to the possibilities that exist at the pan-African level for the resolution of some of the challenges confronting the nation-state project at the national level. In this regard, the promotion of rights on the basis of the residence/site of labour could be integrated into a wider pan-African notion of citizenship that guarantees to all Africans in Africa a package of political, economic, social and cultural rights, including fundamental human rights and civil liberties.

As part of the reconstitution of the nation-state project in Africa, governments have to re-capture their economic policy-making responsibilities from the multilateral financial institutions. This is necessary if the boundaries of local democratic governance, including accountability to the governed by elected representatives are to be extended. Moreover, given that hard economic choices will have to be made by most African countries over the foreseeable future, it is necessary that the economic policy making framework is within the reach of the populace and is open for their input and scrutiny. This way, the people of Africa will be able themselves to determine the kinds of social costs they are ready or willing to pay for correcting temporary economic difficulties and restoring growth. It should also be possible to redress the alienating and repressive political components of the current economic crisis management approaches which have done a lot to undermine the quest for the sustenance of the post-colonial national unity project in much of structurally adjusting Africa. It is not conceivable that the current challenges to the nation-state in Africa could ever be fully addressed if control over the destiny of the countries of the continent and their economies rests with multilateral agencies exercising unaccountable transnational power.

The disproportionate influence which the IMF and the World Bank have been wielding over the content and direction of economic policy in much of Africa since the early 1980s has raised concern about the dangers of re-colonisation facing the continent. This concern has been reinforced by journalistic comments in some of Europe's leading newspapers calling for an active reconsideration of the option of re-colonising Africa in order, *inter alia*, to prevent the potential human tragedy and Westward migration of people which the political disintegration of the continent might bring about. But within Africa itself, debates have been going on about re-colonisation and its desirability. In this regard, Ali Mazrui has provoked an intensive exchange with his calls for a benign re-colonisation of Africa under a trusteeship system that derives from African consent and is presided over by the United Nations or self-colonisation whereby some of Africa's regional powers like Nigeria, South Africa, Egypt, Ethiopia, and perhaps Zaire take over control of other problematic African states (*CODESRIA Bulletin*, No. 2, 1995).

One thing that is common to all of the proposals about the re-colonisation of Africa is the view that it is a viable and necessary solution to the current crisis of the nation-state and the chaos that threatens to engulf the continent on account of state collapse and socio-economic decay. For us however, the sheer abhorrence of any colonial rule, whether benign or not, internal or external is sufficient a basis to rule out the re-colonisation option as a viable solution to the challenges facing the nation-state in Africa. Those who are genuinely interested in addressing Africa's political future must premise themselves on options that are democratic and which do not tolerate the subjugation of one people by another in any form or under any guise. That, after all, has been the essence of all human struggle over the ages for a better, more just and egalitarian society.

CONTRIBUTIONS TO THE BOOK

There is broad agreement among the contributors to this book about the need for the promotion of a participatory, democratic political framework for the resolution of the crisis of the nation-state in Africa. The authors of the country case-studies see a direct connection between the National Question and the political and social question. The decentralization of power and the recognition of minority rights would have to be integral to the democratisation project. For Jibrin Ibrahim and Wamba-dia-Wamba, this could, in the respective cases of Niger and Zaire, take the form of a federalist project on which clear democratic demands are made from the outset. This position is carried over into the analy-sis of the increasingly contested Nigerian "federal" experience by Olukoshi and Agbu. For his part, Mutahi Ngunyi underlines the problems posed by a top-heavy federalist project promoted by the ruling KAMATUSA elite that domi-nates the affairs of KANU as part of its strategy for responding, *inter alia*, to popular pressures for democratic reform. In all of the chapters, issues of how the exercise of power can be made more accountable are discussed and a common view among the contributors is that the political reforms that have been introduced so far in Africa leave room for vast improvements that can decisively turn the tables on authoritarianism.

BIBLIOGRAPHY

Adekanye, J.B., 1995, "Structural Adjustment, Democratization and Rising Ethnic Tensions in Africa", *Development and Change*, Vol. 26, No. 2.

Ake, C., 1994, "A World of Political Ethnicity", (mimeo), Port Harcourt, Nigeria.

Anderson, B., 1991, *Imagined Communities: Reflections on the Origin and Spread of Nationalism*, Verso, New York.

Bangura, Y., 1994a, "The Search for Identity: Ethnicity, Religion, and Political Violence", *Occasional Paper* No. 6, November, UNRISD, Geneva.

Bangura, Y., 1994b, "State and Civil Society: Institutions in a Changing World", (mimeo) UNRISD, Geneva.

Bangura, Y., 1994c, "Economic Restructuring, Coping Strategies and Social Change: Implications for Institutional Development in Africa", *Discussion Paper* No. 52, July, UNRISD, Geneva.

Bangura, Y., 1995, "The Pitfalls of Recolonisation: A Comment on the Mazrui-Mafeje Exchange", (mimeo), Geneva.

Bangura, Y., and B. Beckman, 1991, "African Workers and Structural Adjustment with a Nigerian Case-Study", in D. Ghai (ed.), *IMF and the South: Social Impact of Crisis and Adjustment*, Zed Books, London.

Beckman, B., 1988, "The Post-Colonial State: Crisis and Reconstruction", *IDS Bulletin*, Vol. 19, No. 4.

Beckman, B., 1992, "Empowerment or Repression? The World Bank and the Politics of Adjustment", in P. Gibbon *et al.* (eds.), *Authoritarianism, Democracy and Adjustment: The Politics of Economic Reform in Africa*.

Beckman, B., 1993a, "The Liberation of Civil Society: Neo-Liberal Ideology and Political Theory", *Review of African Political Economy*, No. 58.

Beckman, B., 1993b, "Economic Reform and National Disintegration", (mimeo) Uppsala.

Colclough, C., and J. Manor (eds.), 1991, *States or Markets? Neo-Liberalism and the Development Debate*, Oxford University Press, Oxford.

Cornia, G., R. Jolly and F. Steward (eds.), 1987, *Adjustment with a Human Face*, Clarendon, Oxford.

Davidson, B., 1992, *The Black Man's Burden*, James Currey, London.

Diamond, L., 1988, "Roots of Failure, Seeds of Hope", in Diamond, L., J. Linz, and S. Lipset (eds.), *Democracy in Developing Countries, Vol. 2, Africa*, Lynne Rienner, Boulder, Colorado.

Gellner, E., 1983, *Nations and Nationalism*, Basil Blackwell, Oxford.

Ghai, D. (ed.), 1991, *The IMF and the South: The Social Impact of Crisis and Adjustment*, Zed Books, London.

Gibbon, P., Y. Bangura and A. Ofstad (eds.), 1992, *Authoritarianism, Democracy and Adjustment: The Politics of Economic Reform in Africa*, SIAS, Uppsala.

Gibbon, P., 1992, "Understanding Social Change in Contemporary Africa", (mimeo) SIAS, Uppsala.

Gibbon, P., 1993, "The World Bank and the New Politics of Aid", *The European Journal of Development Research*, Vol. 5 No. 1.

Havnevik, K. (ed.), 1987, *The IMF and the World Bank in Africa*, SIAS, Uppsala.

Haynes, J., 1995, "Popular Religion and Politics in Sub-Saharan Africa", *Third World Quarterly*, Vol. 16, No. 1.

Herbst, J., 1990, "The Structural Adjustment of Politics in Africa", *World Development*, Vol. 18, No 7.

Himbara, D., and D. Sultan, 1995, "Reconstructing the Ugandan State and Economy: The Challenge of an International Bantustan", *Review of African Political Economy*, Vol. 22 No. 63.

Martin, G., 1995, "Continuity and Change in Franco-African Relations", *The Journal of Modern African Studies*, Vol. 33, No. 1.

Mamdani, M., and E. Wamba-dia-Wamba (eds.), 1995, *African Studies in Social Movements and Democracy*, CODESRIA, Dakar.

Mkandawire, T., 1995a, "Beyond Crisis: Towards Democratic Developmental State in Africa", (mimeo), Dakar, Senegal.

Mkandawire, T., 1995b, "Democratisation and Economic Liberalisation in Africa", (mimeo), Uppsala, Sweden.

Neo-Cosmos, M., 1995, "National Elections and State Form in the BLS Countries: A Comparative Historical Approach", (mimeo), Maseru and Helsinki.

Oman, C., 1993, "Globalization and Regionalization in the 1980s and 1990s", *Development & International Cooperation*, Vol. 9, No. 16.

Olukoshi, A., 1995, "The Impact of Recent Reform Efforts on the State in Africa", (mimeo), Uppsala.

Olukoshi, A., and L. Wohlgemuth (eds.), 1995, *A Road to Development: Africa in the 21st Century*, SIAS, Uppsala.

Onimode, B. (ed.), 1989, *The IMF, the World Bank and the African Debt*, 2 Vols., Zed Books, London.

Osaghae, E., 1995, *Structural Adjustment and Ethnicity in Nigeria*, Research Report No. 98, Nordiska Afrikainstitutet, Uppsala.

Roche, M., 1992, *Re-thinking Citizenship: Welfare, Ideology and Change in Modern Society*, Polity Press, London.

Sandbrook, R., 1985, *The Politics of Africa's Economic Stagnation*, Cambridge University Press, Cambridge.

Schlyter, A., 1993, "Social Movements for Democracy and Women's Rights: Community Organization in a Poor Urban Area during the Transition from a One-Party to a Multi-Party Democracy in Zambia", Paper to the Nordic Conference on Social Movements in the Third World, University of Lund, August.

Schraeder, P., 1995, "Elites as Facilitators of Impediments to the Democratization Process? Some Lessons from Africa", in L. Laakso (ed.), *Development and Its Discontents: Proceedings of the Second Finnish Africa Days*, IDS, University of Helsinki, Helsinki.

Simon, D. *et al.* (eds.), 1995, *Structurally Adjusted Africa: Poverty, Debt and Basic Needs*, Pluto Press, London.

UNRISD, 1995, *States of Disarray: The Social Effects of Globalisation*, UNRISD, Geneva.

World Bank, 1989, *Sub-Saharan Africa from Crisis to Sustainable Growth: A Long-Term Perspective Study*, World Bank, Washington, DC.

Zartman, I. William, 1995, *Collapsed States: The Disintegration and Restoration of Legitimate Authority*, Lynne Rienner Publishers, Boulder, Colorado.

NEWSPAPERS AND PERIODICALS

Africa Confidential, London.
CODESRIA Bulletin, Dakar.

Chapter 2

Changing Notions of the Nation-State and the African Experience: Montesquieu Revisited

Liisa Laakso

INTRODUCTION

Recent political developments in Africa have generated questions which are compelling political scientists to extend their analysis beyond the particularities of the intensive political competition which has taken/is taking place in individual states between different leaders, parties, and ethnic groups. This has resulted, *inter alia*, in reflections among political scientists on the basic perceptions that flow from the theories that dominate their discipline. Few will doubt that the reflections are both necessary and welcome if the continent-wide crisis of the nation-state in Africa is to be fully understood. For many commentators, what this process of reflection has led them to conclude is that the post-colonial nation-state project in Africa can no longer be taken for granted, and its crisis has to be understood from the vantage point of its socio-historical meanings and evolution. It is a key contention of this chapter that the crisis of the nation-state has its roots in the very manner of the constitution of the nation-state project itself. Subjecting that project to a detailed analysis whilst simultaneously trying to understand recent political experiences should move us away from the earlier approaches towards interpreting politics and the state in Africa.

Researchers on the left and right of the ideological spectrum have generally focused their analysis of the African state on its capabilities and strategies in different policy areas, and not on its explicit characteristic as a project or on its form and content. This has to be understood in the context of the ideological impact which the Cold War had on the analyses of political and economic development in Africa and elsewhere. Those who favoured liberal democracy paid little theoretical attention to the state because for them "the less state the better" was an ideologically given premise. Their interest in the state was focused on how to marginalize it. Just as the ideological right assumed that the state was "bad" and the less of it the better, the left assumed that the state was an instrument of oppression that had, ultimately, to be done away with. Thus even the socialist state was intended to be a temporary, transitional one. In this framework, the state institution was treated as being far less important than the class status of those who controlled/dominated it. Strangely enough, the perceptions of the state by the left and the right ultimately converged insofar as they considered the state to be a nuisance, historically necessary but, as dictated by ideology, to be got rid of/severely curtailed as soon as possible. In most writings on the state, there was little or no real effort to understand its functioning in a detailed manner (see for example Chazan *et al.*, 1988; Nyang'oro and Shaw, 1989 and Bayart, 1993).

The fear of ethnocentrism contributed to the development of research approaches on the state in Africa that had no clear points of reference or explicitly presented and discussed models. For example, the separation of powers in the state was seen, as far back as the 1960s in the West, as an ethnocentric, Anglo-American conceptualization of the state (Almond & Powell, 1966). As a consequence, researchers concentrated on an analysis of political behaviour, political culture, political systems, political development, and political economy in Africa, while the state institution was dealt with only in a descriptive way. It is no wonder, therefore, that the more perplexing the African state seemed, the more unspecific the interpretation of its character became. The African state was labelled "patrimonial", "a lame leviathan", (Callaghy, 1986:31–36), "structurally superfluous from the point of view of the individual producer" (Hyden, 1983:7), giving no safety and security to the individual, and leading "to the strengthening of kinship ties" (Ekeh, 1990:693), or having a "capitalist nature" and a "neocolonial task" (Nzongola-Ntalaja, 1987:107). Political scientists, representing various ideologies and nationalities, almost systematically failed to see the African state as the sphere of certain kinds of political institutions that derived from explicitly definable power structures with clear socio-historical origins and consequences.

In this chapter, my intention is to go beyond labels deriving from the form of the state and to address substantive issues connected with the power structures of the state. This is done through an attempt to uncover and deconstruct some aspects of the early meaning of the nation-state project not only in Africa but in the modern world as a whole. I seek to undertake this task through a rereading of Montesquieu, a much neglected political philosopher whose works are however still relevant to the current discourse on the nation-state in the contemporary international system.

ISSUES OF STATE AND GOVERNMENT IN MONTESQUIEU'S
PHILOSOPHY

Montesquieu's work is both inspiring and irritating, sometimes very logical, sometimes extremely contradictory. Montesquieu was, in his time, radical in his diatribe against all arguments offered to justify slavery. But he was also conservative in his defence of the monarchy and the nobility—his own class. Still there is no doubt that Montesquieu's contribution to political and social theory was innovative and very influential in many ways. It was the course of history, the American and French revolutions and the Enlightenment in particular, that made Montesquieu's works acquire a significance. In the formulation of the American constitution, Montesquieu was one of the most important influences on both the federalists and anti-federalists. He also had a strong impact on the radical political thoughts associated with the French revolution.

It is, of course, important to remember that Montesquieu came before the American and French revolutions; in a sense, he also came before the Enlightenment. The latter point may sound odd since Montesquieu's name always appears without fail on the list of those who gave critical, reforming and revolutionary content to the Enlightenment. Nevertheless his thinking differed in one fundamental sense from that of the Enlightenment—a difference that should neither be ignored nor exaggerated. Whereas the Enlightenment was saturated by "the belief that human history is a record of general progress" (*The New Encyclopædia Britannica*, 1991), Montesquieu was interested in issues of corruption and the decline of human civilizations. This is evident in his arguments in *The Spirit of the Laws* (1748) dealing with the English Constitution that he admired very much. There, Montesquieu wrote about the buying and selling of votes: "Since everything human must end, the state discussed here will lose its liberty and perish. Rome, Sparta, Carthage—all have perished. This state will perish when its legislative power becomes more corrupt than its executive" (Montesquieu, 1990:191).

However, Montesquieu's recognition of the human tendency to corruption is not the most salient theme when one reads him with the current conditions of the African nation-state in mind. More striking is the general importance Montesquieu gives to government and to what he calls "a principle of government". According to him, government must be based on a principle that is concomitant with the general spirit of the nation: "Every nation is dominated by a general spirit, on which its very power is founded. Anything undertaken in defiance of that spirit is a blow against that power, and as such must necessarily come to stop" (*Considerations on the Causes of the Romans' Greatness and Decline* [1734] quoted in Richter, 1990:35).

It is interesting to note that this spirit was by no means metaphysical for Montesquieu as it later became for German romanticism. Montesquieu understood the general spirit of a nation empirically through the upbringing of its members in families, in schools, and through social practice. He emphasized morality, religion, economy and trade. A present-day reader might have difficulties only with his notions of climate and terrain (see Richter, 1990:45). This means that the Hegelian idea of the nation-state as the highest level of objective mind is incompatible with Montesquieu's thinking. For Montesquieu, there was nothing metaphysical in the spirit of a nation that would be part of an intelligible historical progress and *world-mind* as it became epitomized by Hegel.

Even the idea of the *general will* was not a part of Montesquieu's political theory. It was Jean-Jacques Rousseau who radically conceptualized the general will in accordance with democratic ideas and popular participation. For Rousseau, legislative power could only belong to the people. It required the existence of a general will to which all the citizens had to contribute. "The constant will of all the members of the state is the general will; it is through it that they are citizens and free" (Rousseau, 1968:153). Montesquieu was interested in the state and government as something that captures the *spirit* (not the will) of the nation into its basic principle. Since he thought that this spirit was embedded in the foundation of power in the society, its capturing by the government meant the empowering of that government and the state. For Montesquieu, the state was, if not a source of political power, at least a singular sphere of the expression of that power. The state was not about historical progress or freedom of nations, it was not even about human will. For Montesquieu the state was about power.

Montesquieu's distinctive classification of governments and their principles further clarifies this point: *republic* had *virtue* as its principle, *monarchy* had *honour* as its principle, and despotism had *fear* as its principle. None of these principles was equal to power as such, but all of them could be empowering when employed skilfully by the government. Furthermore "[t]he corruption of every type of government almost always begins with the corruption of its principles" (Montesquieu, 1990:161). No doubt, virtue, honour and fear still exist in the contemporary world. Perhaps they exist even as sign posts giving content to something that can be called the general spirit of nations or societies. But we can doubt whether this kind of spirit could form the most important foundation of power in contemporary societies, whether in Europe or in Africa.

GLOBAL CAPITALISM AND THE NATION-STATE PROJECT IN AFRICA

In the course of history, the nation-state project as understood by Montesquieu had to give way to another project in the modern world: that of capitalism. Capitalism as an economic mode, with its notions of competition, accumulation, exploitation and technocratic, instrumental rationality, without doubt has become the most important source of power in contemporary society. As we know, capitalism started to expand in a peculiar way within the nation-state project. More importantly, it eventually conquered an arena that was larger than the territorial space which any nation-state actually controlled. As Immanuel Wallerstein puts it, "[t]his gives capitalists a freedom of manoeuvre that is structurally based. It has made possible the constant economic expansion of the world-system, albeit a very skewed distribution of its rewards" (Wallerstein, 1974:348).

The significance of the expansion of capitalism as a mode of production was quickly remarked by those thinkers theorising about the state. What happened was that both in practice and in theory, the nation-state was no longer treated, exclusively, as a *source* or *sphere* of political power but as a *means* of power, and particularly as a means of economic power. This, of course, is very clear in the writings of Karl Marx and Friedrich Engels, who characterised the state in terms of class domination, as "the form in which the individuals of a ruling class assert their common interests" (Marx & Engels, 1976:90). But it was also clear in the earlier writings of liberal theorists. Jeremy Bentham, for example, put forward the idea of *universal interest* and the utilitarian notion of the state as aggregating the interests in society. For Bentham the "general end" of a good constitution was to promote "the greatest happiness of the greatest number" (Bentham, 1978:298). Those interests, in turn, necessarily got their meaning in the context of the capitalist mode of production—even so that a common nationalist culture in a state became a facilitator for mass production and mass consumption and a facilitator for interest aggregation, interest articulation, conflict and compromise in purely economic terms. By the same token, the spirit of the nation became only indirectly empowering for the state. It was transformed into a static nationalist ideology that was functional in the fragmentation of political power into fixed nation-states, and more or less, in the free expansion of capitalism. In this framework, the strength of the nation-state was subordinated to its strength in the capitalist world economy.

This, of course, is a simplified picture. But generalizations are useful in order for us to understand the foundations and propellers of complicated and contradictory, but nevertheless universalized, processes like the nation-state project in the modern world. Some aspects of the complicated and contradictory content of the nation-state project can be approached precisely through the fact that capitalism, as the foundation of power in modern societies, functions through the agency of state institutions rather than providing the means for empowering those institutions. Thus, unlike virtue, honour and fear which in Montesquieu's thinking were not only sources of power but were also empowering, capitalism acts more as a source of power and less as a source of empowerment for state institutions. Of course, in a general sense, it can be argued that capitalist economic organization could also define the spirit of a nation, and that what is needed, following Montesquieu's thinking, is the creation of a new type of government, that of a technocratic facilitator of economic processes with a corresponding apparatus which copies the principles of capitalism into its own rationality. And indeed, production and consumption are terms that are increasingly used by state agencies to legitimate public policy and political choices as the 20th century draws to a close. Even universities are having to grapple with productivity standards. Political leaders speak increasingly in terms that contain strong notions of policy production and consumption, including the "the consumption of security" and its "production". References are made to the need to balance "the production" and "consumption" of security and other state policies. It becomes increasingly difficult and absurd to defend non-material values in the language of production/consumption. Still, this rhetoric of capitalist rationality cannot put the state in command of that rationality. Capitalism as such does not empower anyone or any kind of social relations: it has its own logic and it is tied to one particular institution—the business enterprise. Its power is not essentially social but anonymous.

Nowhere has the state's subordination to capitalist rationality been more obvious than in Africa, where modern state apparatuses were often even literally introduced by private European enterprises. It is all too well known how contradictory and complicated the economic processes during colonialism were, and how little they contributed to the creation of strong national economies. Still, most significant for the development of the form and content of nation-states in Africa, was the fact that during colonialism, they were not designed to get their power from those societies that were ruled. Their institutions were not arenas of decision-making but control apparatuses serving external interests. In the context of the changing nature of the capitalist project, this pattern of state institutionalization was to have important consequences for the actual form of the African state and the process of post-colonial nation-building.

As far as capitalism is concerned, the "enterprise state" that strives to be more and more effective in the global power structures, can never do much more than adjust to economic imperatives. Nowadays, this means adjusting to an increasingly globalized, anonymous power. The globalization of economic processes has contributed to a situation in which decisions that decisively shape public policies are made in distant places, by agents and forces hardly known. This leads, inevitably, to a trivialization of political activity in the nation-state in a manner and on a scale unforeseen by modern political theorists. If the state was a singular sphere of political power (as it was for Montesquieu), if the state was about general will (as it was for Rousseau), if the state was a means at the disposal of a dominant class (as it was for Marx), if it was a sphere of interest aggregation (as it was for Bentham), political action or participation in this sphere or vis-à-vis this class or these interests would be meaningful. Quite a contrary situation prevails in contemporary Africa. Under structural adjustment policies, sources of power affecting people's daily lives appear increasingly remote and to some extent anonymous such that they seem very difficult to challenge and are not easily made accountable within the parameters of normal national political discourses. The World Bank, the International Monetary Fund (IMF) or the headquarters of transnational corporations are not accountable to those people whose lives their decisions affect in a very profound manner. Even worse, the rationality of their decisions is not dependent on the conditions of those people. What we are left with is a set of undefined, law-like principles of capitalism and the discontents which they generate. Increasingly, the message that is created is no longer about the exploitation of Africa and its working people but about the marginalization of the continent from the mainstream of global capitalism and the collapse of the bargaining/negotiating power of the people vis-à-vis global economic imperatives.

Concomitant with the actual disempowerment of the African state itself are the consequences of this development for the political mobilization of citizens and for their political identities. The politicization of ethnic and regional identities derives its meaning precisely from this context of disempowerment—in the same way as clientelism and complicated loyalties provided material security and dignity for Africans that faced the uncertainty of colonial interventions, externally imposed exploitation, and "modernization". By definition, this politicization of ethnic and regional identities is not concerned with public decision-making, but with identities, human dignity and honour. Because it is centred around social relations, it is in a sharp contrast with the rationality of the modern state, and so it either "escapes" this state or challenges its very foundations.

On the other hand, the form of the African state has made it extremely insensitive to the needs and pressure of its own citizens. Here I will turn to Montesquieu again, focusing particularly on that part of his work that is perhaps best known and which has been canonized in Western political thought and the constitutions it inspired, namely, the separation of powers. The single institutional fact that distinguished despotism from monarchies and republics (which Montesquieu further divided into democracies and aristocracies) was separation of powers and checks and balances. According to Montesquieu, "[p]olitical liberty exists only when there is no abuse of political power... To prevent the abuse of power, things must be so ordered that power checks power" (Montesquieu, 1990:181). These checks of power have to be distinguished from the actual location of power. Power can be used in a concentrated and arbitrary manner at all levels: starting from the state to districts and villages. Power in a despotic government does not solely lie in one office. On the contrary, "[a] government cannot be unjust without putting some power in the hands of its agents"; by the same token "it is impossible that they not profit from their position" (Montesquieu, 1990:156).

It is surprising how little attention political scientists have paid to the concentration of power in post-colonial states in Africa. Politicization of the security apparatus, governmental interference in the judiciary either through political nominations or pardoning of convicted state officials, and governmental control over the media have created monolithic power structures in most African states. These means of control are typically inherited directly from colonialism. They have survived the popularly-supported independence struggles and the elements of Western parliamentarism that were hastily introduced when the colonialists left Africa. Soon after independence, the constitutions were almost automatically altered in favour of a concentration of power in the executive, accompanied by the onset either of one-party states or military regimes. For instance the emergency powers act which the post-colonial state inherited from colonialism and with which it was possible to detain people without reason or trial, was hardly discussed in the independence parliament which, in theory, was accountable to the "independent nation".

To the extent that the current African state reminds us of Montesquieu's definition of despotism, its principle is fear: fear of criticism, fear of disloyalty. There is no doubt that this kind of fear severely constrains the space available for a politically active civil society and crystallises the character of an oppressive state. However, in the contemporary international system, this fear does not make the *government* powerful in the sense Montesquieu thought. It is not used to rule the public sphere and to serve the public purpose. It is used to protect the interests of the ruling elite and its quest to accumulate capital "primitively". Fear is also used as an instrument in privatizing the state. Therefore state power in Africa becomes very attractive; its exercise on the basis of terror also delegitimises the state. Political competition—even in the form of multi-partyism—does not seem to promote the political organization of the masses so that their voices can be heard at the national level. In its extreme form politics becomes warfare. It consists of a zero-sum competition among the elites, where the loser loses everything and the winner takes all. It knows no tolerance, no compromise and no accountability. It also leads, inexorably, to the concentration of power.

The twin phenomena of the globalization of anonymous economic power and the consolidation of an inherited oppressive state have contributed to the emergence of a state form which is, at best, quite far from the ordinary people and, at worst, life-threatening. The trivialization of multi-party democracy into an intensive power struggle is a logical outcome of a globally weak but domestically concentrated state power. It brings issues like ethnicity and party leadership to the political arena as central elements in the political mobilization of the voters. There is little room for discussing alternatives to economic policies that are directed by the IMF and/or the World Bank. With the president having a lot of unchecked power, it is natural that the president's personality and the relations of individuals and groups to that person become crucial. Politicized ethnicity and a "dear leader" mentality are not reflections of an authoritarian political culture *as such*, but reflections of the peculiar characteristic of the nation-state project in Africa. Similarly when politics is not about decision-making but about loyalties, it often becomes violent—the other end of the continuum being frustration, cynicism and apathy.

CONCLUSION

The critical re-evaluation of the nation-state project in Africa presented in this chapter does not lead us to easy solutions. However, it might move our attention away from romantic hopes concerning the potential of multi-partyism or the civil society to check the power of the oppressive state to the necessity of transforming the state institutions themselves. In order to promote meaningful political participation in Africa, the nation-state must be reconceptualized as a sphere of power. Certainly this reconceptualization cannot be done solely with

Montesquieu in mind. But his works offer a theoretical starting point, imperfect though it may be. Beyond this reconceptualization is the urgent need to the globalized power of capitalism through concerted international efforts. As the recent crisis in Mexico shows us, the power of global financial capital is no longer beneficial for any political actors. It benefits only the speculators who can "play the game".

In Africa, the reconceptualization of the state must start from the constitution, security apparatus, the judiciary etc.—not only to prevent the privatization of state power but also to make possible and promote the identification of the citizenry with the constitution. Montesquieu understood this essential prerequisite when he equated the love of one's native land [*la patrie*] with the love of equality. He called this love virtue, thus developing a politically dynamic definition of the source of power and its nature in republics. And after all, his statement that "[s]uch virtue is neither moral nor Christian, but political" (Montesquieu, 1990:106) implies the necessity for an institutional framework for decision-making rather than a distinct, parochial or static spirit of the nation. This implies that the focus of our attention should be on finding political solutions to the crisis of the nation-state and the heightening of fragmented political identities not only in contemporary Africa, but all over the world.

BIBLIOGRAPHY

Almond, G.A. and G.B. Powell, Jr., 1966, *Comparative Politics: A Developmental Approach*, Little, Brown and Company, Boston.

Bayart, J-F., 1993, *The State in Africa: The Politics of the Belly* (transl. by Mary Harper, Christopher and Elizabeth Harrison), Longman, London.

Bentham, J., 1978, "Leading Principles of a Constitutional Code" in Bramsted, E.K and Melhuish K.J. (eds.), *Western Liberalism: A History in Documents from Locke to Croce*, Longman, London.

Callaghy, T.M., 1986, "Politics and vision in Africa: the interplay of domination, equality and liberty", in Chabal, P., (ed.), *Political Domination in Africa: Reflections on the Limits of Power*, Cambridge University Press, Cambridge.

Chazan, N.; Mortimer, R.; Ravenhill, J. and Rothchild, D., 1988, *Politics and Society in Contemporary Africa*, Lynne Rienner Publishers, Boulder, Colorado.

Ekeh, P., 1990, "Social Anthropology and Two Contrasting Uses of Tribalism in Africa", *Comparative Studies in Society and History*, Vol. 32, No. 4.

Hyden, G., 1983, *No Shortcuts to Progress: African Development Management in Perspective*, University of California Press, Berkeley and Los Angeles.

Marx, K. and Engels, F., 1976, "The German Ideology", in *Collected Works, Volume 5, Marx and Engels 1845-1847*, Progress Publishers, Moscow.

Montesquieu, 1990, *Selected Political Writings*, translated and edited by Melvin Richter, Hackett Publishing Company, Cambridge.

Nyang'oro, J.E. and Shaw, T.M. eds., 1989, *Corporatism in Africa: Comparative Analysis and Practice*, Westview Press, Boulder/San Francisco/London.

Nzongola-Ntalaja, 1987, *Revolution and Counter-Revolution in Africa: Essays in Contemporary Politics*, Zed Books, London.

Richter, M., 1990, "Introduction" in Montesquieu, pp. 1-53.

Rousseau, J-J., 1968, *The Social Contract*, Penguin Books, Harmodsworth.

Wallerstein, I., 1974, *The Modern World-System I: Capitalist Agriculture and the Origins of the European World-Economy in the Sixteenth Century*, Academic Press, San Diego.

Chapter 3

The Weakness of "Strong States": The Case of Niger Republic

Jibrin Ibrahim

INTRODUCTION

Niger, like other African countries, attained independence in 1960 on the basis of a secular, centralised and in fact Jacobin state framework. For thirty years, the orientation of the state was shaped by the primacy of enforced nation-building. Niger was virtually a prototype of the African state form that denied the existence of differences and contradictions between the component units of the political community. A very strong concern was nurtured within the Nigerien elite about the necessity of promoting a strong state that has effective authority that cannot be contested by regions, ethnic groups, social movements or indeed individuals. Most members of the elite spoke a unitary language, that of the Jacobin state that was assumed not only to express the will of all the people but also to be the sole source of legitimacy. For three decades, it appeared as if Niger was indeed a success story in nation-building because political differences and opposition were not expressed openly. It appeared as if the myth of the Nigerien nation had been internalised. Appearances are however often far from reality. While the doctrine of national unity might have become a Jacobin dogma, not all those who articulated it actually believed in it. The widespread concerns of the Nigerien political elite about developing and maintaining a strong and united state have not and are not, therefore, producing the desired effects. Indeed, the reality of the country is the development of widespread challenges to the secular national territorial state framework centred around ethno-regional, religious, and national, and international economic factors.

THE ETHNO-REGIONAL CHALLENGE

Niger has a long history of authoritarian rule which made it very difficult for ethnic perceptions or differences to manifest themselves politically. In such authoritarian contexts, the transition to more democratic political forms provokes the decomposition and/or disarticulation of the coercive apparatuses of the state and opens the possibility for ethnic mobilization and even conflagration. Ethnic pluralism is in itself not a dangerous feature in multi-ethnic states. It only becomes problematic when ethnicity assumes the status of an object around which discrimination is perceived and interpreted in the cognition of groups (Otite, 1990). Inter-ethnic conflicts tend to emerge at moments when groups perceive that they are being excluded from access to what they consider to be their rights be they linguistic, economic, administrative, commercial, religious etc. The most important question is, therefore, the perception of domination by a group. Not surprisingly, violent ethnic conflicts are usually linked to perceptions of group domination in the absence of channels for articulating demands (Osaghae, 1992:219–220). The articulation of ethnic aggression however needs a relatively open or democratizing environment. For Niger, the concern which the movement towards more open political forms and structures throws up centres around the possible effects which the country's democratic transition might have on ethnic conflicts.

The establishment of an educational infrastructure was one of the major instruments used in trying to forge a new national space in Niger. The first regional school was established in Zinder, the then capital, in 1913 and the first set of students and teachers were recruited in that Hausa speaking region (Tidjani Alou, 1992:332). The decision to move the capital from Zinder to Niamey was a conscious political move aimed at preventing the evolution of a Hausa political elite that might be too closely allied to their cousins in northern Nigeria. The colonial authorities believed that building a Zarma/Songhai educated elite would be easier to handle politically because they were culturally closer to the French-controlled Songhai population in what are now known as Mali and Burkina Faso. The impressive study by Tidjani Alou shows that with the movement of the capital, Niamey became the centre of production of the educated elite especially with the establishment of the first regional school there in 1930. That was the school from which students could go for higher education in the Ecole Normale William Ponty in Dakar. It was not an accident that the first graduates of William Ponty from Niger were all Zarma/Songhai and they became the first political leaders of the country, their political importance closely following their seniority and year of graduation in Dakar—Boubou Hama (1926), Hamani Diori (1933), Djibo Bakary (1938) and Seydou Djermakoye (1943).

In pre-colonial Niger, identities were usually defined territorially and not on an ethno-linguistic basis. An early colonial survey by Abadie listed 39 ethnic groups in the country. Indeed, Niger is composed of a number of communities that had already constituted their macro and micro identities in the pre-colonial period. The largest of these communities, constituting about 53 per cent of the population, are the Hausa. They occupy the south central part of the country from Dogondouchi to Zinder and were organized in smaller political communities or states. The main ones were Adar, Arewa, Konni, Gobir, Katsina and

Tsotsebaki states. The Zarma and the Songhai speak the same language and are tied historically by their common appurtenance to the Mali and Songhai empires. Nonetheless, they consider themselves to be two distinct peoples and since the collapse of the Songhai Empire, they have lived in numerous princi-palities in the western part of Niger. They constitute about 21 per cent of the population.

The Fulani, both the exclusively nomadic Bororo and town Fulani, live in almost all parts of the Republic of Niger. Territorially, they were organized in many principalities, the largest being the Say theocracy. They form about 10 per cent of the population. The Tuaregs are also a nomadic group and they too constitute about 10 per cent of the population and occupy the northern desertic fringes of the country. They had a number of centralized political communities such as the Air and Adar Sultanates and Damargu. The Kanuris (Beriberi), make up about 5 per cent of the population and occupy the far south-eastern part of Niger. They are a constellation of different groups with a majority living around the Lake Chad area. They had a number of Kingdoms such as Kanem, Bornu, and Damagaram. The Gurmance constitute about 3 per cent of the popu-lation. Other smaller groups include the Toubou, who like the Tuaregs are a desertic nomadic group based in the Tibesti and having a strong warrior tradi-tion, the Budumas, the Arabs etc.

These ethnic categories constitute macro levels of identification in contem-porary Niger. The real picture of ethnic identities is, however, somehow more complicated than that:

> Most observers agree that ethnicity is an important factor in contemporary Nigerien society, but, it is difficult to be precise about the country's ethnic identi-ties. Fearing greater divisiveness, the governments of Niger since independence have strongly discouraged research into ethnicity, and this type of classification is also difficult because the people of Niger use it so imprecisely to serve their own purposes. General ethnic groupings such as Hausa, Zarma or Beriberi, mask a great deal of diversity because they group people whose origins and cultural practices can be quite varied. (Charlick, 1991:8)

Even the most politically visible distinction, that between the Zarma and the Hausa, could become problematic in some instances. The study by Mahamane Karimou of what he calls the "Mawri Zarmaphones" is an interesting example in this regard. The group in question changed their identity from Hausa to Zarma in the 19th century. The impetus for their change of identity was mate-rial—seeking protection from attacks from Tuareg and Zarma groups by inte-grating into neighbouring communities.

The genesis of the ethnic problem in contemporary Niger is linked essen-tially to the association that has been made in the public mind between the Zarma/Songhai ethnic group and the monopoly of political power on the one hand and the Hausa ethnic group and the control of commerce and the smuggling network with Nigeria on the other. The origins of Zarma/Songhai political control, as we have said, are linked to the history of colonial elite formation which favoured it. The problem deepened after independence because the Zarma power elite developed a highly authoritarian system that virtually excluded all others from joining the summit of the political hierarchy. The origins of the control of smuggling and commerce by the Hausa are related to geographical proximity created by the over 1,000 kilometre boundary that separates Niger and Nigeria and the consequent rise of Maradi as the major commercial town in Niger following the imposition of colonial rule and the decline of the commercial status of Zinder in the wake of the destruction of the trans-Saharan trade.

The Republic of Niger became independent on 3 August 1960. By that time, the democratic experiment that had been initiated in French West Africa following the installation of the Fourth Republic in Paris had already ended for the people of Niger. In the two years preceding independence, rival political parties had been outlawed, trade unions had been disbanded and an all-powerful President, Hamani Diori, had been installed in office. According to a constitutional chronicler of Niger, Jean-Jacques Raynal (1991:13-14), the Constitution of the First Republic invested virtually all the authority of the state in the hands of the President. He had complete executive powers and was not accountable to parliament. He had powers to make ministerial appointments without scrutiny by any other authority, as well as powers of appointment and termination in the armed forces and the civil service. He had the authority to veto parliamentary bills (by perpetually suspending the second reading), and at the same time had the power to enact legislation by ordinance. In addition to these powers, he was also the Secretary General of the ruling party and therefore controlled the party machine. There was no pretence of trying to practise a liberal democratic model.

The first stage of the construction of authoritarianism in post-colonial Niger involved the establishment of the single party regime that was able to eliminate rival parties and adversary trade unions. The party of President Hamani Diori, the Parti Progressiste Nigérien (PPN), was formed in June 1946 by a small group of *évolués* most of whom were from the Zarma ethnic group and who had studied at the Dakar Teachers' College (Ecole Normale William Ponty). The party was formed in response to the decision by the newly inaugurated French Fourth Republic to allow "natives" of the colonies the right to elect territorial representatives. The PPN affiliated with the regional political confederation, the "Rassemblement Démocratique Africain" (RDA), when it was established in 1947. At the political level, all other parties were forced to dissolve themselves and join the ruling party, the result being that, even before independence, Niger had become a *de facto* one party state. Those in the leadership structures of the other parties were, however, never fully integrated into the top hierarchy of the party or the state and the core group that formed the politburo of the PPN in 1956 remained the barons of the party until the *coup d'état* of 1974.

One of the specificities of the French colonization of Niger was that, from the very beginning, the French seemed to have a preferred choice among the various ethnic groups:

> The French decided to turn their backs on the East and the North to some extent, and to focus their attention on the West and on the Zerma/Songhay, whom the French probably considered more malleable than the traditionalist Hausa ... The Hausa were also suspect in the eyes of the French because of their Northern Nigerian, i.e. British, "connection". This shift of emphasis is in a way symbolized by the transfer of the capital from Zinder to Niamey in 1927. (Fuglestad, 1983:125)

The result of this choice was that most educational facilities and development projects established during the colonial era were located in the Zarma/Songhai zone in the far western part of the country. It was thus not surprising that the vast majority of the educated elite that established political parties in the 1946-1960 era were of the Zarma/Songhai ethnic stock, and the same category remained in power until the National Conference in 1991.

Virtually all the founders of the PPN were Zarma/Songhai and the other major groups—Hausa, Kanuri, Fulani, Toubou and Tuareg were effectively absent. This situation did not change for a long time and, over an 18-year period (1956–1974), no non-Westerner was admitted into the 12-member politburo of the party. From 1956 to 1990, the top two office-holders were always Zarma/ Songhai: Diori Hamani-Boubou Hama; Seyni Kountché-Sani Sido; Seyni Kountché-Ali Saibou; Ali Saibou-Ahmadou Maiga. According to Soulay Adji (1991:234), in terms of political control, the only contest in Niger politics in thirty years has been between aristocrats and commoners of the Zarma/ Songhai group while the elites of the other ethnic groups have been uneasy onlookers. He adds that even in the army, the Zarma/Songhai had at least 70 per cent of the officer corps. This ethnic control had repercussions on the dis- tribution of national resources. The survey carried out by Adji (1991:296) in 1990 revealed that 62.7 per cent of development projects were in Zarma/ Songhai areas and only 22.7 per cent in Hausa areas. The conclusions of Finn Fuglestad, the chronicler of Niger's political history, are without ambiguity in this regard:

> Niger had fallen victim of the "sub-imperialism" of the Zerma/Songhay and the nascent political awakening of the Hausa had been cut short. In a sense the Diori government pursued exactly the same policy as the French after 1922, that of trying to sterilize all political activity to silence the voice of the average Nigerien. (1983:187)

The PPN, as the party in power, was incapable of widening its power base and became the focus of nation-wide grievances.

The regime of Hamani Diori was overthrown on 14 April 1974 in a *coup d'état* led by Lt. Col. Seyni Kountché. Neither the authoritarian nature of the regime nor its narrow ethno-regional base were at issue in provoking the change of government and both characteristics not only continued but were aggravated under the military regime. The major factor that seemed to have precipitated the change of regime was France's concern over Diori's attempt to make her pay more for uranium. The military regime was extremely harsh and repressive to its own people. Soulay Adji (1991:279), explains that the coup was greeted with popular acclaim because people were fed up with the coercion of the PPN regime. However, the new regime of Seyni Kountché soon installed a system of blind terrorism, starting with the top members of its own Supreme Military Council. In fact, the members of the council were never announced and, within a year, most of them had been killed or put in prison. On 4th August 1975, President Seyni Kountché made a radio broadcast in which he declared:

> From today, the ship that is the Nigerien State has only one captain; I am the captain and I shall remain the captain." (Raynal, 1991:18) (Author's own translation)

The military regime had turned into a one-man tyranny that only ended with his death in 1987. President Kountché turned the whole country into a virtual military cantonment with gendarmes controlling the movement and activities of people. In the capital, for instance, he employed 10,000 political police to control a population of only 400,000 people (Adji, 1991:280). Niamey was also closed to traffic as from 6 pm each night. People disappeared for having made a careless comment and silence became the "watchword" for survival. Only nomadic Tuaregs and students were able to put up some element of resistance to the state terrorism organized by President Seyni Kountché.

ETHNO-REGIONALISM AND THE CHALLENGE OF DEMOCRATISATION

Niger's Second Republic was inaugurated on 6th October 1989, with the promulgation of a new constitution which had been massively approved (99.3%) in a referendum a month earlier. The process of return to democratic rule was a long and elaborate one and was initiated on 3 August 1983, when President Seyni Kountché announced a programme of gradual return to constitutional rule and grassroots democracy. The first stage was the drawing up of a National Charter that would define the operational principles of the future constitution as well as the instrument for democratization—the National Council for Development (CND). The objective of the CND was to dynamise and integrate neighbourhood, village and ward associations, known as *samariya*, into organs of democracy and development. The first draft of the Charter was circulated in April 1986 and adopted by the Council of Ministers in May 1987 after a national debate. It had no provisions for the transfer of power to elected representatives but it proposed the establishment of the rule of law in the country (Raynal, 1990:379-381). The death of Seyni Kountché and his succession by Ali Saibou as Head of State in November 1987 accelerated the process of political change. On assuming power, he declared that he would pursue the process of democratization but would not accept multipartyism so as to preserve stability and national integration.

President Saibou transformed the CND into a single party, the MNSD (National Movement for the Development of Society). The Constitution that was adopted and the elections that were held in 1989 were aimed at the institutionalization of the idea of single party "democracy" in the country (Maidoka, 1991). The directing principle of the Second Republic was to "restore democracy while maintaining order" (Raynal, 1990:382). Apart from these institutional changes, President Saibou also considerably mellowed the authoritarian grip of the state. He disbanded the political police and lifted the night curfew in major towns. He released over a hundred political prisoners from detention (including Hamani Diori and Djibo Bakary) and allowed political exiles to return to the country (Adji, 1991:329). He also initiated a policy of *decrispation* by making the regime less austere, more open and friendly. On 10th December 1989, Ali Saibou was elected President of the Republic with 99.6 per cent of the vote and 93 members of the National Assembly were elected with 99.52 per cent of the vote, all in a very orderly and successful manner (Niamdou-Souley, 1990:249).

Two months after the election of the President, on 8 February 1990 to be precise, university students started a boycott of lectures over the adoption and implementation by the government of International Monetary Fund-inspired structural adjustment policy measures that were pushing the state to undertake substantial reductions in funding levels for the educational sector. The following day, they organized a peaceful march into town to express their grievances and press the government to reverse its policies. As they got to the Kennedy bridge on the outskirts of the capital, soldiers attacked them and at least 14 unarmed and defenceless students were killed (Niamdou-Souley, 1990:268). This massacre of students on Friday 9 February became a major turning point in Niger's history. It was a great shock to people that a government that claimed to be democratizing society could massacre unarmed students without provocation.

Immediately after the massacre, the central labour organization, the Union des Syndicats des Travailleurs du Niger (USTN), was shocked out of 30 years of lethargy and collaboration with the government in power. It withdrew from the governing council of the ruling MNSD party and began to openly agitate against the MNSD state. It played a major role in organizing a massive demonstration the following Friday (16 February), after prayers at the mosque, which turned out to be the biggest protest march since independence. Souley Adji (1991:333) argues convincingly that the massacre on what has come to be known as Black Friday signalled the birth of civil society in Niger. The slogans at the demonstration were a clear indication—"Down with whisky" (in reference to the well known drinking habit of Saibou), "Down with the Second Republic", and "Down with the IMF". The fear of gendarmes that is so characteristic of Francophone African socio-political culture was reversed and the people signalled their desire to define their own democracy rather than operate the one proposed by the state.

With the birth of civil society, the edifice of state-organised terror and repression collapsed in Niger. The state even started to lose its capacity for manipulation. The Minister of Internal Affairs was removed to calm the situation but people wanted more. The Council of Ministers was dissolved and a non-Zarma (Hausa) Prime Minister was appointed to serve under Saibou. A new Council of Ministers which, for the first time, represented the country's ethnic diversity was appointed but it was too late. Four months after Black Friday, *Haske*, the first independent newspaper since independence, was launched. From its first edition, it started a debate on the necessity for multi-partyism and a National Conference. The trade unions moved from calling for respect of the Constitution to demanding its abrogation. In a speech on 20 July 1990, President Saibou appealed to the Nation in the following terms:

> We must not copy for the sake of copying. Multipartyism will come at its own time but not through street pressure or in confusion. (Adji, 1991:337)

It is a familiar refrain that has been repeated in many African countries over the past five years. However, nobody was ready to listen. From 5 to 9 November 1990, a general strike was organized in support of a National Conference and multiparty democracy and an estimated 100,000 people marched on the streets of Niamey. It was the end of an era. The days of the Zarma/Songhai authoritarian oligarchy were apparently numbered. The people had imposed a linkage between *democratization* and popular multiparty participation. It is to Ali Saibou's credit that he accepted the people's verdict and agreed that a National Conference be convened.

The National Conference in Niger was declared open by President Saibou on 29 July 1991. It sat for four months and was composed of over 1,200 delegates representing trade unions, students' unions, 30 political parties, chambers of commerce, voluntary associations, and the civil service. As was the case in Benin Republic, the National Conference ruled from the very beginning that its decisions were sovereign and would over-ride all pre-existing institutional powers. It, in fact, dissolved the government and asked Directors General of Ministries to report directly to it, thus turning President Ali Saibou into a ceremonial Head of State. It even removed the Chief of Army from office. What was most striking about the National Conference was the spirit of liberty it fostered all over the country. The security forces were removed from the streets and confidence seemed to return to the people. The National Conference generated very wide interest in politics and its proceedings (from 8 o'clock in the morning to 10 o'clock at night, Monday through Saturday) were broadcast live on radio, and the whole nation was virtually glued to the radio.

The Conference also became a forum for public complaints. Policemen in uniform, for example, came up to present evidence that the Director of Police had misappropriated fuel vouchers that were meant for public use while customs officials attended to explain how the "dictatorial leadership style" of their director had forced them to go on a national strike. Even the press developed very rapidly. After *Haske*, three other independent newspapers, published in French, emerged within months. These were *Le Républicain, Horizon 2000*, and *Expresse Nigerien*. In addition, a Hausa language newspaper, *Kakaki*, was launched. The press openly discussed questions that had never been posed previously in any public arena. Among the questions that were openly debated were state repression, ethnicity, and democracy. Only the official government newspaper, *Le Sahel*, seemed to have had problems of production at that time. The National Conference reversed the marginality of the population and the will and determination for popular participation in politics became the order of the day. It was indeed a major cathartic moment that helped release the spirit of liberty lurking in Nigeriens.

Three issues attracted particularly intense and passionate debate during the National Conference. The first was the history of political crime in the country, starting from state-directed political assassination in the 1960s and 1970s, through to the massacre of Tuaregs, especially the mass murder of Tuareg families by the gendarmerie in 1990, and of course the attack on students on 9 February 1989. The Commission on Political Crimes and Abuses (La Commission Crimes et Abus Politiques) became the most controversial one in the National Conference as the result of a barrage of vociferous demands to "punish the murderers" it received, and its inability to punish the alleged offenders due to the insufficiency of legally binding proof.

The second issue was that of corruption. The vast majority of Niger's political and technocratic elite have evolved in a culture of widespread corruption that had never been previously questioned or punished because of the highly authoritarian nature of the state. Major revelations were made in the National Conference on various deals and the public was shocked at the extent of the "theft" of public resources in such a poor country. A tribunal was subsequently established to try the accused persons and recover the moneys misappropriated.

The third issue that provoked intense debate was that of the economic and financial crises facing the country. From its inception, the National Conference was confronted by the fact that the state was virtually bankrupt. Officials of the International Monetary Fund and the World Bank were actually in attendance at the Conference as observers to explain that the only viable option for the country was their version of a structural adjustment programme (SAP). The Conferencees were unimpressed by the arguments for SAP and voted to reject it. They were, however, unable to develop a coherent alternative that could steer the country out of its dire economic condition. In fact, most of the issues raised in the National Conference were not resolved but the Conference itself provided a valuable political forum. For the first time, serious national issues were openly and honestly discussed in a public forum thus setting the agenda of issues that a democratic Niger would have to resolve in the next few years.

At the end of its deliberations on 29 October 1991, the National Conference established transitional institutions that would rule the country for fifteen months, after which fully democratic elections would take place. The transitional institutions were the office of the President of the Republic, which would only have protocol functions, having been stripped of executive and legislative powers by the National Conference; a "High Council of State"/Haut Conseil de la Republique (HCR) that had legislative powers as well as supervisory powers over the executive; and finally, the Prime Minister and his ministers, who had executive powers. General Ali Saibou remained as President of the Republic, Andre Salifou, the President of the Presidium of the National Conference, was elected President of the HCR while Tcheffou Ahmadou was elected Prime Minister. All these elections were conducted in the National Conference which also decided that none of the three transition officers could contest the forthcoming presidential elections.

The transitional institutions were considered the final phase of the National Conference and their main function was to lead the country to democratic rule. In fact, the National Conference did not succeed in drawing up a constitution, only a "Fundamental Act" (Acte Fondamental No. 21 de 1991) which was to guide the transitional institutions in their task. The HCR adopted the new constitution on 30 September 1992 and Nigeriens accepted it in a referendum which took place on 26 December 1992. The Fundamental Act did not spell out the functions and prerogatives of the transitional institutions very clearly, resulting in many conflicts of interpretation and clashes of personality during the transition. Notwithstanding, the institutions were able to overcome the difficulties and lead Niger towards the adoption of the constitution and successful legislative and presidential elections in 1993. The expansion of political space and the dynamics of *democratization* that occurred in Niger also opened up the possibilities for the "ethnicisation" of the political process as the elites struggled for the control of political power.

Following the series of demonstrations and strikes to which we referred earlier, President Saibou and his government were forced to accept the principle of multiparty politics on 15 October, 1990. The establishment of parties opened the floodgates to widespread and open ethnic mobilisation in the country Thirty political parties participated in the National Conference. Most of them were formed in haste and did not represent any real political force and have since faded away. Some of them however had deep roots in Niger's politics, in particular, the ethno-regional dimensions we have been discussing. Let us now discuss some of these parties more closely.

i. Movement National pour la Societé de Développement (MNSD-Nassara)

The MNSD was the single party that had, hitherto, ruled the country during the "failed transition". It was a party of notables and virtually all the top military bureaucratic and business people in the country were members and the Head of

State, Ali Saibou was the President of the party. Saibou withdrew from the party leadership in 1991 and a congress was convened to elect a new leader. Two "military notables", who were leading power brokers under President Seyni Kountche, retired colonels Adamu Djermakoye and Tandja Mamadou contested the leadership at the March 1991 congress. Djermakoye is a scion of the Zarma ruling oligarchy in Niger and had in fact tried to take over power following Kountche's death. Tandja was also a part of the top politico-military leadership of the country and had been a prefect in Maradi and Tahaoua, interior minister and ambassador to Nigeria. However, unlike most of the rest of the top leadership, he was not Zarma. He is of mixed Kanuri and Fulani parentage from Diffa, in the south-east.

The leadership contest was won by Tandja Mamadou, mainly because the non-Zarma party cadres teamed up to support him. Bala dan Sani, the very wealthy Hausa businessman, perhaps the richest person in the country and baron of the most densely populated region, Maradi, threatened to take Maradi out of the MNSD if Djermakoye was elected leader. The election of Tandja as party leader saved the MNSD from being considered an ethnic party. He had a wide network of supporters, especially among the business community and being neither Hausa nor Zarma assured him even wider support. He is generally considered the most "de-tribalized" politician in the country. He also had very close connections with the military leadership in Nigeria, Niger's major economic partner and was openly supported by the then military ruler of Nigeria, General Ibrahim Babangida.

It was a party that assumed that it was "destined" to win the elections because it had within it the people of wealth and influence in the country, hence its party slogan of *nassara*, meaning victory. Its campaign platform was the necessity to re-establish state authority, seriously compromised by the Tuareg rebellion and the "libertarian atmosphere" introduced by the National Conference. The party's presidential campaign train was in fact attacked by armed Tuareg rebels at Abala (Filingue District) on 9 January 1993 and in the ensuing battle, Tandja led the successful army defence and counter-attack. The MNSD is the most national of Niger's political parties. It not only won the most seats in the elections (29 out of 87) but also had the widest national spread, with at least two seats in all districts. Its candidate won the first round of the Presidential elections and its main rival, the CDS had to form an alliance with other parties to win the second round of the elections. The Alliance formed by the MNSD won a majority of seats in the January 1995 parliamentary elections and is currently running the government. The capacity of the MNSD to transform itself from an authoritarian sole party to an effective player in the democratic game is indeed remarkable.

ii. Convention Démocratique et Sociale (CDS-Rahama)

The CDS is strongly associated with the interests of the Hausa bureaucratic elite and some elements of the Hausa commercial class that have felt excluded from political power. Its origins have been traced to a regionalist cultural association, AMACA (Association Mutuelle pour la Culture et les Arts), established in Zinder, the centre of Hausa resistance to Zarma hegemony, in 1982. Not much is known about AMACA except that it was formed as the Hausa political response to "energie de l'ouest" a secret organization, established in 1976 as a think-tank for the preservation of Zarma political hegemony in the country. AMACA metamorphisised into the CDS in 1990 with a clear intention of relying on the Hausa majority for its electoral success. Although the party has a strong Hausa nationalist orientation, many of its top leadership are not "ethnically" Hausa. President Mahamane Ousmane for example considers himself to be Kanuri and the 1st Vice President of the party, Sanusi Jackou is of Tuareg origin. Hausa identity has however never been a narrow "ethnic" issue and these leaders are as Hausa as anyone else. The party was led by Mahamane Ousmane, the current President of Niger. The party won 22 seats in the legislative elections, 14 of them in the Hausa strongholds of Maradi and Zinder.

iii. Parti Nigerien pour la Démocratie et le Socialisme (PNDS-Tarayya)

The PNDS is a socialist party formed by a broad cross section of the Nigerien left. Most of its cadres had been active in clandestine Marxist revolutionary groups and in the students' movement (USN) and the teachers' union (SNEN). Many of these militants such as the party leader, Mahamadou Issoufou, had however risen to the top hierarchy of the civil service and public corporations and had become "bourgeoisified", at least in their material conditions of existence. The PNDS is widely acknowledged as the most ideologically committed and non-ethnic party in Niger. The party however got 5 out of its 13 seats in Tahoao, the home region of its leader although it also got seats in all other districts, except Niamey, the capital. It was a major surprise that it was unable to get any seats in the intellectual and political centre of the country. The PNDS however did not have major financial backers so its campaign was rather low key.

iv. Alliance Nigeriene pour la Démocratie et le Progrès (ANDP-Zaman Lahiya)

The ANDP is the personal party of its leader, Moumouni Adamou Djermakoye who lost control of the MNSD to Tandja Mamadou. His objective seemed to have been to take the Zarma vote away from the MNSD. Immediately after the MNSD Congress, he formed the Club des Amis de M. A. Djermakoye or Club of Djermokoye's Friends (CAMAD) to help him establish a party network. He had been ambassador to the United States and was conversant with modern campaign tactics which he used effectively when CAMAD was transformed into the ANDP. His party was considered a great personal success because he stood against the huge MNSD party machine and won 11 seats, most of them in the

Zarma area. He got his revenge against the MNSD by denying it the extra Zarma votes that would have assured it of complete victory.

v. Parti Progressiste Nigerien (PPN-RDA)

The party represented an attempt to recreate the ruling party of the First Republic. It is led by Youssoufou Oumarou, an old diplomat and it got two seats in the heart of Zarmaland in Dosso and in Tilaberi. Its prized candidate, Abdullahi Diori, the son of the former President however lost his bid for a parliamentary seat.

vi. Union Démocratique des Forces Progressistes (UDFP-Sawaba)

The party is a reincarnation of Djibo Bakary's radical nationalist's SAWABA (Liberty) party of the 1950s. It was founded on a non-ethnic platform but was however stillborn because on his release from prison, Bakary compromised with the military regime and even joined the MNSD. Nigeriens seemed to feel that although he is a national hero, he had lost touch with political reality due to his long incarceration and his advanced age. The party managed to get two seats, in the traditional Hausa strongholds of Maradi and Zinder but Djibo Bakary himself did not succeed in getting elected to parliament in his Zarma place of origin.

vii. Union des Patriots Démocrates et Progressistes (UPDP-Chamoua)

A small Zinder party opposed to the CDS and formed under the inspiration of Professor Andre Salifou, President of the Constituent Assembly and of the HCR. It is led by Illa Kane and has two seats in the National Assembly, one in Zinder and the other in Maradi.

viii. Parti Social Démocrate Nigerien (PSDN-Alheri)

A small Kanuri party whose founder, Wazir Mallam Adji, died in 1992. It is now led by Kazelma Omar Taya and got one seat in Diffa,

ix. UDPS-Amana

The UDPS got only one seat in the elections but it is potentially one of the most politically explosive parties in the country. It is the legal political wing of the Tuareg rebellion. In addition, it has one clear political demand, the establishment of federalism in Niger.

The second and decisive round of the presidential elections in Niger took place on 27 March, 1993. A day later, the loser, Tandja Mamadu, visited his rival, Mahamane Ousmane to congratulate him for winning the elections and promised him a vigorous but loyal opposition in the parliament of the country's

Third Republic. The next morning the 120 foreign observers that had covered the elections declared them to have been free and fair although a few problems had been observed in the Agadez region where the Tuareg uprising was strong. The results of the elections were confirmed by the electoral commission COSUPEL or Commission Nationale de Controle et de Supervision des Elections less than 48 hours after the end of voting. There were no complaints about rigging or electoral fraud. It was a very smooth and genuinely successful operation.

The legislative elections were conducted on the principle of proportional representation at the level of the eight departments of the country rather than on the basis of a national list. There were 618 candidates representing 12 political parties. The candidates contested 83 seats in the elections but only nine parties were able to obtain seats. The results of the 83rd seat (Tesker) were cancelled as only 1,203 out of 8,785 voters had the possibility of voting due to serious logistical problems. New elections were organized for Tesker and the PNDS eventually won.

14 February 1993 and 12 January 1995 Legislative Elections

Party	Slogan	Seats (1993)	Seats (1995)
MNSD	Nassara (Victory)	29	29
CDS	Rahama (Bounty)	22	24
PNDS	Tarayya (Togetherness)	13	12
ANDP	Zaman Lahiya (Peace)	11	9
PPN/RDA		2	1
UDFP	Sawaba (Liberty)	2	0
UPDP	Chamoua (Stork)	2	1
PSDN	Alheri (Grace)	1	2
UDPS	Amana (Trust)	1	2
PUND	Salama (Peace)	0	3

The major revelation from the 1993 elections was that the MNSD, the single party established by the military, was the leading party in Niger with 29 out of 83 seats. Although it did not have an absolute majority, it seemed on the way to capturing the forthcoming presidential elections. The second party in the elections, the Social Democratic Convention/Convention Démocratique et Sociale (CDS) took off with the handicap of being widely considered as the party of the Hausa. It was however, able to partially transcend the ethnic label by embarking on a campaign strategy of presenting itself as the party for *change* and for the *new breed*. The fact that influential Hausa businessmen and notables such as Bala dan Sani of Maradi, teamed up with the MNSD and campaigned against the CDS also helped downplay the fear of a "gang-up" of the Hausa people. On 16 February, two days after the legislative elections, the CDS spearheaded the formation of the Alliance of the Forces of Change/Alliance des Forces de

Changement (AFC) composed of nine parties—CDS, PNDS, ANDP, PPN/RDA, PSDN, UDPS, PRLPN, PUND and UDP.

The Alliance had 49 of the 82 seats already declared. In addition, the participation of Djermakoye's ANDP in the Alliance assured them of substantial Zarma support while the presence of the socialist and nationalist PNDS broadened its progressive orientation. The Alliance adopted a minimum programme of action aimed at promoting democracy, social justice, national unity and integrity as well as a peaceful resolution of the Tuareg problem. The parties also agreed that they could all present candidates in the first round of the presidential elections but that they would all support the candidate with the highest votes during the second and decisive round. That was how Mahamane Ousmane, the leader and presidential candidate of the CDS became the candidate of the AFC in the 27 March 1993 final round of the presidential elections. Thanks to the Alliance, he won the elections with 54 per cent of the votes, leaving his rival, Tandja Mamadu with an impressive 46 per cent of the votes. A ruling triumvirate was established with Osmane of the CDS as President, Issoufou of the PNDS as Prime Minister and Djermakoye of the ANDP as President of the National Assembly.

THE CHALLENGE POSED BY THE TUAREG REBELLION

All over the world, the modern state has always had problems with nomadic populations who refuse to recognise its boundaries and Niger is no exception. The Tuaregs are currently the major challengers of the national territorial state framework in contemporary Niger. They belong to the family of the veiled Berber people who live in small isolated tribes, ranked along noble and vassal lines and spread out across the Sahara. They have sought to maintain their cultural unity through a common language, the Tamacheq. In fact, they define themselves as Kel Tamacheq, those who speak the Tamacheq language. Their history has been one of constant southern migration. The Tuaregs have often been accused of terrorising and raiding their neighbours and stealing their camels and cattle. Their traditional value system, organized around the warrior traditions of heroism, bravery and honour, has made it difficult for them to accept being subjugated. The result has been continuous attempts by the colonial and, later, the post-colonial armies to "pacify" them, attempts which they have always tried to resist.

During the regime of Seyni Kountché, the government even banned nomadism and decreed that all nomads would henceforth be considered ordinary animal rearers with no right to free movement (Adji, 1991:282). This was a direct and deliberate move to control the Tuaregs. Perhaps not surprisingly, the Tuaregs have suffered neglect by the state—very few among them are educated and their areas have benefited from very few amenities. Climatic changes have also been very devastating on their habitat. Thus, they have serious problems with both the state and nature. Matters are not helped by the fact that the political and ecological zone within which the Tuaregs operate is vast, over 1,500,000–2,000,000 square kilometres spread across five countries—Niger, Chad, Mali, Algeria and Libya (Baroun, 1985:17; Salifou, 1993:12).

There is a racial dimension to the Tuareg problem as many of them are light skinned. They have a long history of raiding their more dark skinned sedentary neighbours for slaves and booty. They have destroyed many political communities and left deep scars of resentment among many peoples. Historical memories play a large part in the widespread contemporary belief that they are the resident terrorists of the Sahara. These historical memories were jolted in 1992 by the publication of a book in Paris—*Touaregs, La Tragedie* and effective international press propaganda by Mano Dayak, a Tuareg nationalist hitherto engaged in ferrying French tourists to visit the beautiful deserts over which his compatriots commute. The book brought out in sharp focus the political and socio-economic marginalisation to which the Tuaregs are subjected. A reasoned academic response to the book was published by Andre Salifou in 1993—*La Question Touaregue au Niger*. Since then, the war of words has escalated at the same rate as the armed conflict.

In February 1994, the armed wing of the Tuareg rebellion, Coordination de la Resistance Armee (CRA), published its programme in which it argued that French nuclear power and most of Niger's resources are derived from uranium which is mined exclusively in Tuareg territory and the people of the area are completely marginalised. CRA (1994:3) claimed that two-thirds of the Nigerien land mass was Tuareg territory and announced the intention of Tuaregs to "reconquer their liberty" and punish those who had been massacring their people. They also called for an essentially federal arrangement. Since then, a number of respected Nigerien historians and academics have started a demolition job on the Tuaregs, some of which were published in a volume by their academic staff union, SNECS, under the title *Info Special* (Niamey, June 1994). In that volume, Djibo Hamani for example argues that Tuaregs are no longer real Berbers because they have been contaminated by Sudanese stock. He adds however that they cannot be accepted as autochtonous to the Central Sahara and Sudan because that is the land of the Blacks and they are of Berber origin. He adds that they have never been African nationalists because they failed to do much in the battle against French imperialist incursion at the turn of the century.

The relationship between the state and Tuaregs in Niger has deteriorated to a level of open and bitter warfare. In May 1990, there was a major military operation against the Tuaregs in which there were speculations that over 400 were massacred (*Marchés tropicaux*, 22 June 1990). The Official Report to the National Conference admitted that during one attack at Tchintabaraden, 19 people were summarily executed, 50 others were tortured to death and a considerable number of Tuareg women were raped (*Salifou, 1993:63* and *Haske*, 16 September 1991). The National Conference sought an immediate solution to the problem by dismissing the army officers involved and detaining them. A section of the army however revolted on 28 February 1992 and released the officers involved. In addition, pressure was put on the Prime Minister of the transition, Tcheffou Amadou, to remove his Tuareg Minister of the Interior, Mohammed Moussa, and on 23 March 1992, the whole cabinet was dissolved because of the crisis. The two Tuareg ministers and other high state officials were not only relieved of their functions but also detained. Amnesty International adopted one of these high Tuareg officials as one of its "Prisoners of Conscience" for 1992. He is Moctar El Incha, one of the "responsible" Tuareg elite who was appointed Prefect of Agadez in an earlier reconciliatory move which included deliberate efforts to appoint the Tuareg elite into positions of authority so they could calm down "their people". He was however detained by the army and kept in the Agadez military barracks without trial.

The Tuareg insurrection is led by a number of organizations: Front de Liberation de l'Air et de l'Azawak (FLAA), Front de Liberation du Tamouste (FLT), the Front Populaire pour la Liberation du Sahara (FPLS) and an umbrella organization, "Coordination of Armed Resistance" (CRA). The government has been negotiating with the CRA but the attempts to work out a compromise in February 1994 failed over the issue of federalism, with the government refusing to accept a federal solution. In October 1994, a partial accord was reached between the Tuaregs and the government that allowed for the negotiation in the future of a new territorial framework. Also, a three-month cease-fire which was in force was extended for another three months in January 1995. In March 1995, a crisis of leadership occurred among the Tuaregs and Dayak was removed as leader and CRA was replaced by Organisation de la Resistance Armee (ORA) under the leadership of Rhissa Ag Boula, a more radical leader with more maximalist demands. ORA reached a temporary accord with the Nigerien Government in April 1995 but the prospect of a peaceful settlement of the conflict remains bleak.

The very strong reflex which exists in Niger for a unitary state and against a federal structure has been a major stumbling block in efforts at seeking a negotiated settlement of the Tuareg problem. A major part of the political and intellectual elite in Niger refuses to take the Tuareg problem seriously. Tankoano for example dismisses Tuareg complaints about political marginalisation and constant persecution and accuses them of demanding autonomous management of their space as if autonomy is bad in itself. He adds that:

> The federalism of the rebellion is aimed at "ethnic purification" as in Bosnia. In fact, from the standpoint of territory, population and political power, the objective is the establishment of an ethnically based state in which rights and privileges are restricted to those who are considered autochtonous. (1994:59)

Others see the Tuareg problem as an illegitimate one created by foreigners Ganda, for example, has been peddling the position that:

> The so-called Tuareg rebellion is an imperialist war of destabilisation led by France with the objective of controlling the rich mineral resources of the area such as

> petroleum, natural gas, uranium and precious metals and the regions significant underground water resources which could be used for agriculture. ...The support for the rebellion was fabricated by the French intelligence service with the help of millions of French francs. (Ganda, 1994:44 and 49

He describes the leaders of the rebellion as dishonest, politically immature, racists and bandits, adjectives that are unlikely to encourage dialogue. The concern of the Nigerien elite is that the Tuaregs would try to create an autonomous Saharan state along the lines of the Organisation Commune des Regions Sahariennes (OCRS) once proposed by France.

The problem of regional autonomy and federalism cannot, however, be wished away in Niger. In October 1994, a new front was opened by the Front Démocratique du Renouveau (FDR) which started an armed uprising in the Diffa region near Lake Chad. The FDR is fighting for a federal Niger as the only solution to the marginalisation suffered since the colonial times by the eastern region in general and Kawar and Manga districts in particular. The FDR seems to be well armed, is linked to some Chadian armed factions, and has carried out a number of attacks since its formation (*Haske*, 29 November 1994).

THE FUNDAMENTALIST CHALLENGE TO THE NIGERIEN STATE

Virtually the whole population of Niger is considered Muslim with only a tiny minority of the people classified as Christians and followers of traditional African religions. Most Nigeriens share a number of social and cultural practices linked to their Islamic heritage. However, many Nigeriens are relatively recent converts to Islam, for although Islamisation started in the 8th century, it did not become widespread until the 18th and 19th centuries. Thus, many nominal Muslims have retained aspects of pre-Islamic "pagan" practices such as *bori*, the Hausa spirit possession cult. The tradition of Islam in Niger is linked largely to the tolerant mystical Sufi brotherhoods, mainly the Tijjaniyya and Quadiriyya. Most ordinary Muslims depend on religious intermediaries or *Marabouts* (Mallams) to coach them on religious practices and interpret religious texts. As is the case in Nigeria, there is a high level of competition between brotherhoods for followers.

The authoritarian regimes that have controlled Niger from the time of independence to the inauguration of an elected government closely monitored the religious establishment and allowed the various brotherhoods virtually no autonomy. The first Islamic organisation that was allowed to register was the Association Islamique du Niger (AIN) which was established in 1974 with state support. In 1988, the *decrispation* regime of Ali Saibou allowed the registration of the first Islamic magazine in the country, *Iqra*. The same year, the Iranians got state permission to open an embassy in the country. Shortly afterwards, the regime allowed the formation of autonomous Islamic associations in the country.

Islamic Organisations in Niger

Name	Date	Leadership
Association Islamique du Niger (AIN)	Sept 1974	Traditional Marabouts and "Arabisants"
Association Nigerienne Pour l'Appel et la Solidarité Islamique	July 1991	Intellectuals; "Arabisants"
Association Pour le Royanne-ment de la Culture Islamique	March 1992	Tijjaniyya Sheikhs
Association Nigerienne Pour l'Appel a l'Unite et a la Solidarité Islamique	July 1992	Traditional Marabouts
Association Pour la Diffusion de l'Islam au Niger	January 1993	Merchants
Association des Etudiants Musulmans de l'Université de Niamey	January 1993	Students

From A. M. Fari "L'Islam au Niger" in *Haske Magazine*, April 1994, p. 50.

Another important association that has recently been formed is *Adini Islama*, popularly called *Yan Izala*. It defines itself as a movement against heterodoxy and for the *Sunnah* (orthodoxy) and is similar to the Nigerian variant. Its major focus is the struggle against the mystical practices of Islamic Brotherhoods such as Tijjaniyya and Quadiriyya.

The objective of these associations is to contribute to the spread of Islam and Islamic knowledge. The major political question which this poses relates to the attitude of the organisations to political power. According to A. M. Fari (1994:48), the oldest one, the AIN, has no political objectives and is simply interested in promoting Islamic practices. It has always been close to the authorities and has been financed by succeeding governments. The other organisations which are products of democratisation, Fari argues, are much more radical and want to play a role in the direction of the affairs of state. Some of them tried to constitute themselves into political parties during the transition but the secular character of the constitution excluded them. They however managed to make an input into the constitution. On 6 September 1992, four Islamic associations sent a memorandum to the Haut Conseil de la République demanding the abrogation of the secular clause in the constitution and the insertion of a provision that reserves the posts of the Presidents of the Republic, of the National Assembly, and of the Supreme Court for Muslims. Subsequently, the word "secular" was withdrawn from the Draft Constitution and a phrase stating that all religions would be protected was substituted in its place (Kotoudi, 1993:68-71).

Some of the associations, especially the Association Nigerienne Pour l'Appel et la Solidarité Islamique (ANASI) and the Association des Etudiants Musulmans de l'Université de Niamey (AUMUN), vehemently contest the secular constraints imposed by the constitution. Radical Islam has a political project to replace the democratic regime with an Islamic polity. For the moment however, their major campaign has been against the use of condoms and allegedly sexually suggestive dressing by women. All the associations are against the "Family Code" and against family planning. On 17 November 1994, seven Islamic organisations issued a joint communiqué condemning adverts for condoms, pornography as well as birth control which they said are being encouraged in Niger as part of "a satanic plot by secular enemies of Islam" (*L'Avenir* 27 December 1994).

Religious activists have started engaging in militant activities. In January 1992, violent clashes occurred in Maradi and Zinder between Tijjaniyya and Izala militants. In April 1992, Islamic associations in Niamey led a demonstration to the City Council because the Mayor had issued a strong warning against the violent activities of religious militants. On 30 June and 17 July 1992, female students and prostitutes in Zinder were beaten up and stripped naked after being accused of being the cause of drought. The offices as well as the vehicle of the Association des Femmes du Niger were also destroyed. Throughout 1994, Islamic associations were busy dismantling billboards promoting the use of condoms.

The school system is a major centre of Islamic revivalism in Niger. The paradox is that although the country has a largely secular educational system, revivalism is very strong among the Western educated elite, especially the student community. The students' association AUMUN, argues that Islam is the sole alternative to other decadent ideologies, especially after the collapse of communism. Marxism which was the dominant ideology on campus for twenty years is fast receding and its place is being occupied by Islam. The books, magazines and cassettes now circulating on campus are green rather than red.

Over the past thirty years, there has been an attempt to integrate Western and Islamic education through the establishment of Franco-Arab schools that teach in the two languages and combine secular and religious education. There are one hundred such primary schools with 20,000 students but there is only one secondary school located in Niamey with a student population of two thousand (*Haske Magazine*, April 1994). The majority of the youth in Niger are outside the Western school system although they attend Islamic schools. There are over 45,000 Islamic schools in Niger with most of the youth in the country between the ages of five and fourteen years attending them (*Haske Magazine*, April 1994). So far, there is no link between the project of radical Islam and these children. If and when such a link occurs, the fundamentalist challenge to the secular state of Niger would be a major one. A significant part of civil society in the country is located in the religious arena. It was repressed for a long time by authoritarian regimes and has been liberated by the forces of democratisation. It is now offering an increasingly effective challenge to the liberal democratic state that is emerging in Niger.

CONCLUDING REMARKS

Niger has so far succeeded in its transition from an austere, ethnically-based and authoritarian military regime to a civilian, democratically elected pluralist regime. Nonetheless, this success does not imply the establishment of a stable and non-problematic form of liberal democratic politics in the country. There are a number of important problems which remain and which could destabilise both the state and the democratization process.

Niger is virtually bankrupt and major aspects of economic and social life have come to a standstill due to financial difficulties. Over the past two years, the state has been in arrears with salary payments in the public sector. The newly elected government was unwilling to carry out, and may be incapable of doing so, the massive cuts in salaries or in the size of the public workforce that is being demanded by international financial institutions. At the same time, new sources of funds are hard to come by. The non-payment of salaries is provoking serious social agitation as most workers in Niger are on the government wage bill. Disruptions in the educational sector have led to the cancellation of the academic year (the so-called *année blanche*) in secondary schools and the primary and tertiary sectors have also been affected. There have been major student demonstrations in May 1993 and January 1994 and there are fears that the anger of the youth might disrupt the entire democratization process.

Serious ethnic and regional tensions have accompanied the democratization process and the facade of national unity imposed by military fiat has disappeared. Ethnic groups have emerged as major political actors fighting for the control of state power and the ideal of "le Niger pour tous les Nigeriens" is under threat. However, in the long run, ethno-regionalism might play a positive role in strengthening the nation-state by broadening participation and pluralism and establishing rules for running the country. At the same time however, religious militants are actively trying to subvert the secular state and replace it with an Islamic one, a project that has not progressed much, but which has a lot of potential. Religious conflicts might become more serious than the ethno-religious one because what is at stake is not only the re-definition of the state, but also of citizenship.

The current Tuareg uprising has already imposed serious strains on the democratization process and on the stability of the state. The Tuaregs are determined to get at least a federal system and at most an independent state and the most the state is offering so far is a fairly vague promise of decentralisation. The obvious compromise between the forces of disgruntled tribes and Tuareg irredentism is federalism but too many forces are unwilling to accept that. The Tuareg rebellion, like ethno-regionalism, might play into strengthening the state by mobilising public opinion against secession and the threat of a long drawn out civil war.

The ruling Alliance collapsed in October 1994 and legislative elections were held in January 1995 in which President Ousmane's Alliance lost its parliamentary majority. The President has been very reluctant to accept the implication of this loss and has been trying to scuttle the French style cohabitation that follows the loss of parliamentary elections. The political climate is highly charged in a context in which the country's experience of democratic governance is very limited. Four different governments have already emerged in the short life of the Third Republic.

The problems confronting the Nigerien state and the democratization process are serious but not insurmountable. Niger's Third Republic has produced the first democratically elected government in the country's history. The people of Niger have suffered from dictatorship for a long time and they have learnt to hate it. More importantly, they have learnt to fight against dictatorship and for democracy. They have started learning that democracy is difficult to operate but that it is a worthwhile venture. We cannot but end on the positive note that whatever problems arise, the people of Niger will struggle to retain and advance their democratic gains.

BIBLIOGRAPHY

Adji, Souley, 1991, *Logiques Socio-communautaire et Loyautés Politiques en Afrique: Essai d'Analyse de la Construction de l'Etat au Niger*, Ph D Thesis, Bordeaux II.

Adji, Soulay, 1992, "Les Successions Politiques Legales: Mechanismes de Transfert du Pouvoir en Afrique, l'Exemple du Niger", CODESRIA Conference on Democratic Transition in Africa, Lusaka, May.

Adji, Soulay, 1994, "Approche Sociologique des Mutations au sein de la Societe Tuareg" in SNECS, *Info Special*, Niamey.

Baroun, Catherine, 1985, *Anarchie et Cohesion Sociale chez les Toubou*, Cambridge University Press, Cambridge.

Baulin, Jacques, 1986, *Conseiller du Président Diori*, Eurofor Press, Paris.

Charlick, R. B., 1991, *Niger: Personal Rule and Survival in the Sahel*, Westview Press, Dartmouth.

Coördination de la Résistance Armée, 1994, Programme–Cadre de la Résistance.

Dayak, Mano, 1992, *Touaregs, la Tragedie*, Lattes, Paris.

Fari, A. M., 1994, "L'Islam au Niger" in *Haske Magazine*, April.

Fuglestad, F., 1983, *A History of Niger: 1850–1960*, Cambridge University Press, Cambridge.

Ganda, A. W., 1994, "La Rebellion "Touaregue": Genese et Solutions" in SNECS, *Info Special*, Niamey.

Gervais, Myriam, 1993, "Etude de la pratique des ajustements au Niger et au Rwanda", *Labour, Capital and Society*, Vol 26, No 1.

Guillaument, Patrick and Sylvianne (eds.), 1991, *Ajustement Structurel, Ajustement informel: le cas du Niger*, Harmattan, Paris.

Hamani, Djibo, 1994, "Une Gigantesque Falsification de l'Histoire" in SNECS, *Info Special*, Niamey.

Hamani, Djibo, 1994, *Au Carrefour du Soudan et de la Berberi: Le Sultanat Touareg de l'Ayar*, IRSH, Niamey.

Ibrahim, Jibrin, 1992, "From Political Exclusion to Popular Participation: Democratic Transition in Niger Republic" in B. Caron et al. (eds.) *Democratic Transition in Africa*, CREDU, Ibadan.

Ibrahim, Jibrin, 1994, "Political Exclusion, Democratization and Dynamics of Ethnicity in Niger", *Africa Today*, Vol. 41, No 3.

Karimou, Mahamane, 1977, *Tradition orale et histoire: Les Mawri Zarmaphones des origines a 1898*, IRSH, Niamey.

Kotoudi, Idimama, 1993, *Transition a la Nigerienne*, Nouvelle Imprimerie du Niger, Niamey.

Koudize, Aboubacar Kio, 1991, *Chronologie politique du Niger de 1900 a nos jours*, Niamey.

Maidoka, Aboubacar, 1991, "La Constitution Nigerienne du 24 september 1989", *Revue Juridique Africaine*, No 1.

Martin, G., 1989, "Uranium: A Case Study in Franco-African Relations", *Journal of Modern African Studies*, Vol. 27 No. 4.

Niamdou-Souley, A., 1990, "Le Niger après Seyni Kountché", *Année africaine 1989*, Pedone, Bordeaux.

Osaghae, E. E., 1992, "Managing Ethnic Conflicts under Democratic Transition in Africa" in B. Caron et al. (eds.) *Democratic Transition in Africa*, CREDU, Ibadan.

Otite, O., 1990, *Ethnic Pluralism and Ethnicity in Nigeria*, Shoneson, Ibadan.

Prazauski, A., 1991, "Ethnic Conflicts in the Context of Democratising Political Systems", *Theory and Society*, No. 20.

Raynal, J.-J., 1990, "La Deuxième République de Niger: une démocratie bien ordonnée" in Penant: *Revue du Droit des Pays d'Afrique*, No. 804, October.

Saibou, Ali, 1988, *Discours et Messages, Agence Nigerienne de Presse*, Niamey.

Salifou, Andre, 1993, *La Question Touaregue au Niger*, Karthala, Paris.

Tankoano, A. and Dagra, M , 1994, "Le Programme Cadre de la Résistance et le Droit" in SNECS, *Info Special*, Niamey.

Tidjani Alou, M. S., 1992, *Les Politiques de Formation en Afrique Francophone: Ecole, Etat et Societe au Niger,* Ph D Thesis, Bordeaux.

Chapter 4

The Deepening Crisis of Nigerian Federalism and the Future of the Nation-State

Adebayo O. Olukoshi and Osita Agbu

INTRODUCTION

Will Nigeria survive? This is a question which would have sounded too academic, even subversive and unpatriotic in the thick of the euphoria that greeted the end of the Nigerian Civil War in 1970 and amidst the promise which the growth, in the 1970s, of a boom in petroleum exports and revenues generated. Indeed, following the end of the Nigerian Civil War (1967–1970), many commentators and public policy makers were to intone that the question of Nigeria's unity and territorial integrity had been solved once and for all. Typical of the confident optimism of the period was the comment by the prominent political scientist, Ali D. Yahaya, who argued that "The political future of the country as one indivisible nation is resolved with the end of the civil war ... The major political issue today is, therefore, not the unity of the country" (1982:8). For Yahaya, as for many Nigerians, the Civil War was, above everything else, Nigeria's war of national unity. The victory of the federal forces was, therefore, seen as a victory for national unity. By the beginning of the 1990s however, the mood in the country had swung decisively from one of optimism to extreme pessimism as many wondered aloud whether the "dilemma" called Nigeria can or even deserves to survive as one sovereign entity and if it does on what terms (Wright, 1986).

The renewed interest in and concern about the future unity and territorial integrity of Nigeria came to a head in the early 1990s, particularly following the annulment by the military regime of General Ibrahim Babangida (1985–1993), of the 12 June 1993 presidential elections that were supposed to mark the final stage of the Nigerian transition from military to civilian rule and into the Third Republic. But even before the 1990s, especially as the civilian-led Second Republic (1979–1983) neared its end, it was clear that Nigerian unity, or at least the basis for it, could not be taken for granted in spite of the Civil War experience of the 1960s. It was indicative of this sharp reversal in outlook and expectation that debates began to flower in academic and political circles about ways in which the country's federal system could be effectively re-structured in order to promote greater local autonomy and provide for a politically and financially weaker centre. These debates were not so much concerned with the creation of more states and local governments as with a significant reduction in the powers of the federal government in order to allow for a greater equality of access to power and resources by federating units that enjoy substantive autonomy. In other words, at the heart of the debates was the National Question especially at it pertained to the twin issues of political power and revenue allocation (Mustapha, 1986).

But beyond the debates that began to take place, events during the course of the 1980s such as the incessant disputes over the application of the principle whereby all public appointments were supposed to reflect the "federal character". conflicts, especially in the geographical north of the country, between Christians and Moslems resulting in massive destruction of property and loss of life; increasingly frequent clashes that pitched minority ethnic groups against each other and against majority groups (some of these clashes, such as the one between the Tivs and the Jukuns, became low intensity wars claiming thousands of lives); the acrimony and extreme chauvinism that accompanied the 1983 general elections (witness the "No Nation, No Destiny" broadcast on the federal radio in Kaduna); the increasing resort by the highly profligate political elite of the Second Republic to ethnic, religious, and regional forms of mobilisation; the growing centrality of religion (Islam vs. Christianity, Christian Association of Nigeria vs. Jama'atu Nasril Islam) to the national political discourse; and the return, in 1983, of the military to the centre-stage of national politics through coups and counter-/palace coups served, among other developments, to underline the continuing fragility of Nigerian unity and of the basis on which the federation has been built (Mustapha, 1986; Otite, 1990; Albert, 1993).

Reflecting on the main political trends that emerged in Nigeria during the course of the 1980s, A.R. Mustapha was to note, with justification, that, contrary to the popular perception that prevailed in the early 1970s, "The Civil War did not resolve the National Question in Nigeria. What is true is that the Nigerian state was able to overcome a specific challenge to its integrity. This does not, however, mean that no future challenges are probable, or that the state would always have the capacity to overcome such challenges" (Mustapha, 1986). This position was given concrete vindication when on 22 April 1990, a group of middle-ranking Nigerian military officers, mostly made up of ethnic minorities from northern and southern Nigeria, attempted, unsuccessfully, to overthrow the increasingly authoritarian Babangida regime and expel seven states, predominantly populated by Hausa-Fulanis, from the Nigerian federation allegedly because of their unwillingness to live and work with other members of the federation as equals. The arbitrary annulment of the 1993 presidential elections by the military regime of General Babangida and the repercussions of that action served to further exacerbate the political tensions that had been building

up in the country from the end of the 1970s and which increasingly got concrete
expression in the massive resurgence of ethnic, regional, and religious forms of
popular political identity and in the growth as well as emboldening of movements either for ethnic separatism or for the drastic reconfiguration of the Nigerian federation as it is presently constituted. The crude despotism of the military junta of General Sani Abacha and the fascistic, chauvinistic malevolence of
his regime have served to further complicate matters. Clearly, at no time since
the end of the Nigerian Civil War has there been so massive a loss of faith in the
Nigerian nation-state as in the period leading up to and following the annulment of the 1993 presidential elections.

Our objective in this chapter is to identify and analyse some of the concerns
that have arisen about the nation-state in Nigeria in the period since the annulment by the Babangida regime of the 12 June 1993 presidential elections. In
doing this, we will also attempt to assess the response by the state to the challenges which it has had to contend with since the cancellation of the election
results. While many of the challenges pre-date the 1993 elections, the cancellation of the election results and the return of the country to full military rule after
the overthrow, on 17 November 1993, of the Interim National Government set
up by Babangida on 26 August 1993, served to give them greater focus and
relevance. We argue that against the background of the numerous problems of
governance that have afflicted post-independence Nigeria, problems which
have tended to accentuate the National Question and undermine the country's
fragile unity, it is entirely misplaced to view with negative suspicion, as
Nigeria's rulers instinctively do, all demands for a possible restructuring of the
nation-state. With the failure of administrative fiat and military force to oblit-
erate the National Question from the national political discourse, and with the
social question gaining in significance as the continuing national economic
crisis takes its toll, we also argue that only a democratic solution, pursued in a
political framework that is open, unfettered by the state, fully representative,
and based on elected governmental power holds any promise of enabling the
country to manage the deepening crisis of its federalism.

THE NATIONAL QUESTION AND NIGERIAN FEDERALISM

No discussion of contemporary Nigerian politics in general and the deepening
crisis of Nigerian federalism in particular can be complete without close attention to the National Question. Indeed, many students of Nigerian history and
politics have argued, with justification, that at the root of the country's recurring and worsening crisis of governance and development is the failure to
evolve an effective and democratic mechanism for managing the National
Question (Toyo, 1975; Nnoli, 1980; Usman, 1980; Mustapha, 1986). As a multi-
ethnic society characterised by deep-seated social inequality, uneven territorial
development, and a variety of other forms of potentially destabilizing popular

identity, including, especially, religious identities (Islam and Christianity each have a wide following), it should not be surprising that the National Question occupies so central a place in the national political process (Otite, 1990; Nnoli, 1980; Onoge, 1993; Udogu, 1994).

Prior to the arrival of the forces of British colonialism in the area that they were later to constitute into Nigeria, the various nationalities that are today part of the country were at various levels of development ranging from the communal to the feudalistic. They were organised into a variety of polities that were based increasingly on territoriality and occupation and less on simple blood ties and language (Mustapha, 1986). The shabby welding together of the different nationalities by the British first into the Protectorates of Northern and Southern Nigeria and then, in 1914, following the amalgamation proclamation, into one united colony which was administered from Lagos took place in a framework in which competing ethnicities, regionalisms, and religious identities flowered without an adequate structural mechanism for managing them. This was partly a result of the colonial policy of divide and rule which was as important to the sustenance and prolongation of direct British rule as to the creation and maintenance of British neo-colonial influence. But it was also the result of the extremely arbitrary and inherently unaccountable exercise of power by the colonial authorities. Thus, by 1960 when Nigeria attained independence, it did so in a context in which there were influential and competing centres of power whose perception of one another and of national matters was increasingly coloured by ethnic, regional and religious considerations as the struggle for access to and control of resources intensified. These considerations and the concrete political forms which they took culminated in the collapse of the First Republic (1960–1966) and in the onset of the Civil War.

As we noted earlier, the Civil War did not resolve the National Question in Nigeria. In fact, in many important respects, the attempt by the political elite and the state to prevent the recurrence of such a bloody conflict merely fudged the Question and complicated it further with the consequence that today, Nigeria appears to be far less united politically than ever before and the spectre of disintegration continues to haunt the country with dire consequences for its developmental prospects. Mustapha (1986) has identified a series of eight overlapping contradictions by which the National Question manifests itself in contemporary Nigeria. They include the contradiction between Nigeria and imperialism; the contradiction among the three major nationalities (Hausa, Igbo and Yoruba) which each dominated the tripodal regional structure that served as the basis for the First Republic and which are in the forefront of the struggle for the control of federal power; the contradiction between the three major nationalities on the one hand and the smaller nationalities on the other, i.e., the majority versus the minorities; the rivalry and sometimes bitter disharmony among the ever-growing number of states that have made up the federation in the period since the dissolution of regional administrations in 1967; inter-ethnic rivalries in states of the federation with a mixture of ethnic groups such as between the Nupe and Hausa in Niger State or the Tiv and Idoma in Benue State or the Urhobo and Itshekiri in Delta State; inter-sectional rivalries within the same ethnic group or nationality, such as between the Egba and Ijebu or Ife and Modakeke or Kano and Sokoto; and inter-clan rivalries within particular provinces or districts as is common in parts of south-eastern Nigeria.

These contradictions have been reproduced as an integral part of the capital-ist class formation process in post-colonial Nigeria, serving to mediate and temper the integrating effects of the capitalist development process itself and of the construction of a national market. Thus, to cite one example, the construc-tion of the north-south rail link during the first two decades of colonial rule resulted in a flow of population in various directions as a national market began to emerge. However, the pattern of settlement that accompanied this develop-ment resulted in the creation in various parts of the country of a host of *sabos* which served to distinguish the "new" settlers from the host/"indigenous" communities. Thus in northern Nigeria, *sabon garis* were created and predomi-nantly settled by non-Hausa populations. In the west and east of the country, the *sabos* were mostly inhabited by settler Hausa trading communities. In the worst cases, these *sabos* became almost enclave-type settlements that took on definite ethnic/religious patterns which made them easy targets during periods of political unrest; they have been the main theatres of inter-ethnic and religious clashes in Nigeria since the 1950s.

If the capitalist development process in Nigeria has been mediated and influenced by the content and pattern of the National Question, the capitalist accumulation process has, in turn, shaped and re-shaped the contradictions that underly the Question itself, sometimes giving them new meanings and contexts. The contradictions have also been exacerbated by the very uneven process of capitalist development in the country, the deepening social inequalities that have been a defining feature of the capitalist accumulation process, and the extremely poor and deteriorating quality of leadership and governance in post-independence Nigeria. As we shall argue later, nothing better underlines this crisis of leadership and governance than the fact that the military have ruled the country for most of the post-independence period. The fallout from this has, *inter alia*, included the increasing concentration and centralization of power in the federal centre and, in the period since the onset of the national economic crisis in the early 1980s, the growing personalization of that power in a succes-sion of despotic military rulers.

Furthermore, the contradictions that lie at the heart of the National Question in Nigeria have been complicated by the increasing centrality of religious iden-tities to the political process (Ibrahim, 1991; Williams and Falola, 1995). This has been particularly so in cases and situations where contradictions between members of a major ethnic group and a minority nationality have been rein-forced by religious differences. The example of the repeated and very costly clashes between the Moslem Hausa and Christian Kuteb in the Zangon Kataf area is a case in point. But there are also cases where Igbo traders, who mostly claim a Christian religious identity, have been pitched against Moslem Hausas in such urban centres as Kano (Albert, 1993). Intra-Moslem factional fights have also been frequent occurrences in northern Nigeria involving members of the same ethnic group. More recently however, tensions have built up to dangerous levels between Moslem Yorubas in/from south-western Nigeria and Moslem Hausas. The religious factor also plays a part in reinforcing the North-South contradiction and has been deployed in the arguments over the secular status of the state as well as the nature of the federal judicial structure. As we shall see later, the 12 June 1993 presidential elections and their subsequent annulment by the military government of General Babangida contained elements of most of the major contradictions that underly the manifestation of the National Question in post-colonial Nigeria. It also had/acquired a religious dimension.

BACKGROUND CONTEXT TO THE 1993 PRESIDENTIAL ELECTIONS

In order for a full understanding to be gained of the deepening crisis of Nigerian federalism which the annulment of the 12 June 1993 presidential elections brought to a head, it is necessary to have a proper appreciation of the background context that increasingly shaped political attitudes in the country from the early 1980s onwards. In this regard, two major and inter-related factors appear to us to be the most crucial. They are the sharp deterioration from 1981 onwards in Nigeria's economic fortunes and the worsening crisis of governance in the country most vividly symbolised by the return of the military to power in 1983. To forestall a misunderstanding: Many of the problems that lie at the heart of Nigeria's federal crisis pre-date the 1980s and although the post-Civil War euphoria that enveloped much of the country as well as the revenue explosion of the oil boom years helped, temporarily, to sweep them under the carpet, they were always there, waiting to re-assert themselves. In our view, the onset of a major crisis in the Nigerian economy in the early 1980s combined with the increasingly authoritarian and clientelist structures of political governance that were consolidated during the 1980s in the framework of diminishing state legitimacy helped to accelerate the process by which the hitherto latent contradictions in Nigeria's federal structure re-asserted themselves forcefully.

Economic Decline, Structural Adjustment and the Crisis of the Federal State

The origins and dimensions of the Nigerian economic crisis which began in the early 1980s have already been fully debated in Nigeria and so need not detain us here Olukoshi, 1990, 1991, 1993b; Usman and Bangura, 1984). Suffice it to note that it is generally agreed that the crisis is by far the most serious which the country has experienced. Its most direct manifestation has taken the form of a drastic fall in federal receipts from oil exports, from an average of some 10 billion dollars annually in the 1970s to about five billion dollars annually in the 1980s and 1990s, at a time when the country had become a virtual monocultural economy depending on oil exports for over 90 per cent of its foreign exchange earnings and revenues. The collapse of the receipts accruing to the state from oil exports not only created a major fiscal crisis for the state by undermining the revenue base of the federal and state governments, it also severely disrupted all sectors of public and private economic activity in the country given the economy's heavy dependence on imported inputs. In time, the economic difficulties facing the country also triggered an external debt and payments crisis which has led to frequent boycotts of the country by the international financial and donor communities. Furthermore, the economic crisis exacted massive social costs not only in terms of the gradual decay of social institutions but also in terms of collapsing incomes and rising unemployment.

Various attempts were made during the course of the 1980s to contain the deepening economic crisis culminating, by 1986, in the adoption by the military government of General Babangida of an International Monetary Fund (IMF) / World Bank structural adjustment programme (SAP). At the heart of the adjustment programme was the quest for national economic stabilisation and recovery through the simultaneous liberalisation of the market and the retrenchment of the state. This entailed the drastic and repeated devaluation of the naira as well as the floating of the currency, the liberalisation of prices, the liberalisation of interest rates, the abolition of commodity boards, the withdrawal of real and imagined subsidies, the liberalisation of trade, the privatisation and commercialisation of public enterprises, the rationalisation and reform of the civil service, and the introduction of user charges, among other measures. It is widely recognised by students of the Nigerian political economy that, for a variety of reasons, the adjustment programme not only failed to stabilise the economy but also quickly became an integral part of the unfolding dynamic of Nigeria's economic decline. Indeed, structural adjustment served, in many important respects, to complicate the problems of the Nigerian economy (Olukoshi, 1993b).

Insofar as the consequences of the dynamic of economic crisis and structural adjustment for Nigerian politics are concerned, it is possible to point to a number of inter-related trends whose combined effect was to deepen the crisis of the country's federalism. At one level, the diminishing revenue base of the federal government and, therefore of the other layers of government, following the collapse of the world oil market immediately triggered pressures for a drastic revision of the country's revenue allocation formula in order to ensure that those states/communities that contributed the most to the centrally collectible revenue (in this case the oil producing states of mid-western and south-eastern Nigeria) got a greater share of revenue than those that were regarded as contributing little or nothing. This position was further justified not only on the grounds of "natural justice" (those communities under whose soil oil is found should get a "fairer", if not a greater share of the petro-dollars accruing from the exploitation and exportation of the resource) but also on the basis of the fact that the process of oil exploration and production was wreaking environmental havoc in the oil-producing states and destroying all other forms of economic activity, especially fishing and farming. This view was successfully canvassed by the defunct Bendel State government at the Supreme Court, resulting in the nullification of the revenue allocation formula adopted by the Shagari regime following the submission of the Okigbo Commission report. During the course of the 1980s, it became closely linked to a perceived marginalisation from national political affairs and patronage by many of the peoples of the south-east and the oil delta.

By the early 1980s, the oil communities, most of them peopled by the minority ethnic nationalities of south-eastern Nigeria, had become restive, pressing the federal government for a greater share of the country's diminishing oil revenues, a halt to their marginalisation from the federal political/power structure, compensation for increasing environmental damage, and a halt to all exploration and production activities with a potential for causing more damage. They declared themselves to be totally dissatisfied with the token gestures made by the federal government to address their concerns and grievances, such as the formation of an Oil Mineral Producing Areas Development Commission (OMPADEC). One outcome of the mobilisation of the oil producing communities was the creation of the Ethnic Minorities Organisation of Nigeria (EMIRON) and a host of other minority ethnic associations. The most important of these associations is the Movement for the Survival of the Ogoni People (MOSOP) which not only successfully got itself recognised by the United Nations as a representative of an endangered ethnic minority but also directly took on the federal government and the oil multinationals, led by Shell, which are active in Ogoni land. EMIRON and MOSOP were to be at the forefront of the debate in the 1990s about the reconfiguration of the Nigerian federation.

Apart from the intensification of the struggle among the different constituent political units and nationalities in Nigeria for greater access to the revenues accruing to the federal state from oil exports and the challenges to the existing structure of the nation-state which this gradually entailed, the drastic decline in the economic fortunes of a majority of Nigerians and the vigorous attempts made at retrenching the state, including especially its social expenditures, had the effect of further de-legitimising a state whose legitimacy has, for most of the colonial and post-colonial periods, been a fragile one. SAP initially made its entry into the Nigerian economic crisis management strategy, as elsewhere in Africa, on the basis of a distinct anti-statism which cared little about national public institutions and the role they could play not only in quantifiable developmental terms but also in the formation of national identity and consciousness. Rather, public institutions and state capacity were assailed and consciously undermined on the basis of the flawed perception that they were the privileged domain of urban "parasitic" and "vested" interests that had to be mercilessly dismantled or neutralised. Not surprisingly, the main social actors associated with the Nigerian public sector, especially workers and professionals have borne the brunt of the adjustment process not only in terms of the collapse of their incomes and the deterioration of their working environment, but also in terms of their retrenchment on a large scale and the diminution of opportunities for them to realise their aspirations. As Bangura and Beckman (1991) have noted, the assault on these groups as part of the adjustment process was simultaneously an assault on the project of nation-building since the groups "tend to belong to the most nationally-oriented segments of society, concerned with the unity of (the) national territory..." (Beckman, 1993).

The legitimacy of the post-colonial Nigerian state, closely interwoven with the anti-colonial nationalist project, rested in part on the promise of the delivery of core social services to the generality of the people. The social expenditure of the state which increased dramatically during the oil boom years came under severe attack during the 1980s both before and especially after the adoption of SAP (Ihonvbere, 1993). Furthermore, the introduction of all manner of cost recovery measures even as the country's social infrastructure declined combined with the increasingly authoritarian/despotic mode of governance in the country to alienate many Nigerians from the state and its institutions. Matters were not helped in this regard by the worsening problems of corruption and clientelism in the framework of a frenetic "primitive" accumulation of capital. As the national economic crisis deepened and the military government of General Babangida attempted to push ahead with an adjustment programme that was unpopular and which was widely seen as a foreign imposition, so too did the authoritarianism of the regime, which SAP helped to reinforce, tend to narrow the space for a national participatory debate on the country's economic and political direction and future. Many Nigerians felt increasingly alienated by this state of affairs and from the affairs of their country.

Reflecting on the drastic decline in the social expenditure of the state and the virtual collapse of public institutions generally and social institutions in particular, Ihonvbere (1994) and Ekekwe (1988) concluded that the Nigerian state had become an "irrelevant" state insofar as the social aspirations of most Nigerians are concerned. Elsewhere, scholars like Azarya and Chazan (1987) have written about a process of "disengagement" by a variety of groups from the state in a process which is seen as strengthening civil society and thus democratisation or its projects. Setting aside the conceptual difficulties that inhere in the notion of the "irrelevant" state and "disengagement" and the contentious conclusions which their advocates have drawn from them (Gibbon, 1992; Gibbon *et al.*, 1992), it is clear that the resurgence of ethnic and community associations which has been observed in Nigeria during the 1980s is partly a response to the social crisis associated with economic decline and structural adjustment in the 1980s (Adekanye, 1995; Osaghae, 1995). So too is the rapid mushrooming of Christian pentecostalist and Moslem revivalist groups as a variety of people seek to fill the increasing emptiness which they feel in their lives and cope with the challenges of a process of rapid social fragmentation/

dislocation that has taken its toll on the family and national solidarity (Bangura, 1994; Marshall, 1991; Williams and Falola, 1995).

A host of non-governmental organizations has also emerged in the social arena in Nigeria to fulfil functions which the state has abandoned wholly or partially or which it is increasingly incapable of effectively undertaking. Informal sector strategies and frameworks for alternative social provisioning have, in addition, been in evidence (Mustapha, 1992b; Meagher, 1995). The adoption by a variety of social actors of multiple modes of livelihood which lead them to straddle the formal and informal sectors has also had implications for conventional forms of popular mobilisation that entail a strong reliance on full time formal sector employees. Multiple livelihood strategies in the context of increasing social fragmentation and the flowering of ethno-religious identities have tended to undermine national territorial political forms whilst encouraging particularistic tendencies.

The strengthening of ethnic and religious identities in the framework of the social consequences of economic crisis and structural adjustment has exacerbated the legitimacy crisis of the state. Inter-ethnic clashes, with very costly consequences in terms of lives lost and properties destroyed, have been a recurring feature of politics in Nigeria during the 1980s and 1990s. So too have challenges to the authority of some state governments (especially in northern Nigeria) and the federal government by Moslem groups that mobilise their followers (mostly unemployed youths, lumpen proletariats, and poor peasants) to reject all temporal authority and directives and laws emanating from them. The authoritarian response of successive Nigerian governments, from the civilian government of Shehu Shagari (1979–1983) to the military governments of Muhammadu Buhari (1983–1985), Ibrahim Babangida (1985–1993) and Sani Abacha (1993–), to the challenges posed by growing ethnic and religious identities has only served to worsen the legitimacy crisis of the state. Matters have not also been helped by the increasingly narrow ethnic /regional base on which successive governments have either rested from the outset or retreated into in the face of political pressures. This, in turn, has heightened the sense of exclusion, marginalisation, isolation, and discrimination among some ethnic and religious groups in the country.

Deepening Crisis of Governance and the Problems of Nigerian Federalism

Beyond the consequences which economic crisis and structural adjustment have had for Nigerian federalism and the nation-state, the worsening problem of governance in the country has been another major factor in the build up of pressures for the reconfiguration of the federation (Mustapha, 1992a). The crisis of governance in Nigeria has manifested itself not just in terms of the fact that the military have ruled the country for 25 out of 35 years of independence and seven out of the ten heads of government/state which the country has had have been serving military officers, but also in terms of the increasingly dysfunctional effects of a burgeoning system of "primitive" accumulation in which public officials and private sector economic agents with access to the state take extreme liberties with the public purse at the local and national levels. Corruption, an integral but by no means exclusive factor in the bourgeois class formation process, has, in the public perception at least, seemingly acquired the status of a directive principle of Nigerian state policy as a succession of elected and unelected/self-appointed rulers have looted public funds and, in a lot of cases, siphoned most of their loot out of the country, spending whatever they have retained in the country on luxuries (Ibrahim, 1988; 1989). It is not difficult to see the de-legitimising political effects of "primitive" accumulation in a situation where an increasing number of households are faced with the daily task of eeking out a living from their diminishing real income. "Primitive" accumulation, widely called "settlement" or *egunje* in the popular political parlance of the Nigeria of the 1980s and 1990s, was developed into an art form by the Babangida regime which, of all post-colonial Nigerian governments, was also seen as creating one of the most elaborate structures of patron-clientelism in the institutions of the state and in society, further weakening them in the process.

One fallout from the crisis of governance in Nigeria has been the increasing concentration and centralization of economic and political power and responsibility in a country which attained independence in 1960 as a fairly loose federal system. The independence constitution provided for three strong regional governments with wide economic and social powers as well as a significant political leverage. The federal government's only areas of exclusive jurisdiction were defence, the printing and circulation of a national currency, and the conduct of foreign policy. In the period from 1967 onwards, this division of responsibility and powers between the federal government and the other units of the federation, imperfect though it was, was gradually eroded until all effective power became centralized and concentrated in the federal centre. At the heart of this process of concentration and centralization was the state creation exercise that began in 1967 and which was repeated in 1976, 1987, and 1991.

Initially aimed partly at blunting the secessionist pressures that were building up in the old Eastern Region and at meeting legitimate minority ethnic pressures for an autonomous space of their own within which they could promote their developmental aspirations unencumbered by the tyranny of the majority ethnic groups that dominated the independence regional system, state creation soon became a self-multiplying exercise that gradually negated the basis for an effective federal system. In addition to promoting the centralization/concentration of power, the exercise failed increasingly to resolve the minority problem for the simple reason that the effort to solve the minority problem by creating states created new majorities and minorities in the new states. The "solution" increasingly became a problem that was assuming the dimensions of a vicious circle as no attention was paid to the development of a framework for the protection of minority rights in the states that were created, a major irony as it was this omission in the regional system that fuelled minority opposition to its continuation.

The state governments that replaced the regional structures on the basis of which Nigeria was ushered into independence are a miserable shadow of their predecessors, enjoying no effective autonomy and being almost all totally dependent on federal budgetary handouts for their survival. Whereas the regional governments of the 1960s could survive financially without federal financial allocations, the state governments that replaced them found themselves relying on the federal authorities to pick up their wage and salary obligations to their workers. As the scope of the federal might expanded, so too did the arena of state government power shrink. Every round of state creation in post-Civil War Nigeria resulted in a further centralization of the country's governance and the diminishing viability of the state government as an effective and genuinely representative unit of governance in a federal system. It is needless to say that in this situation, the system of local governance was, for all intents and purposes, non-existent even though many new local governments have been created in the country since the mid-1970s. In effect, post-Civil War Nigeria increasingly became a unitary state or, at least, a federal state more in appellation and less in essence.

The increasing centralization and concentration of power in the federal centre is, as we noted earlier, partly a result of the attempt first, to weaken the secessionist pressures that eventually led to the Nigerian Civil War and then of the conscious bid that informed post-Civil War political engineering to prevent the re-emergence of powerful regional centres that could challenge the federal state. The logic of the oil economy that emerged and boomed in the 1970s also contributed to the dynamic of centralization and concentration, providing the federal authorities, under a re-constructed revenue allocation formula that favoured them,with the resources which they required to finance their ever-growing scope of responsibility and the increasing pressures for federal patronage. So too did the imperatives of the process of the "primitive" accumulation of capital contribute to the logic of the centralization and concentration of power in the federal goverment.

One other factor which has been much ignored in the literature on Nigerian federalism but which is very crucial both by itself and in terms of its impact on the political engineering of the immediate pre- and most of the post-Civil War period is the fact of prolonged military rule in Nigeria. It is not often sufficiently recognised in most analyses of post-Civil War Nigerian politics that the military have wielded power for 21 out of the 25 years since the end of the war. This reality has left its imprint on the polity generally and on the attempts to re-model the federal structure inherited at independence in particular. In brief, the various attempts at re-modelling Nigerian federalism have been undertaken almost exclusively by a succession of military regimes all of which were completely oblivious of the need to devolve power and enhance accountability and representativeness in a multi-ethnic, multi-religious society. Where they had to tackle important socio-economic and political problems, their overall response was simply to strengthen the hand of the federal centre and, in so doing, weaken the other administrative units of the federation (Suberu, 1993; Olowu, 1991).

Like the military in most parts of the world, the Nigerian armed forces operate a centralized command structure which their years of involvement in the political arena has transferred into the administration of the country. The structure of governance which they have encouraged is one which is based on a hierarchy of tiers of government in which the federal government is pre-eminent and the state and local governments are subordinate. The chain of command in the federal arrangement they promoted assumed the flow of instructions and mandates from the top to the bottom. This centralized approach to managing the federal set up inevitably meant that local autonomy and attempts at building/strengthening it were viewed suspiciously and stifled. Local/community initiatives, especially those that appeared to have political undertones, were discouraged as part of the military's self-appointed role of being the guardians of national unity. The authoritarianism that inheres in the promotion of a project of centralization was reinforced by the equally authoritarian nature of military rule itself. Military rule in Nigeria built on and extended the repressive legacy of British colonialism in the country. With the onset of a national economic crisis that resulted in an acute fiscal payments, and debt crisis for the federal state, and with the diminishing capacity of the federal state to carry out its self-assigned social and economic obligations even as the various state and local governments sank into an even worse economic quagmire, the over-concentration of power and responsibility in the federal government and the high centralization of the federal system became increasingly suffocating and dysfunctional, obstructing the attempts by various groups to recapture some space for themselves (Suberu, 1993).

Attempts during the 1980s to pass back some responsibilities to state and local governments by the federal government were driven more by the desire of the federal authorities to lessen the financial burden which they had to carry and less by the need for a far-reaching reform of the federal system. With the state and local governments so financially weak as to be practically insolvent in many cases, the federal government was compelled to claim back some of the responsibilities and provide supplementary funds to the two other tiers of government to enable them to meet the cost of primary and secondary school education, for example. In effect, even as the Nigerian economic crisis deepened, the centralized essence of the country's structure of governance was reinforced. Federal power therefore remained the main attractive and profitable power in the country worth struggling over and, increasingly, it became a bitter struggle to the finish. Struggles for access to federal power and for the retention of federal power as well as the privileges of office therefore intensified even as those nationalities that felt marginalised from the federal centre campaigned, increasingly openly, for autonomy and the reform of the federal system. We have already cited the example of EMIRON and MOSOP. A whole host of other groups was created under a variety of umbrellas with agenda that, to a greater or lesser extent, aimed to draw attention to the perceived marginalisation of some nationalities from the federal centre and federal patronage and canvass reforms that they felt would redress the situation.

Group Disaffection and the Quest for a Re-Structuring of the Federation

Among the many groups that were created to promote either regional or ethnic interests or a wider, more secularly-based reformation of the federal set up were the Middle Belt Forum, the Eastern Mandate Union (EMU), the Western Consultative Group, the Northern Elders Forum, the *Egbe Afenifere*, the Movement for National Reformation (MNR), the *Ndigbo*, and, of course, MOSOP and EMIRON. The issues which dominated the discourse of most of the groups included ways of ensuring that federal political power is equally accessible to all Nigerian nationalities which should also be allowed to have their own political and economic space in a radically restructured federation in which the power of the federal state is reduced. Vociferous demands were also made for a greater balance between the north and the south of Nigeria in the leadership of the country, in the distribution of political and parastatal offices, and the economic benefits accruing to the country. Furthermore, arguments for and against a secular federal system and federal judiciary were tabled as were demands for a greater balance between the Christians and Moslems both in the headship of the federal government and in key military command appointments. Some groups even went so far as to canvass the re-regionalisation of the Nigerian Police Force as well as the regionalisation of the armed forces as part of a strategy both for giving substance to regional autonomy as well as preventing the all too frequent intervention of the military in politics. Strong views were expressed in support of and against the use of the principle of derivation as the sole or main criterion for the allocation of revenue.

There is much in the plethora of views that were canvassed that was both useless and useful, democratic and anti-/non-democratic but whatever view we may hold of them, they reflected the changing mood in the country for a far-reaching programme of reform. The financial profligacy and political wrecklessness of the Babangida military regime only served to reinforce the necessity for reform and, in time, a host of professional associations and interest groups whose members still had an objective interest in defending a pan-Nigeria national-territorial agenda began publicly to push the case for the convening of a sovereign national conference to discuss the entire basis on which the Nigerian federation is built and to reform it in such a way that it would promote democratic accountability, greater participation in national and sub-national affairs by a majority of the people, the creative channelling of the energies of the people for national reconstruction and development, and the enhancement of the basis for national unity. Among the interest groups and professionals which were at the forefront of the campaign for a sovereign national conference were those represented by the Nigeria Labour Congress (NLC) and a majority of its 42 affiliate unions, the National Association of Nigerian Students (NANS), the Academic Staff Union of Universities (ASUU), the National Association of Democratic Lawyers (NADL), the Civil Liberties Organisation (CLO), Women in Nigeria (WIN), the Constitutional Rights Project (CRP), the Concerned Professionals (CP), the Nigerian Medical Association (NMA), and the Committee for the Defence of Human Rights (CDHR), among others. Several of these groups were affiliate members of the Campaign for Democracy (CD) that was at the forefront of the struggle against the continuation of General Babangida and the military in power following the annulment of the 1993 presidential elections (Olukoshi, 1993b, 1994).

The campaign by professional associations and interest groups (like labour, students, and academics) with a national-territorial agenda was taken up by some of the organizations that had been set up to canvass the reformation of the federal system on the basis of autonomous nationalities in a political arrangement that involves a reduction in the powers, competences and responsibilities of the federal centre. Particularly prominent in this regard were the MNR (1993) and EMIRON/MOSOP. The various groups and interests were united, partly at least, by an extreme distrust of the military government of General Babangida in whose programme of transition to civilian rule they had little or no faith. This loss of faith in the Babangida regime related as much to their distrust of its intention to hand over federal power to an elected federal executive as to their loss of faith in the capacity of the regime particularly, and the Nigerian military in general, to champion a systematic reform of the federation to permit a greater input in decision-making by the people. The tempo of the campaign for a sovereign national conference grew with the increasing arbitrariness with which the Babangida regime conducted the transition programme. The programme itself was cumulatively discredited with every round of postponement of the date for the handing over of executive power to an elected president. Such was the extent to which the tempo for genuine reformation of Nigerian politics, economy, and society had built up that not even the election of a civilian president could have blunted the demand for a national conference of one sort or the other.

It was a mark of the groundswell of pressures that had built up in favour of the restructuring of the federal arrangement in the country that a group of retired senior civil servants (the so-called super-permanent secretaries) from the Yakubu Gowon years (1967–1975), who could justly claim to be as much a part of the task of keeping Nigeria united during the Civil War years as the military commanders who conducted the combat operations of the federal war effort, teamed up with some senior technocrats and influential private sector managers to also argue the case for a national conference to be superintended by a transitional government of some sort. Unlike the professionals and popular interest groups to which we referred earlier, they did not however insist on a sovereign status for the conference they were calling for, a point which marred efforts to produce a common agenda and platform between these "technocrats" and the "radicals". The response of the increasingly discredited regime of General Babangida was first to ban all public debate on Nigeria's political future and then to appoint a "transitional" government after the highly un-popular and bitterly contested postponement, for the third time, of the terminal date for the disengagement of the military from power. Some of the "techno-crats" were absorbed into the transitional cabinet but this did not deter the "radicals" from carrying on with their campaign for a sovereign national conference.

Thus it was that by the time the 12 June, 1993 presidential elections were taking place, Nigeria was confronted by the resurgence of the National Question with all of the contradictions by which it manifests itself, including a deepening social crisis. Inevitably, the Question loomed large over the manoeuvring in various parts of the country for the succession to the presi-dency even as the possibility of that succession was repeatedly called into question by the increasingly clumsy management of General Babangida's "hidden agenda" to cling on to power. Among other moves, General Babangida and his military and civilian aides sponsored a variety of shadowy groups, not least among them the Association for a Better Nigeria (ABN) led by Arthur Nzeribe, to disrupt and discredit the only remaining part of the already heavily manipulated transition programme, namely, the election of a president. The failure of General Babangida's manoeuvrings to prevent the election from taking place after the National Electoral Commission (NEC) decided, on the basis of existing legislation earlier enacted by none other than General Babangida himself, that it was not bound by a late night court ruling given after regular court hours stopping the elections, set the immediate context for the subsequent annulment of the vote. The suit that sought to prevent the election from taking place was filed at the request of Arthur Nzeribe and the ruling by the judge was given less than 24 hours to the polling day although the presiding judge added in her written judgement that NEC was not bound by her ruling.

THE 12 JUNE 1993 PRESIDENTIAL ELECTIONS

The 12 June 1993 presidential elections were meant to be the last stage in a tortuous, heavily manipulated, and increasingly dubious transition from mili-tary to civilian rule (Olukoshi, 1993b; Campbell, 1994). The transition process began in 1986 with the launching of a political debate in the country, the subse-quent convening of a constituent assembly to write a new constitution, and the holding of some elections on the basis of a two-party system designed and imposed by the military regime of General Babangida. Not only did the government create the two parties which were allowed to contest the election, it also wrote their constitutions and manifestos, gave them their names—Social Democratic Party (SDP) and National Republican Convention (NRC), built their offices, funded their activities, and provided their initial secretariat staff. By the time the presidential elections were held in June 1993, the majority of the electorate had grown weary of the gimmicks of the Babangida junta and their cynical manipulation of the entire transitional process as part of General Babangida's elaborate but increasingly not-so-hidden bid to hold on to power and office. In pursuit of his ambition to remain in power, General Babangida had not only postponed the terminal date for the transition to military rule three times, he had also repeatedly banned and unbanned many politicians with every round of postponement of the terminal date for the inauguration of the Third Republic until the criteria for participation and non-participation in the electoral process became completely blurred.

Against the background of a deepening national economic crisis, a transition to civil rule programme from which many Nigerians increasingly felt alienated, a military regime that had shown itself to be even more corrupt than the politicians who dominated the Second Republic and which by the sheer scale of its corruption discredited the military as an institution, and a political elite that remained steeped in its opportunistic ways, Nigerians of various classes began to seek alternative avenues for promoting change in the country. We have already referred to the growing movement for a national conference of one kind or the other and to the pressures that had built up for a radical re-structuring of the federation. One common denominator of all of the pressures that were building up for change was the increasing determination, shared across the country, to ensure that General Babangida and his clique did not perpetuate themselves in power. More generally, on account of the record in office of General Babangida, the military came increasingly to be perceived as a veritable obstacle to national political and economic development. It was widely agreed that Nigeria could only begin to get out of the political and economic morass into which it had sunk with the departure of the military from power (Nwolise, 1990).

If the national mood for change was strong, there was no nationally acceptable consensus on how the succession to the military would be undertaken. In particular, there was disagreement among the political elites on the part of the country from which the successor to General Babangida should come. Among politicians from the south of the country, the position was widely canvassed, through a host of consultative fora, that the time had come for the south to be given a chance to field candidates for the presidency. This was thought to be necessary because six out of the eight heads of government/state that the country had had in the period up to the end of 1992 were from the defunct Northern Region. In the most influential political circles in northern Nigeria, however, the idea that it was the turn of the south to produce the next president was stoutly rejected. Instead, some northern Nigerian politicians took the view that the position should be left open to whoever was best qualified for it irrespective of his place of origin. Of course, in their calculations, this position offered them the best chance of winning the struggle for the highest political office in the country on account of the fact that the north had more constituency seats and enjoys a slight demographic/electoral advantage over the south based on the census figures that were in use in the country. The view was also expressed that since the south of Nigeria is more economically developed/advantaged than the north, the latter has to play a leading role in the political terrain. Both in the north and in the south, politicians from the minority ethnic groups also staked their own claim to the presidency, insisting that it was their turn to lead the country. For this purpose, the northern and southern minorities formed their own consultative bloc and presented themselves as the credible alternative that could save Nigeria from the interminable bickerings of the big three ethnic groups, bickerings that had brought the country to the brink several times.

At the conventions of the SDP and the NRC to select their candidates for the presidential election, M.K.O. Abiola was chosen by the former while B.O. Tofa was selected by the latter. For running mate, Tofa, who is a self-professed Moslem from Kano, in the geographical north, selected S. Ugoh, a self-professed Christian from the east while Abiola, a self-professed Moslem from Ogun State in the southwest, selected B. G. Kingibe, a self-professed Moslem from the northeast. The NRC's Muslim-Christian, north-south ticket replicated the pattern adopted by the National Party of Nigeria (NPN) which was the ruling party of the Second Republic and many of whose stalwarts went into the NRC. The SDP's Moslem-Moslem, north-south ticket was however vigorously criticised by some leaders of the Christian Association of Nigeria for its insentivity to Christians, and by some Igbo political leaders for its marginalisation of their ethnic group. There were also apprehensions expressed as to whether the SDP ticket, headed as it was by one of the richest men in Nigeria, would be sufficiently sensitive to the interests and needs of the poor. Abiola and Kingibe had to reach out to labour, church leaders, and some Igbo political elites in order to sooth their anxieties (Olukoshi, 1993b).

In the event, on 12 June 1993, the problems that appeared initially to dog the SDP ticket did not seem to matter much with the electorate as Abiola and Kingibe headed for an emphatic triumph in all the geographical regions and in a majority of the states of the federation. The spread of electoral support for Abiola and Kingibe was fairly even across the country, suggesting a pan-Nigerian electoral mandate in the making for the first time in the history of Nigeria. Even in Tofa's home state of Kano and in his electoral ward, Abiola and Kingibe managed to beat the NRC ticket. For many Nigerians, it was an unexpected but welcome sign that regionalism, religion, and ethnicity were finally being consigned to the dustbin of history in national electoral politics. Almost every pre-conceived notion, myth, and reality about Nigerian politics was shattered by the pattern of voting and the emphatic nature of the victory of the SDP ticket. More realistically however, it was a popular vote against the continuation of military rule as the Abiola-Kingibe ticket, for all its weaknesses, was seen as offering a marginally better chance than the Tofa-Ugoh ticket of steering the country away from the bileful legacy of the Babangida years. In annulling the elections, the military government of General Babangida set back the hands of the political clock in Nigeria, unleashing a floodgate of ethnic, regional, and religious recrimination on a scale not seen since the mid-1960s and paving the way for the return of the military to power. Much of this recrimination was spontaneous and autonomous but much of it was also deliberately promoted by the military government and its allies among the politicians as part of their bid to ensure that the annulment was upheld. There was also some hope among General Babangida's supporters in government that he could, in the midst of the national confusion created by the annulment, somehow cling on to power whilst the ground was being prepared for fresh presidential elections. It was a forlorn hope and in the end Babangida was forced, very much against his desire, to surrender the presidency.

Thus it was that what could, in the view of many a commentator, have been an electoral outcome that had all the potential for helping to strengthen the already badly weakened basis for Nigerian unity at a time of great economic and political trial for the country, was transformed by the ambitions of a General and the junta he headed to cling on to power and the anxieties of power groups unable to come to terms with the electoral outcome, into a major factor for division and for the further weakening of whatever was left of Nigerian unity. It was a sad paradox whose consequences are bound to haunt Nigerian politics for a long time. As we noted, in the recrimination that followed the annulment, the Babangida regime, and those who openly and clandestinely supported its action, spared no effort to fan the embers of ethnic, regional, and religious disharmony and hatred. The north was pitched against the south, the Hausas against the Yorubas, Christians against Moslems, the southeast against the southwest, minorities against majorities, minorities against minorities, and friends against friends as the platform for a national dialogue narrowed and inflammatory threats and counter-threats were lobbed across the series of lines that increasing divided the peoples of Nigeria.

In time, even the protests which greeted the annulment and which were co-ordinated by the CD as part of its effort to re-focus the rapidly degenerating national political discourse on issues of democracy and democratisation were to be reduced to questions of ethnic, regional, and religious partisanship. In part, this was the result of the unrelenting propanganda in the state-owned media about the "hidden" ethnic motives of the principal leaders of the CD, a propaganda buttressed by the fact that the organization was most active and effective in the south west from where Abiola comes. However, some blunders and unguarded statements by a few of the leaders of the CD and the narrowing of the channels of consultation within the organisation also fed into the negative propanganda against it by the state and weakened the internal cohesion of the group as did growing differences over the strategy and tactic for prosecuting the pro-democracy and anti-military campaign. With the CD in decline, the national political terrain became even more widely open for the political forces with the greatest interest in promoting ethnic, regional and religious hatred to enjoy a field day. Many of them did so with the tacit encouragement of a federal military government intent on maintaining the political grip of the military on the country.

ATTEMPTS BY THE STATE TO MANAGE THE POST-12 JUNE NATIONAL POLITICAL CRISIS

Following the forced exit of General Babangida from power on 26 August 1993, an exit which the CD and its affiliates did so much to precipitate, an unelected Interim National Government (ING), hand-picked by the military, was imposed on the country. It was, from birth, a lame duck at the head of which was a colourless figure, Ernest Shonekan, who was widely seen, with justification, as a puppet of the military. Discredited by his failure as the nominal head (Babangida retained real effective power and control) of the "transitional" gov- ernment which the military junta set up in January 1993 after the postponement for the third time of the terminal date for the disengagement of the military from power, Shonekan had no chance of succeeding in office. Even the instru- ment of his appointment was not categorical as to whether he was merely the "Head of Government" or "Head of State" and it was silent on who the com- mander-in-chief of the armed forces was. It took the amendment of the "Interim Constitution", after contradictory statements from the Attorney General, for the formal title of Head of State and Commander-in Chief to be conferred on him. The titles were however nominal and real effective power rested with the mili- tary faction represented by General Sani Abacha, one of Babangida's longest serving associates who held the defence portfolio in the ING. Abacha was eventually to shove Shonekan aside ignominiously in a palace coup staged on 17 November 1993.

Some of the bitterest opposition to Shonekan came from southwestern Nigeria. An Egba like Abiola who had won the annulled election, Shonekan's right to rule the country was bitterly contested by the Egba and wider Yoruba elite on account of the fact that he was not elected into the office he was occupy- ing, was playing the role of a usurper, and was a pawn in a complex power game which he did not appear to fully understand or appreciate. For the dura- tion of the 84 days for which Shonekan paraded himself as head of state, southwestern Nigeria, whose political elite had invested much in the quest for the leadership of the country, not only treated him as a pariah but was also in the grip of strikes and disruptions which were aimed at bringing down the ING. Rioters set his property ablaze in Abeokuta; they did the same with the properties of those they felt were collaborators with the ING. On top of this, a Lagos High Court judge, ruling early in November 1993 on a suit brought by

Abiola challenging the legality of the ING, declared the process by which Shonekan and his team were appointed as irregular and the interim government illegal. It was the final death blow that brought the ING to an end.

With the host of problems that the ING was confronted with and its legitimacy, which was always dubious, wiped out by the Lagos High Court ruling, it became clear that Shonekan had absolutely no chance of carrying out the mandate which Babangida had handed to him, namely to conduct fresh presidential elections by the end of March 1994. Armed with the Lagos High Court ruling, Abiola was himself making open moves to form a government even as some politicians, especially from southwestern Nigeria, declared that they would boycott any fresh elections that sought to bypass the actualisation of the results of the 1993 presidential poll. A host of other politicians drawn from various parts of the country and inspired by the High Court ruling, called for the formation of a government of national unity led by Abiola to replace the ING and to convene a national conference to discuss the crisis of Nigeria's federalism. Demonstrations and strikes intensified in Lagos and the key urban centres of southwest Nigeria against the ING. It was increasingly clear that the issue was no longer whether the ING would fall but when and how. On 17 November 1993, senior military officers led by General Sani Abacha announced that the ING had been dissolved and with it all the elected local government councils, state houses of assembly, and the National Assembly. All the elected civilian governors of the 30 states of the federation were also dismissed and replaced with military administrators.

The agenda of the military regime of General Abacha was to launch a fresh transitional programme starting from scratch. This process was to begin with an elected constitutional conference which the regime initially claimed would be given "full constituent powers". The Abacha regime's approach to tackling the national political crisis, its disappointment of the expectation of those who thought, naively, that the government was going to de-annul the 1993 presidential elections, and its unwillingness to commit itself to a specified period in office at a time when many Nigerians had grown weary of military rule eventually provoked an angry response as much from many members of the political elite as from various sections of civil society and the trade unions. Pressures were mounted on Abiola to proclaim himself president and announce an alternative government as the first annivesary of the 12 June 1993 elections drew closer. As the challenges to the regime built up, it became increasingly repressive and barbaric and it hastened the "election" of some people into the constitutional conference which it convened. The election was held amidst widespread calls for its boycott. The boycott was most effective in southwestern Nigeria but even in other parts of the country, the turnout of voters was on average below 10 per cent. The regime moved against its leading opponents, including Abiola who had proclaimed himself president in June 1994, clamping a majority of them in detention without trial and under conditions that were , to put it mildly, inhuman.

The constitutional conference which the Abacha regime convened was bedevilled from the outset by a host of problems which are bound to affect its outcome. For a start, the authority and legitimacy of the government which convened it is dubious and contested, a fact which underlies the extremely repressive and barbaric approach of the government. This legitimacy problem is reinforced by the fact that the principal figures in the miltary regime are heavily tainted by the excesses of the Babangida years which they were central players. In the case of some of them at least, there is no doubt that they were privy to the annulment of the 1993 election. Privy or not, they displayed an astonishing lack of interest in probing the circumstances that led to the annulment of the election. Furthermore, the popular perception of the leading members of the regime is of extremely corrupt military officers and politcians who are not motivated by the public purpose. But apart from the legitimacy crisis of the regime, the conference is limited by the fact that the election of its members was boycotted in parts of the country and the turnout of voters was pitifully low. Moreover, as a consequence of the boycott of the election in southwestern Nigeria and places like Ogoniland and the Niger delta area, those parts are not represented in the conference by people who are seen as legitimate spokespersons for their group interests and who have a reasonable chance of delivering on whatever deal that is hammered out at the conference.

The decision of the military government to nominate one third of the delegates to the conference and the calibre of some of the nominees cast additional doubt on the capacity of the conference to serve as a genuinely useful and autonomous platform on which the problems of Nigerian federalism could be discussed. The rules which the regime drew up for the workings of the conference provided for a quorum which could be formed by one third of the members. The implication was that the nominees of the government could on their own form a quorum if for whatever reason those of the conferencees that could claim to be elected felt dissatisfied with the proceedings. What is more, the military government also appointed the chair and deputy chair for the conference and debarred it from discussing or negotiating issues pertaining to the unity and territorial integrity of the country. The prevention of the conference from debating the unity of the country was not only a reversal of the pledge which the government made at its inception that the conference would be free to discuss all issues of concern to Nigerians, it also underlined the fact that the conference had neither "full constituent powers" nor the scope to discuss the substantive issues that have undermined the quest for an enduring basis for national survival. The military government has also made clear that it would have the last say on the constitution which the conference will produce.

With the limited confidence which the shackled constitutional conference has generated, it is clear that the crisis of Nigerian federalism is not about to abate. To be sure, with a combination of vicious repression, widespread intimidation, and crude manipulation, the government may go ahead to "successfully" launch a new transitional programme but it would only have succeeded in sweeping key issues under the carpet and postponed the day when Nigerians would have to confront the problems that lie at the heart of their wobbly federalism. The extreme repression, bordering on an officially sponsored pogrom, perpetrated at the behest of the Abacha junta against the people of Ogoniland and Ekpoma may have restored a semblance of order; it certainly has not addressed the genuine grievances of the peoples of the oil-producing areas of Nigeria. The arrest and detention of the key activists in the forefront of the campaign for a reconfiguration of the federation may, on the surface, appear to have taken the wind out of their sail; it has not addressed the essence of their demand. The incarceration and attempts at humiliating and breaking M.K.O. Abiola or his supporters made up of disaffected politicians, some retired military officers, and human rights activists organised under the banner of the National Democratic Coalition (NADECO) may appear to have taken the heat out of the clamour for the actualisation of the results of the 12 June 1993 elections; it has neither obviated the necessity for a full-scale national re-appraisal of the circumstances that led to the criminal annulment of that poll nor the necessity for building confidence measures that can help to assure that nationally acceptable elections can be held in Nigeria in the future. The imposition by the military of themselves on the Nigerian people and the extreme repressiveness of the Abacha regime, a repressiveness that is tainted with vindictiveness and malevolence, may have created the impression of silence in the land; in fact, it only underlines the centrality of the democratic question to any sustainable effort at tackling the National Question in Nigeria. For, the military have become the single most important obstacle to the prospect for the realisation of a democratic path to national development and to the resolution of the crisis of Nigerian federalism.

CONCLUDING REMARKS: BEYOND THE CONSTITUTIONAL
CONFERENCE

It is necessary to recognise that no effort to come to grips with the crisis of Nigerian federalism will succeed if it starts from a premise which seeks to rig or constrict the agenda. However desirable it is to keep Nigeria united, and we are fully convinced that Nigeria will be far better off as one country and that any efforts to split it up are bound to be extremely messy (witness the state of affairs in the former Yugoslavia), it is essential not to foreclose discussions about the country's unity in any attempt to tackle the National Question. For although unity may be desirable, it can neither be taken for granted or assumed away nor can it be treated as something static or too sacrosanct to be openly negotiated. While the use of force and state terror may create the semblance of unity, it can never provide an enduring basis for it. In essence, if unity is to be sustainable, it has to be based on consent, rooted in the existence of a legitimate state and government to which people freely give their allegiance in return for certain basic socio-economic and political rights.

Happily, none of the principal forces at the forefront of the campaign for the reconfiguration of the federation has seriously advocated the complete dismemberment of the country or the dissolution of Nigeria as a country although insensitivity to the demands of aggrieved groups may well make this a political option. What most groups have called for is the re-designing of the basis for national unity to permit greater autonomy to nationalities as well as greater equality among them in national political, economic, and social affairs. Some have also called for the right of nationalities to secede which is not necessarily the same thing as the advocacy of secession and which does not assume that the constitutional requirements for the exercise of that right (which have to be negotiated any way and which, definitely, cannot be exercised unilaterally) will make secession as simple as it sounds. Furthermore, it is often forgotten that a community of interests and inter-dependencies already bind the peoples of Nigeria together to such an extent that it would be wrong to take an instinctively negative attitude to debates about the structure of the federation. For all the factors and issues which divide its peoples, and these are many and real and should not be underplayed or underestimated, Nigeria has, in many important respects, not least economic, ceased to be a mere geographical expression.

In our view, no effort at addressing the crisis of Nigerian federalism and the National Question which underlies it can go too far which does not seriously attempt to resolve the democracy question. At a minimum, this will imply in the context of contemporary Nigeria that the military are made to give way to elected civilian politicians and that a process is set underway to elect a national conference with sovereign powers and which reflects not only the interests of the nationalities that make up the country but also the main professionally- or socially-based interest groups that are also central to the national political process or what is left of it. In other words, it is also necessary to recognise that the crisis of Nigerian federalism is not just about bickering "tribes" but also about social injustices that are rooted in cross-national class and gender conflicts. The conference will, therefore, have to win the confidence of all categories of Nigerians and its proceedings would have to be conducted in the open. In the end, national unity can only endure where the various units and interest groups in the country have both a stake and a basic faith in the country and the way it is constituted and administered. In other words, unity endures where diverse groups feel themselves to be part and parcel of an existing national bargain, do not feel discriminated against in the existing socio-economic and political order, and can tap credible, representative, and responsive channels for the resolution of their grievances.

Because the Nigerian military has shown itself to be the single greatest threat to democracy, and because the mainstream of the political elite is tainted by the repeated opportunism of its members, it would seem that the task of mobilising the Nigerian people for a genuinely open and democratic national debate on the future of the nation-state will have to fall on those groups, weakened though they might be, that can still claim, with some credibility, to have an objective interest in national-territorial politics and the survival of the country. These groups include labour, the student and youth movement, and the professionals generally and their progressive/radical component in particular. Although they are themselves not immune to the prejudices that divide or have been used to divide the country, they, unlike the increasingly bankrupt ruling class and military oligarchy can claim, on account of their political history, to be the more credible guardians of the national interest at this crucial juncture in Nigeria's history.

It would not be sufficient however simply to convene a sovereign national conference which merely discusses how power should be shared in a multi-ethnic, multi-religious society. Nigerians would also have to seriously address issues of economic management with a view to containing the national economic crisis, tackling corruption, ineffiency and inequality, re-establishing a civic culture in the country and checking the problem of uneven socio-economic development. In our view, this process will have to include a set of deliberate policy measures aimed at re-inventing the structures of the state and the key institutions of society with the main objective of enhancing the prospects for a more effective system of governance that is sensitive both to the requirements of economic rationality and the social welfare of the people. No re-configuration of the federal state will succeed which merely devolves power in a new power-sharing arrangement without re-inventing the structures of governance in order to increase popular participation and enhance transparency and accountability. In essence, structures and processes that enhance effective democratic governance will have to be built into the quest for national reformation if self-serving potentates are not to dominate a re-configured system of national administration. What this calls for is a developmental state with an enhanced capacity and which is also, in definition, democratic from the outset. This would involve the jettisoning of the essentially anti-state philosophy and practice of structural adjustment and the significant tempering of the zero sum approach of the market.

The issue of the protection of the rights of minorities in a reconfigured Nigeria is one which has to be tackled seriously. Given the vast number of groups that can stake a legitimate claim to some space of their own, and given the many internal divisions that afflict even those groups that are defined as the majority ethnic groups in the country, it is clear that separate political/administrative sub-units cannot be established for all potential claimants. Nor would that be a desirable approach to tackling the country's federal crisis; a more useful path would be to encourage the creation of multi-ethnic and, where appropriate, multi-religious sub-units that encourage cross-ethnic, cross-religious, cross-regional, and cross-cultural socio-economic and political engagement. What this means is that the issue of the protection of minority rights is one which would have to be integrated into the quest for the re-structuring of the country. This could form part and parcel of a re-definition of citizenship rights which would have to be defended and protected in all parts of the country. It would also entail a departure from a definition of citizenship that is tied too narrowly to the place of origin of Nigerians to one that is related more closely to their place of residence/site of labour. Furthermore, women's and children's rights will also have to be built into the definition of the rights of the Nigerian citizen. In the end, the quest for the re-invention of the Nigerian state will stand or fall on the basis of the capacity to manage competing ethnicities and religious identities as well as address problems of social inequality and uneven development in a framework that is both developmentalist and democratic and in which citizenship rights are promoted on the basis of secular criteria and protected vis-a-vis all the structures of power at the various levels of government that impinge on the citizen.

BIBLIOGRAPHY

Adekanye, J. Bayo, 1995, "Structural Adjustment, Democratization and Rising Ethnic Tensions in Africa", *Development and Change*, Vol. 26, No. 2, April.

Albert, I.O., 1993, *Inter-Ethnic Relations in a Nigerian City: A Historical Perspective of the Hausa-Igbo Conflicts in Kano 1953–1991*, IFRA Occasional Publications, No. 2.

Azarya, V. and N. Chazan, 1987, "Disengagement from the State in Africa: Reflections on the Experience of Ghana and Guinea", *Comparative Studies in Society and History*, Vol. 29, No. 1.

Azarya, V. 1988, "Re-Ordering State-Society Relations: Incorporation and Disengagement", in D. Rothchild and N. Chazan (eds.), *The Precarious Balance: State and Society in Africa*, Westview, Boulder, Colorado.

Bangura, Yusuf and Bjorn Beckman, 1991, "African Workers and Structural Adjustment with a Nigerian Case-Study", in D. Ghai (ed.), *IMF and the South: Social Impact of Crisis and Adjustment*, Zed Books, London.

Bangura, Yusuf, 1994, *The Search for Identity: Ethnicity, Religion and Political Violence*, Occasional Paper Number 6, UNRISD, Geneva, November.

Beckman, Bjorn, 1993, "Economic Reform and National Disintegration", (mimeo), Stockholm.

Campbell, Ian, 1994, "Nigeria: The Election that Never Was !", *Democratization*, Vol. 1, No. 2, Summer.

Gibbon, Peter *et al.* (eds.), 1992, *Authoritarianism, Democracy and Adjustment*, Nordiska Afrikainstitutet, Uppsala.

Gibbon, Peter, 1992, "Understanding Social Change in Contemporary Africa", (mimeo), Uppsala.

Ibrahim, Jibrin, 1988, "From the Primitive Acquisition of Power to the Primitive Accumulation of Capital", (mimeo), Zaria.

Ibrahim, Jibrin, 1989, "The State, Accumulation, and Democratic Forces in Nigeria", (mimeo), Uppsala.

Ibrahim, Jibrin, 1991, "Religion and Political Turbulence in Nigeria", *Journal of Modern African Studies*, Vol. 29, No. 1.

Ihonvbere, J. and E. Ekekwe, 1988, "The 'Irrelevant State': Structural Adjustment and the Subversion of Democratic Possibilities in the Third Republic", in S.G. Tyoden (ed.), *Democratic Mobilisation in Nigeria: Problems and Prospects*, Proceedings of the 15th Annual Conference of the Nigerian Political Science Association (NPSA), Ibadan.

Ihonvbere, J., 1993, "Economic Crisis, Structural Adjustment and Social Crisis in Nigeria", *World Development*, Vol. 21, No. 1.

Ihonvbere, J., "The 'Irrelevant State', Ethnicity, and the Quest for Nationhood in Africa", *Ethnic and Racial Studies*, Vol. 17, No. 1, 1994.

Marshall, R., 1991, "Power in the Name of Jesus", *Review of African Political Economy*, No. 52, November.

Meagher, K., 1995, "Crisis, Informalization and the Urban Informal Sector in Sub-Saharan Africa", *Development and Change*, Vol. 26, No. 2, April.

Movement for National Reformation, "Position Paper", *The Guardian* (Lagos), 29 January 1993.

Mustapha, A.R., 1986, "The National Question and Radical Politics in Nigeria", *Review of African Political Economy*, No. 37, December.

Mustapha, A.R., 1992a, "Nigeria: The Challenge of Nationhood", *Nigerian Forum*, September–December.

Mustapha, A.R., 1992b, "Structural Adjustment and Multiple Modes of Livelihood in Nigeria", in Peter Gibbon et al. (eds.), *Authoritarianism, Democracy and Adjustment...*, *op cit.*

Nnoli, Okwudiba, 1980, *Ethnic Politics in Nigeria*, Fourth Dimension Press, Enugu.

Nwolise, O.B.C., 1990, "The Military as the Obstacle to Democracy in Nigeria", in S.G. Tyoden, (ed.), *Constitutionalism and National Development in Nigeria*, Proceedings of the 17th Annual conference of the NPSA, Jos.

Olowu, D., 1991, "The Literature on Nigerian Federalism: A Critical Appraisal", *Publius: The Journal of Federalism*, Vol. 21, No. 4.

Olukoshi, A.O. (ed.), 1990, *Crisis and Adjustment in the Nigerian Economy*, JAD Press, Lagos.

Olukoshi, A.O. (ed.), 1991, *Nigerian External Debt Crisis: Its Management*, Malthouse Press, Lagos and Oxford.

Olukoshi, A.O. (ed.), 1993a, *The Politics of Structural Adjustment in Nigeria*, James Currey, London.

Olukoshi, A.O., 1993b, "The Current Transition from Military Rule in Nigeria", (mimeo), Copenhagen.

Olukoshi, A.O., 1994, "The State and the Civil Liberties Movement in Nigeria, 1985–1993", (mimeo), Kampala.

Onoge, O. (ed.), 1993, *Nigeria: The Way Forward,* Spectrum Books, Ibadan.

Osaghae, E. , 1995, *Structural Adjustment and Ethnicity in Nigeria*, Research Report No. 98, Nordiska Afrikainstitutet, Uppsala.

Otite, Onigu, 1990, *Ethnic Pluralism and Ethnicity in Nigeria*, Shoneson, Ibadan.

Rudebeck, Lars (ed.), 1992, *When Democracy Makes Sense: Studies in the Democratic Pattern of Third World Popular Movements*, AKUT, Uppsala.

Suberu, Rotimi, 1993, "The Travails of Federalism in Nigeria", *Journal of Democracy*, Vol. 4, No. 4, October.

Toyo, Eskor, 1975, "Description, Analysis and Prognosis: National Question in Nigeria", (mimeo), Zaria.

Udogu, E.K., 1994, "The Allurements of Ethnonationalism in Nigerian Politics : The Contemporary Debate", *Journal of Asian and African Studies*, Vol. XXIX, Nos. 3–4.

UNRISD, 1995, *States of Disarray: The Social Effects of Globalisation*, UNRISD, Geneva.

Usman, Y.B., 1980, "The Substance of the Problem of National Unity in Nigeria Today", (mimeo), Zaria.

Usman, Y.B. and Y. Bangura, 1984, "Debate on the Nigerian Economic Crisis", *Studies in Politics and Society*, Special Issue, No. 2, October.

Williams, P. and T. Falola, 1995, *Religious Impact on the Nation-State: The Nigerian Predicament*, Avebury, Brookfield.

Wright, Steven, 1986, "Nigeria—The Dilemmas ahead : A Political Risk Analysis", *Economist Intelligence Unit (EIU)*, Special Report No. 1072, November 1986.

Yahaya, A. D., 1982, "Introduction", in B.J. Dudley, *An Introduction to Nigerian Government and Politics*, Macmillan, London.

Chapter 5

Ghana: Violent Ethno-Political Conflicts and the Democratic Challenge

E.O. Akwetey

INTRODUCTION
DEMOCRATISATION AND ETHNO-POLITICAL VIOLENCE

If, as Bendix (1964:18) contends, "the central fact of nation-building is the orderly exercise of a nation-wide public authority", recent events in Ghana would appear to suggest that violent ethnopolitical conflicts are increasingly posing challenges to central state authority in the country. In early February 1994, a full scale ethnic war broke out in the eastern part of Ghana's Northern Region. It all began as a quarrel between three individuals from two different ethnic groups—Konkonba and Nanumba—which rapidly escalated into a full blown inter-ethnic war. Within the brief span of ten days, over 1,000 lives were lost and more than 150 villages were destroyed together with thousands of acres of farmland and millions of cedis worth of produce. Instantly, inter-ethnically mixed populations which had lived closely as neighbours for centuries in areas re-grouped to form seven administrative districts were pulled apart, overpowered by the emotions of revived historical enmities in a "nasty, brutish, and short" war. As fear overtook those who were lucky to escape the spiralling conditions of insecurity, a refugee crisis arose drawing not only national but also international attention to the scale and consequences of the violence. It raised concerns over the likelihood of the barbaric ethnic wars of Bosnia, Liberia and Rwanda also occurring in Ghana.

What led to this ethnopolitical violence? Was Ghana on the brink of bloody and destructive ethnic strife? Clearly, this has not been the case since there is no civil war raging throughout Ghana today. Prompt intervention by the military and police forces effectively localised the violence as law and order was eventually, albeit temporarily, enforced. Once the state demonstrated the superiority of its coercive power over the armed groups, it became clear that there was no crisis, at least for now, over the juridical and territorial integrity of the Ghanaian nation-state. While this may well be the case, the fact that ethnopolitical violence tends to resurge during transitions to democracy raises questions about the rationale for the democratisation process itself. It appears that violent ethnic conflicts in the Northern Region, for example, atrophy during authoritarian regimes only to re-emerge in periods of return to elected government. In 1981 and 1994 respectively, violence resurged under the elected civilian regimes of the Third and Fourth Republics. In the period 1982-90, the violence atrophied under Rawlings' military backed regime. What accounts for this pattern? This is not a question often addressed by those who see democratisation as a process associated with an end to violence, political instability, and insecurity.

There is a point of view which advocates authoritarian rule for the reason that it is necessary for the effective enforcement of law and order and for the creation of the conditions for effective governance (Huntington, 1968). According to this school of thought, in multi-ethnic societies, authoritarian rule, not democratization, is the antidote to ethnopolitical violence. It is however important for us to stress that important though the effective maintenance of law and order is for the smooth functioning of any socio-political system, it would be wrong to value democracy only in terms of this narrow function. Democracy must be understood to make sense also in the context of its potential for creating an enduring basis for the resolution of conflicts, including those that lead to ethnopolitical violence. With this in mind, we seek in this chapter to address three inter-related questions: What is the nature of the challenge that ethnopolitical violence poses to the multi-ethnic nation-state? How can the state effectively and constructively respond to it? How can the association of democratisation with resurgence of ethnopolitical violence be explained?

It will be argued in this chapter that the resurgence of ethnopolitical violence during transitions to democratisation is the result of the failure of authoritarian regimes to develop an adequate institutional-political framework for the peaceful management of social conflicts. While the installation of liberal democratic constitutions tackles procedural issues of conflict resolution at the national level, local level issues are often ignored or are insufficiently treated. The major challenge posed by ethnopolitical conflicts to the multi-ethnic nation-state lies in how to create an enduring framework for the democratic resolution of disputes and for the enhancement of the political integration of diverse political and social cultures. Authoritarian regimes do better than democratic regimes in breeding intolerance of a plurality of cultures with a potential for counter-balancing the power of the state or the ruling/dominant groups. This they do by repressing the open expression of cultural pluralism in a multi-ethnic setting. Consequently, they rely on force to control the outbreak of ethnopolitical violence in order to maintain law and order and political stability. But, invariably, they fail to enhance the peaceful and effective management or resolution of such conflicts on an enduring basis, especially at local levels.

With political liberalisation and the installation of liberal democratic constitutions, two important stages in a process of democratization, issues that have been suppressed and groups that have been oppressed openly re-assert their identities and re-state their claims on the state. This re-assertion of identities and re-stating of claims manifests itself, depending on the prevailing social and political conditions, either as ethnopolitical protests or rebellion. How can these types of conflicts be resolved? Is the choice facing African countries on this matter one between democracy and authoritarianism? The ethnopolitical challenge to the coherence or unity of the multi-ethnic nation and state will be defined in terms of this choice. As I will argue, this challenge consists of how to enhance the resolution of conflicts via democratic political reforms even in the face of resurging ethnopolitical violence.

NATURE AND CAUSES OF ETHNOPOLITICAL CONFLICTS

I define ethnopolitics, as Hettne (1990:190) does, to mean "ethnic identity activated and used for the purpose of political mobilization". Gurr (1993) suggests that all actions taken in support of the collective interests of any communal group which has experienced economic or political discrimination are ethnopolitical. The broad definition offered by Gurr informs my reference to both intra-ethnic and inter-ethnic conflicts as ethnopolitical. These conflicts consist of actions ranging from *non-violent* to *violent* protests and rebellions. Protest typically aims at persuading or intimidating officials to change their policies toward the group experiencing discrimination; rebellion aims directly at more fundamental changes in government and in power relations among the constituent groups of the nation-state. The essential strategy of protests is to mobilise a show of support on behalf of reform; for rebellion, the mobilisation strategy consists in the build-up of coercive power that is threatening enough to governments which are then forced to accept change (Gurr, 1993:1–10).

When protesters use violence it usually occurs in sporadic and unplanned ways, often in reaction to coercive acts by the police and military. In rebellion, however, violence takes the form of concerted campaigns of armed attacks, ranging from political banditry and terrorism to all-out warfare (Gurr, 1993:93). The distinction between protest and rebellion can be analytically rigorous but, in practice, they may be mixed depending on the political objectives of "oppressed" communal groups and the circumstances within which they may feel compelled to act and to react in response to the "deprivation" or "denial" which they experience. These actions are political if they are taken and directed at dominant groups who may be located either at national or local levels of the state and are, generally, identified as the perpetrators of discrimination.

An ethnic identity is objective to the extent that it denotes specific historical, cultural and linguistic traits which distinguish one group from the other. However, the objective attributes of ethnicity are often amenable to subjective manoeuvres accentuated by some real or felt sense of deprivation and denial. They then become politically salient "when aggravated by uneven development, political competition and the self-serving tactics of ambitious politicians"

(Sandbrook 1985:51–52). The rise of ethno-political conflicts is related to a number of factors including economic development, politics, and ideology. Much too often, even if correctly, uneven economic development is the factor that is most emphasised in discussions about ethnic politics in Africa. Hydén (1984), for example, argues that state coherence in Africa has been maintained through ethnic-based distributive economic policies. Consequently, economic crises also imply ethnic conflicts and a crisis for the state. Drawing on Stavenhagen's (1986) suggestion that the specific nature of the "cause and effect" relationship between uneven development and ethnopolitical mobilisation is a "paradigmatic blind spot" in development thinking, Hettne emphasises the importance of analysing central and local factors in a variety of ways in order to specify how the relationship occurs.

The non-availability of relevant economic data for analysing the specific case of Ghana informs the minimal emphasis on the "uneven development" factor in this chapter. This should not, however, imply that the important relationship between state economic policies and ethnopolitical conflict is being under-rated. The strength of the linkage between the two can, however, not be deduced *a priori* from all types and levels of conflict. When an ethnopolitical conflict is clearly directed against the central state and, therefore, appears to be an issue over its manner of resource distribution, economic explanations may be important. Usually, the geo-political location of the group as well as its demands, especially if granted, could fundamentally affect the structure and exercise of central governmental power in the society. Sri Lanka is one country that comes to mind in this regard.

But where the conflict is between two ethnic groups within a region or between different sections of the same ethnic group, uneven development may be a factor but not the most important cause of such local-level conflicts. In such a case, ideology and politics may prove to be the more potent forces. It would be less convincing to attribute communal violence to uneven development when it occurs within an area where one can or should expect to find a feeling of solidarity, loyalty and attachment towards fellow members vis-a-vis the central government. When the conflict is between two ethnic groups both of whom reside in a region, district or village that is generally underdeveloped, the economic factor fails to explain much, even if it defines the general context within which existing contradictions are formed or intensified. Uneven development in that case does not explain much if the levels of development are not strikingly different. Given the different levels and nature of intra-regional and/or intra-ethnic conflicts, would it not be more instructive and appropriate, in such circumstances, to speak of ethnicised class conflicts, rather than just ethnic conflicts? Certainly, the economic factor is important but it does not sufficiently explain all types and levels of ethnic mobilisation and violent social conflicts. That is why ideological and political factors have to be brought back into the explanation.

Ideology and Politics as Factors in Ethnopolitical Mobilisation

Ideology is critical to ethnopolitical mobilisation because of its power to objectify human relations as a means of imposing hegemony by one group over another. Lema (1993) lucidly describes the ideological processes leading to ethnic domination and subordination in the colonial era. The first was the objectification of ethnicity which influenced the perception of individuals/groups with particular ethnic identities as objects rather than as subjective and rational human beings. On the basis of this objectification, one ethnic group was made to feel superior and more human while the other(s) appeared inferior and dehumanised. This process dovetailed into the second, i.e. the ethnicisation of colonial institutional/organisational relations within African society. This was evident in the mode of recruitment into the mining sector as well as the commercial, administrative and political institutions of the colonial state and economy. The inter-related ideological and political mechanisms of ethnicity, i.e. objectification and power, according to Lema, lie at the root of the violent ethno-political conflicts in post-colonial societies like Rwanda.

The broad thrust of colonial rule rested on the active cultivation of the notion that one ethnic group was superior to the other. It was this factor that inspired the colonial policy of recruiting indigenous Africans into the colonial state bureaucracy according to pre-conceived notions held about their ethnic identity. The ethnic basis of colonial recruitment is generally understood to have been part of a "divide-and-rule" strategy aimed at forestalling the mobilisation of a unified multi-ethnic opposition against colonial rule and foreign domination. Thus, the power of the colonial state over colonised society was rendered secure, albeit temporary. Whatever the nature of the prevailing conditions that originally informed and shaped the politicisation of ethnic identities, their effects have effectively outlived colonial rule. Today the mobilisation of ethnopolitical violence occurs as an "action-reaction" response to ethnicised power relations including the distribution and/or allocation of resources.

Exploiting or manipulating ethnic divisions or conflicts by means of "rewards" or "punitive sanctions" administered to ensure "total loyalty" to neo-patrimonial rulers makes patronage a major source of ethnicised politics. Patrimonial power relations in a multi-ethnic society also tend to be authoritarian, giving rise to practical consequences that sustain the build-up to ethnopolitical violence. Some historical and recent evidence may suggest that authoritarian rule tends to be more effective in incorporating different ethnic groups to form multi-ethnic nation-states. Authoritarian regimes are, however, extremely poor in integrating the plurality of groups so incorporated without the exercise of naked coercive power. This is because authoritarian regimes usually do not tolerate autonomous spheres of power which contest or oppose their policies. The tendency among such regimes is to perceive any criticism or acts of opposition as a threat to the security of power holders as well as the artificially cohesive nation-state. For these reasons, authoritarian regimes tend to be divested of the qualities which are required to shape political conduct as a socially civil and rational behaviour. They create conditions which make people debate whether to act as members of the modern multi-ethnic state or according to their narrow ethnic identities. More than anything else, this debate underscores a lack of political integration in post-colonial multi-ethnic nation-states.

For example, authoritarian regimes often lack the institutional or constitutional framework within which opposition and contestation, as a manifestation of conflict, can be translated into acts of deliberation or procedural discourse that can, in turn, lead to the moderation of otherwise extreme and conflictive views. The ideological objectification of certain ethnic groups neither enables the open expression of the ethnic aspirations of groups labelled as "inferior" nor encourages the tolerance and responsiveness of those labelled as incapable of rational deliberations. As these factors tend to feed on each other, the institutional requirements for the effective management of conflicts such as ethno-political protests are ignored, thereby accentuating the translation of protests into rebellion.

It can thus be hypothesised that ideological and political factors are more likely to lead to ethnopolitical violence than uneven development especially in local-level conflicts where the mobilised group does not fundamentally challenge the coherence/integrity of the nation-state. If these factors are perceived to be more dominant, then the resolution or effective management of ethnopolitical conflicts would require institutional reforms. My argument is that a democratic institutional framework congenially fulfils this condition more than an authoritarian regime.

The Democratic Challenge to the Post-Colonial Nation-State

The institutional character of the democratic challenge posed by ethnopolitical violence is more clearly captured when ideology and politics are factored into the relationship between the *nation* and the *state* in multi-ethnic societies. Although the very process of colonial state creation accounted, in part, for the prevalence of ethnopolitical conflicts within post-colonial states, it also gave rise to a shared nationalist, multi-ethnic aspiration for self-determination and self-rule. "Nations", according to Taylor (1993:43–44), have become "states" in order to rule themselves. The *unity* of the nation, however, has often been assumed to be the pre-condition of sovereign statehood and the basis of political legitimacy (Toulmin 1992:139). It is a major source of the strength and effectiveness of the central political unit or sovereign state which has, since the advent of modernity, been perceived as entirely necessary for civilised progress and social development (Davidson 1992). The unity of the state and the nation has not been naturally endowed. It has always been an act of conscious creation which, depending on the mode of its attainment, periodically creates challenges to the nation-state.

The unity or coherence of the nation and state was something which, from the outset, could not be taken for granted in post-colonial societies. Their essentially multi-ethnic fabric was once conceived as the source of threat to the unity, stability and peace of the nation-state. Thus, developmentalist ideology, as Shivji (1992; 1986) argues, once fed the belief that post-colonial societies can develop rapidly only through the proscription of pluralistic politics be they class- or ethnic-based. The craving for national unity led to the imposition of authoritarian regimes and the suppression, for example, of ethnopolitical grievances and mobilisation. The authoritarian framework was consequently institutionalised as the only legitimate space for articulating, mobilising and aggregating diverse demands and claims on the state. Its primary function was to facilitate the mobilisation of juridically equal *citizens* for national development in spite of ethnic diversity. The belief was that the fragile cohesion of the emergent multi-ethnic state and the conditions for strong, effective and decisive governance were best secured by strong "authoritarian" states (Huntington, 1968; Rothchild and Curry, 1978).

It may be true that post-colonial authoritarian regimes cannot be totally written off as failures if the criterion of assessment is "development within a territorially unified and sovereign nation-state", but whatever their achievements, the prevailing socio-political conditions of today make the limitations of the authoritarian strategy of development abundantly clear. It appears to have failed to eliminate ethnic identities as a salient factor of political mobilisation. Because they encouraged the belief that all forms of ethnopolitical mobilisation were prejudicial to national unity, authoritarian regimes either ignored or failed to address the institutional requirements for the effective management of such conflicts. This stance was ideological to the extent that it denied both the saliency of ethnopolitical mobilisation, even under authoritarian rule, and the actual contribution it made to the political mobilisation that enhanced the anti-colonial struggles for the sovereign statehood of former colonies.

As the history of the anti-colonial and nationalist campaign in Africa and other parts of the world shows, ethnopolitical mobilisation contributed positively to the processes that gave rise to sovereign nation-states. The denial of that positive role has been tantamount to a categorical dismissal of all forms of ethnopolitical mobilisation as negative and, therefore, deserving of being repressed. Hence the general lack of an institutional framework within which to manage ethnopolitical protests and to defuse their potential to degenerate into rebellions. The challenge facing much of Africa then is one of creating institutions (where none exist already) or reforming existing ones to enhance their capacity to manage conflicts effectively. Democratisation is the process that enables the fulfilment of these institutional challenges. But how does or can it meet the political challenge of resurgent ethnopolitical violence?

Liberal democracy has, both historically and theoretically, served as the regime or institutional framework which *procedurally* facilitates the expression of both the juridical and political equality of citizens. Although, from a short-term point of view, they also tend to be relatively more constraining to "effective" governance, democratic constitutions offer a better approach to the management of conflicts through the continuous building of institutions. The representative element in liberal democracy, as well as the rules and preconditions for contestation, may well enhance the resolution of ethnopolitical *protests* rather than *rebellions*. But as Beckman (1992) argues, the existence of that legal-institutional framework is the precondition for institutionalising popular democracy. Managing or resolving conflicts through *democratic politics* involves choice, debate, deliberation, negotiations and compromises leading to mutually agreed solutions or decisions which can command voluntary compliance among the citizens of the nation-state.

However, because the experience so far shows that ethnic violence resurges after electoral contests and the installation of liberal democratic constitutions, it has raised questions in the minds of some about the efficacy of the democratic framework for resolving conflicts. But as we noted earlier, the resurgence of ethnicity following the opening up of the political space may be more the result of the suppression of ethnic identities under a previous, authoritarian order and less a commentary on the efficacy of democratic politics in the management of ethnopolitical mobilisation and conflicts. For all of its shortcomings therefore, democracy provides a more effective institutional space within which both ethnopolitical protests and rebellions can be effectively managed, if not resolved. How far democratisation enables the performance of such tasks is contingent upon the specific circumstances within which ethnopolitical conflicts have been historically dealt with. It is to such circumstances that we now turn based on the experience of Ghana.

GHANA: ORIGINS OF THE MULTI-ETHNIC STATE

The modern nation-state of Ghana was formed out of two inter-related processes. The first was connected to the incorporation of diverse ethnic groups, political cultures, and traditions into the territorial colonial state and the second centred around the emergence of a multi-ethnic country which demanded self-determination and a sovereign status in order to rule itself. The first process was accomplished over a relatively short period of time. It began with an act of agreement signed between British officials and some of the chiefs of a number of southern mini-republics in the colony. This process was first formalised in 1844, then intensified as the British engaged the army of the Ashanti Kingdom in 1874, 1896, and 1900. The eventual defeat of the army led, in 1901, to the formal colonisation of the area that was hitherto covered by the Ashanti Kingdom.

It was also in 1901 that Britain extended colonial jurisdiction over the Northern kingdoms which it had earlier annexed in 1898. Then in 1914, parts of former German Togo under the trusteeship of Britain were added to the Gold Coast. By these acts, the British were able to carve the territorial boundaries of modern Ghana out of the different areas mentioned. In 1934 the incorporated areas were subsequently declared the Gold Coast and put under one central colonial state administration. The colonial state was now fully in place. Its effective imposition also meant the final termination of the long process of state formation, dating from the 15th century, and which consisted of the birth, growth, consolidation and destruction of different states (Ray, 1986). Consequently, centralised political systems consisting of kingdoms and mini-republics and acephalous political communities were fused together under one central political authority. Under the system of indirect rule which they devised for the administration of the colony, the British placed hitherto stateless or acephalous political structures under the jurisdiction of the more centralised states or kingdoms. Hence, the acephalous community of the Konkonba was put under the control of the centralised state of the Northern Dagomba Kingdom (Tait, 1964:8–9).

The imposition of the colonial state also drew different ethnic groups together under one political roof. In Northern Ghana, the Mole-Dagbane (14%), Gurma (4%), Grusi (2%), and others (10%) were brought together while in Southern Ghana, the Akan (44%), Ewe (13%), Ga Adangbe (8%), Guan (4%), and Central Togo (1%) were placed together. If these ethnic divisions are assumed to also form the linguistic profile of Ghana, then over eight major languages are spoken in the country. The ethnopolitical conflict in the Northern Region is essentially a conflict between, on the one hand, sections of the Mole-Dagbane of which the Dagomba, Nanumba and Gonja are members and, on the other, sections of the Gurma to which the Konkonba belong.

British colonial development policy made some impact, albeit modest, in strengthening the economic and political cohesion of the Gold Coast. The development of socio-economic infrastructure gathered momentum in the post-1945 era as vast improvements in government revenue, due to favourable export commodity prices, enabled public investments in education, road and rail communication, health care facilities and industries. Limited though these developments were, they facilitated inter-ethnic interaction as rural-urban migration from the various parts of the country led to the emergence of densely populated urban centres.

British colonial rule was essentially authoritarian in the sense that it withheld the franchise from the majority African population and denied them the right to popular representation and elected government. It excluded the educated African elites from the middle and higher levels of the bureaucracy and other related institutions of the state, and implemented policies that discriminated against African merchants and entrepreneurs in the private sector of the economy. Its rule was based more on coercion than on voluntary compliance by the colonised peoples with the policies of the colonial government. The stark realities of racial segregation and discrimination were mitigated, somewhat, by a policy that encouraged the recruitment of Africans on the basis of ethnicity. Thus the southerners (ethnic groups of the south) were recruited into the lower echelons of the public and private sectors, while the northerners were recruited into the lower ranks of the police and military forces. The recruitment policy was also determined by the specific needs of the colonial labour market. Southerners served as the source of skilled and literate labour while unskilled and manual labour especially in the agricultural sector was recruited from among the northerners. Finally, the restricted scope of investment in the economy as a whole limited employment opportunities for the multi-ethnic rural migrants who now resided in the urban townships.

The inadequacies of British colonial policy in virtually all spheres of life created widespread discontent across all the ethnic and class divides in the Gold Coast. The existence of specific and general grievances provided the fertile ground on which political mobilisation in support of the nationalist cause in the post-war era was later to grow. British colonial policy sought to prevent such a "national" mobilisation through measures aimed at defining a restricted legal-institutional framework for interest group articulation in the colonies. Its socio-economic development policies and programmes over the decades resulted in the emergence of occupational groups who perceived their relationships with the colonial state in terms other than ethnic. Professional bodies of lawyers, accountants, journalists, and teachers emerged in the country with members who saw themselves as a middle class with a stake in the colonial judicial and politico-administrative system, rather than as ethnic representatives who aspired to return to the traditional society which they had outgrown. Wage and salaried workers had also emerged and the colonial state, in response to this development, decided to institute a number of labour ordinances which simultaneously legalised the unionisation of workers and imposed measures of state control aimed at restricting the scope of their activities and their right to associate with political organisations or parties.

Between 1942 and 1946, the British gradually introduced a number of political reforms:

> designed to bring into closer partnership with the officials, the two leading groups of local opinion in the country, namely, the chiefs as presidents of the reformed native authorities and the intelligentsia as the representatives of the growing urban population (Austin, 1964:9).

Austin suggests that the British had hoped that the design of a triple ruling *elite* made up of colonial officials, chiefs and the intelligentsia, would form the basis of constitutional reforms which "would meet any widespread demand for political rights before it reached the final point of violent controversy". In 1946 the Burns Constitution was inaugurated as the institutional stage of a reform process which had begun with the liberalisation of political organisation and association. Two years later, violent riots erupted unexpectedly in the Gold Coast as a swell of nationalist sentiment was transformed into mass political mobilisation in support of what later became a campaign for self-determination and self-rule by the multi-ethnic African "Gold Coasters". This was the first major evidence of the close association between democratisation and political violence in the colony that, at independence in 1957, became Ghana. It served as the prelude to the ethnopolitical mobilisation and violence of the 1950s and beyond.

Power Struggle and Nationalist Political Mobilisation (1950–57)

The causes of the 1948 riots may be attributed to widespread "discontent" with the colonial state. However, as Austin (1964:12) persuasively argues:

> The riots themselves were the violent herald of a struggle for power soon to be conducted by new leaders who drew their support from a much broader, more popular level than had hitherto been active in national politics. They carried with them a strident protest not only against colonial rule but against the existing structure of authority in the Colony and Ashanti Chiefdoms.

The demands shortly to be raised by Nkrumah and the mass-based, populist Convention People's Party (CPP) implied a far greater upheaval in local society than earlier struggles between the chiefs and the intelligentsia ever did. Because the CPP stood for the "ordinary people" or commoners, it was perceived as a threat to the power of the chiefs and the intelligentsia and was, therefore, opposed by them. Their opposition tended to be expressed in ethnic-territorial terms.

Prior to the founding of the CPP in 1949, widespread upheavals were reported in the chiefdoms of the Gold Coast. In both the southern and northern chiefdoms, a broad social group of elementary-school leavers, generally referred to as commoners, had become persistent opponents of a native-authority system which held no opportunities for a career suited to their training and skills. They felt the chiefs had become functionaries of the colonial state and no longer derived their power from the native people. In the 1930s and 1940s, the radicalism of the commoners, many of whom attempted to depose the chiefs, prompted the colonial government to introduce a comprehensive native authority ordinance that strengthened the powers of the chiefs way beyond what they possessed under native custom. Faced with the enhanced authority of the chiefs which were invariably underwritten by the coercive power of the colonial state, a large pool of elementary school leavers migrated to the southern urban townships where they began to turn to new forms of political organisation. Local scholars' unions, literary and debating clubs, youth movements and improvement societies which had formed in the state capitals and market centres were revitalised as the educated migrants used them as fora for social and political gatherings.

By 1948–49, as the global wave of nationalist mobilisation in the post-war era spilled over into the Gold Coast, the revived social fora served as one of the active nuclei of an anti-chief, anti-colonial movement. As the CPP attracted its major following from these commoner associations, it crystallised a division between the commoners, on the one hand, and the elites comprising the chiefs and the intelligentsia represented by the United Gold Coast Convention (UGCC), on the other. The CPP effectively seized the initiative, with its radical and mass appeal, to push the agenda for self-determination and self-rule faster than the UGCC and the colonial government had contemplated. Further constitutional reforms were introduced in 1950 and the first general election took place in 1951. From then on, the power struggle that preceded the formation of political parties in the post-war era was transformed into a struggle between the opposition led by the UGCC and the CPP, the governing party of Kwame Nkrumah.

Until 1954, both the colonial administration and, subsequently, the Nkrumah government had strongly affirmed the "fundamentally homogeneous" character of Gold Coast society. Nkrumah, for example, was to declare in 1953 that the people were not "plagued with religious and tribal problems" and, therefore, demanded an acceleration of the process leading to the full decolonisation of the Gold Coast (Austin, 1964:28). Barely eighteen months after that declaration, a violent ethnopolitical conflict swept across the country. It followed the country's second general election which the CPP again won and marked the turning point in the relationship between violent ethnopolitical conflicts and democratisation in Ghana.

Democratisation and Ethnopolitical Violence (1954–57)

By the end of 1954, a violent conflict swept across Ashanti and other parts of the southern colony. This was also at a time when Nkrumah's government was beset by difficulties in the North and the part of Togoland incorporated into the Gold Coast. Austin (1964:28-29) suggests that ethnopolitical mobilisation grew as nationalist aims receded and local interests came to the fore. According to him, the CPP attained its primary objectives—self-government and local government reform—within five years of the party's formation. The party's Africanisation policy gave jobs to the "commoners" in the new ministries and the national legislative assembly. Then a major reform of the local government system in 1952 enabled the party's followers to gain control in the chiefdoms as the unpopular native authorities were replaced by new local authorities.

Two-thirds of the members of the local authorities were elected on an adult suffrage and only one-third were chosen by the chiefs and their elders. Local interests began to be asserted in 1954 when according to Austin:

> religious minorities—notably the Muslims; ethnic groups—the Ewe of southern Togoland; historic units—Ashanti; and administrative units—including the Northern Territories whose people had acquired their own sense of local identity all began to stress the need for prior recognition of their own claims before the country as a whole became self-governing (Austin, 1964:29).

The political significance of local demands ultimately lay in whether or not they threatened the territorial integrity of the Gold Coast which was soon to be declared an independent sovereign state and re-named Ghana on 6 March 1957. The evidence shows that the only such demand that came close to threatening the territorial unity of the country came from sections of the Ewe people of the southern Togoland trust territory who preferred to link themseives with the neighbouring Togo Republic. They attempted a local armed rebellion in March 1957 but that revolt was easily suppressed.

An internationally-monitored plebiscite had earlier been held in 1956 to decide whether the inhabitants of the trust territory would like to link up with Togo or Ghana. The majority voted to remain as part of Ghana. This rendered the rebellion an unpopular action that was easily contained by the state. With the exception of this case, the other demands for autonomy were not threatening to the territorial integrity of the state. The Ashanti, the chiefdom of Akim Abuakwa and the north, for example, formed an alliance with sections of the intelligentsia and jointly demanded constitutional reforms which would restructure the political system as a federation, rather than as a centralised unitary system. The aim, it appeared, was to safeguard regional interests against the centralisation threats which they associated with the CPP. Indeed, the intensity of the local demands of Ashanti and the north translated into electoral losses for the CPP in the 1954 and 1956 general elections.

British neglect of the north eventually led to the formation of the Northern People's Party (NPP) in the early 1950s. The NPP demanded a special development plan which would narrow the socio-economic and infrastructure gap between the north and the south. Among its demands were a rapid increase in the number of schools and specialist colleges, progress in the railway project from Kumasi to Tamale, and rapid agricultural development. In the 1954 elections, the NPP won twelve out of the twenty-one seats in the Region (Rooney, 1988:78-79). Although, the CPP was sympathetic to the development programme of the NPP, it began to perceive the party as a serious threat when regional issues became more prominent in the national political discourse in the period between 1954 and 1957.

In Ashanti, local interests initially converged around the issue of cocoa prices when the National Liberation Movement (NLM) was formed to mobilise farmers in support of a campaign for a higher price. Nkrumah's government had sought to control local prices as a means of maximizing its share of the export revenue which it desperately needed to finance its development programmes. The attempt to regulate prices through the state's Cocoa Purchasing Company and Cocoa Marketing Board offended the Ashanti farmers who felt they were being unduly exploited by the government. This specific grievance acquired a wider political significance because of the time it was raised and the circumstances that prevailed. The power struggle between, on the one hand, the commoners who controlled CPP and, on the other hand, the relatively conservative alliance of chiefs and sections of the intelligentsia gave the cocoa price grievance a broader political hearing beyond the farmers. The NLM also defined for itself a role in "the stamping out of dictatorship and communistic practices" on the part of the CPP. This was more a reference to, and suspicion of the centralisation tendencies of the CPP.

The opposition parties appeared unrestrained in their willingness to root themselves in the multitude of local interests/issues that came up in the various regions of the country. They supported almost every local discontent, including the secessionist pretensions of the Ewes in British Togoland. Their federalist demands provided a challenging alternative to the centrist inclinations of the CPP. The intensity of the conflict between the CPP and its opponents over the structure of the future political framework for governance in Ghana necessitated further constitutional reforms as negotiations between the parties began in earnest. One outcome of this process was the new general election called in 1956 in which the opposition parties won more votes and seats than the CPP in Ashanti and the North. Overall, the opposition won 43 per cent of the poll in 99 contested seats, while the CPP won 57 per cent. On the strength of its performance, the opposition won concessions on the question of constitutional reform. It was dissuaded from pushing the federalist claim any further. Instead, interim regional assemblies were created and measures were introduced to meet its demands for constitutional and minority safeguards. The 1957 Independence Constitution therefore retained effective legislative and executive power in the centre.

The constitutional accommodation dealt effectively with local ethnopolitical protests which appeared not to carry with them any serious threat of secession. Austin suggests that they were more of an infinitely varied conflict in which districts, chiefdoms, and local groups of one kind and another—including the old conflict between the commoners and chiefs—were opposed to each other in party guise. Consequently, the opposition was able to accept the constitutional settlement and to take its place in the 1957 parliament in the unitary independent state of Ghana. The 1957 Constitution preserved broadly liberal democratic rights. Both Nkrumah's CPP and the opposition declared their readiness to respect civil and political rights, including "freedom from arbitrary arrest", a "free press" and "freedom of association". Government and opposition were to share power by strict observance of the rules laid down in the constitution and by establishing a tradition based on the mutual recognition of the rights and obligations of all political groups and tolerance of each other's views. But as events in the period 1957 and 1964 were to prove, these declarations were not meant to be anything more than rhetoric. Violent confrontations were to ensue in the conflict between the CPP and its opponents and, as the ruling party asserted its legal authority to maintain law and order, the passage from a liberal democratic framework of politics to an authoritarian one-party state seemed irreversible.

Ideology and Transition to Authoritarian One-Party State Rule (1957–66)

The power struggles between the ruling CPP and its opponents continued into the independence era, with the opposition not trusting the CPP nationally and the CPP, in turn, not trusting the organised local/regional interests in Ashanti and the North. The regional and local parties in opposition joined forces to form the United Party as a common platform which was to serve as the "loyal opposition" in the parliament of independent Ghana. Strong ideological differences between the CPP and the opposition, however, fed on the lack of trust between them and violence was soon to break out again. Nkrumah's CPP, influenced by its commitment to building a strong centralised state which it perceived as the political precondition for rapid social and economic development, appeared to be in no mood to tolerate the opposition. It advocated a socialist-oriented developmental pattern for Ghana. In pursuit of this goal, it also put forward two arguments. The first emphasised the necessity for a strong centralised government controlled by a single party and the other asserted that a strong and formally organised opposition was alien to Ghanaian and African practice. Its existence only served, therefore, to divide society and threaten the unity of the multi-ethnic society.

On the basis of this belief, the CPP became increasingly intolerant of the opposition alliance's unrestrained willingness to root itself in the multitude of local issues/interests that arose in the constituencies. The opposition, for its part, suspected every step taken by the CPP as part of a wider movement towards centralised authority and socialism. Its leaders perceived themselves as liberal democrats, who, in alliance with the chiefs, felt that they had the "correct" skills and capitalist-oriented policies with which to rule Ghana. They were as intolerant of the ruling party and its ideology as the former was of them. These mistrusts lent a sharp edge to debates in the parliament over the implementation of the constitutional provision for popularly elected regional assemblies. The CPP found the increasingly vociferous regionalist demands in some parts of the country very alarming. In, therefore, responding to the opposition's demand for the greater regionalisation of powers, it decided to abolish the assemblies and replace them with unelected regional houses of chiefs. This particular act breached the spirit of the settlement which the CPP and the opposition reached in the run-up to Ghana's independence, a settlement which entailed a concession or *quid pro quo* whereby in place of the opposition's federalist claim, regional assemblies were to be established. From then on, ethnopolitical violence resurged in Ashanti and the North.

The CPP government acted systematically after independence to weaken the formal opposition, which it finally proscribed in the early 1960s as individual liberties and political rights were suppressed. Austin (1964:44) captures the mood of the times poignantly by observing that:

> Leaders and rank-and-file alike found it difficult to accept the legitimacy of any organised challenge to themselves, and rode roughshod over the opposition, not because they underestimated its challenge, but because they refused to believe that it had the right to exist.

The drift towards a one party-state that began in 1958 culminated in the promulgation of a new Republican Constitution in 1960. Under this constitution, Nkrumah became the first president with extensive powers, including those of preventive detention. An attempt was made to incorporate all major interest groups which had hitherto been autonomous of the state into the ruling party (Lindqvist, 1974:69).

The act of linking all organisations to the CPP and the state led to an artificial fusion between a hitherto vibrant civil society and an increasingly authoritarian state. In addition to the curtailment of civil liberties, minority rights, including ethnic rights, were also suppressed. Yet, the drift to the one-party state hardly secured the political stability and peace which the CPP government desperately sought on the assumption that it was a pre-requisite for the rapid development of the Ghanaian nation. Violent assassination attempts were made to liquidate Nkrumah. After the failure of several of these attempts, the military moved, both for reasons internal to the deteriorating Ghanaian political situation and due to external conspiracy, to overthrow Nkrumah's government on 24 February 1966. One immediate result of the *coup* was the abolition of the one-party state.

Ethnopolitical Protests (1966–92)

The institutional framework for governance in Ghana has, since the 1966 *coup d'état*, alternated between military regimes and brief periods of multiparty-based civilian administration. Both types of regimes have made changes to the structure of the post-colonial state but have not fundamentally moved away from the authoritarian pattern of centralised state power established by Nkrumah. According to Chazan (1983:55):

> Judicial-administrative structures were implanted at the state level at the expense of representative structures and their local government appendages. In other words, the state apparatus was institutionalized in its legal bureaucratic, as opposed to its politico-participatory aspects.

Ideologies, she further asserts, have been of little importance in the shaping of the state apparatus. This observation, she maintains, has been true of the military regimes of the National Liberation Council (NLC, 1966–69), the National Redemption Council/Supreme Military Council (NRC/SMC, 1972–79), as well as of the elected civilian governments of Busia (and the Progress Party (PP), 1969–72), the Limann (and the People's National Party (PNP), 1979–81). The structure of the state has remained relatively untouched by apparent changes at the top in the political direction (Chazan, 1983:57).

Chazan's observation is corroborated by the fact that in spite of the long period of time over which the military has dominated Ghanaian politics, military rule was never legitimated by the very ideologies that split Nkrumah and the opposition. Both the NRC-SMC of 1972–79 and the Provisional National Defence Council (PNDC) which effectively ruled between 1982 and 1992 alluded to some degree of affinity with Nkrumah's ideas. But they also developed their own brands of populist ideologies which, like Nkrumah's, did not tolerate any formally organised opposition. Party political contestations were entirely proscribed. In their place, the military engaged in a shrewd manipulation of the patronage system with a view to linking themselves to local and regional centres of power either through the chiefdoms or strong "local boys" networks. Usually, this happened after they had lost their popular base of support among the students and workers in the urban areas. Turning to the rural or local communities for support often produced a modified alliance between the chiefs and the military-political elites, much to the disadvantage of the civilian-political elites. This re-grouping of elite alliances also informs the repeated attempts made by the civilian political elite and sections of the intelligentsia to promote political mobilisation in the urban areas against military rule. As part of these attempts, the ethnopolitical mobilisation of sections of the electorate has often been resorted to. Little wonder then that ethnicity/regionalism has been a regular feature of politics during periods of transition from military rule to elected civilian or constitutional government.

In the post-1966 era, however, the pattern of ethnopolitical mobilisation, which counterposed Ashanti and northern local interests against the CPP-controlled central state, changed. A more direct inter-ethnic conflict was to emerge between sections of the Akan-twi or Ashanti and the Ewe. Recruitment into national political office is the one issue over which conflict occurs. The civilian PP regime of 1969-72, for example, was the government whose policies of recruitment raised some of the strongest ethno-political protests. Led by Dr Busia, the Progress Party government is on record for not only excluding Ewes from the cabinet but also for dismissing or re-deploying a good number of them from the top ranks of the civil service (Chazan, 1983). The conflict between sections of these two ethnic groups appears to have its roots in the mistrusts that emerged between their elites following their effective co-operation in the *coup* of February 1966 that resulted in the overthrow of Nkrumah. The military junta that overthrew the Nkrumah regime was led by two officers, Colonels Afrifa (an Akan-twi) and Kotoka (an Ewe). Kotoka was later assassinated in suspicious circumstances in a military putsch in April 1967. Afrifa then became the strongman in the NLC and, eventually, took over as Chairman of the Council after skilfully manoeuvring the most senior ranking military officer, General Ankrah, out of that position.

Under Afrifa's leadership of the NLC, recruitment into the army and the politico-administrative apparatuses of the country appeared to take on an ethnic bias in favour of the Akan-twi. This bias spilled over into the electoral politics of 1969 when the Progress Party, perceived as the party of the Ashanti elites, failed to win any electoral seats in the Volta Region which is predominantly Ewe. In the two subsequent general elections held in 1979 and 1992, the total rejection of candidates remotely associated with the Progress Party of the past was repeated. Ethnopolitical protests by sections of the Ashanti elites was loudest throughout the rule of the PNDC in the period 1982-92 when they claimed that recruitment to the top military and political-administrative posts was heavily tilted in favour of the minority Ewes. These protests have not posed any serious, lasting threat to the cohesion of the nation state and seem to have been fairly accommodated within the terms of Ghana's fourth republican constitution.

ETHNOPOLITICAL CONFLICTS SINCE 1993

The February 1994 ethnopolitical rebellion in northern Ghana is, by far, the most violent inter-ethnic conflict to have occurred in the country since it won its independence. Seen in terms of its intensity and the scale of destruction that accompanied it, the conflict appears to be unmatched by previous incidences of political violence in the country. Yet, the fact that it took place in the context of a transition to democracy depicts a familiar pattern, i.e. ethnopolitical violence resurging in a period of (transition to) democratisation. If one looks beyond the North to the other administrative regions in the country, communal violence would also be observed to be widespread. The Eastern, Western, Ashanti and Brong Ahafo regions have been flash-points of communal violence since 1992 (*Uhuru* No. 2, 1994). Although these conflicts have been described as "communal", they also tend to be intra-ethnic, thereby reinforcing the democratic challenges which the explicitly inter-ethnic conflicts of the North draw attention to. Although the duration of the conflicts and the scale of destruction associated with them have not been as extensive in this region as in the North, it is important to stress that the so-called communal clashes are no less significant than the inter-ethnic ones. Both types of conflict underline the potential for the spread of ethno-political disputes and violence in the multi-ethnic Ghanaian nation-state.

Had the violent conflicts in the other regions been as intensive and extensive as those in the North, five of Ghana's ten regions would have been engulfed in ferocious episodes of violence with a distinct potential for creating serious problems of national security with far-reaching consequences for the territorial integrity of the nation-state. The danger that these types of conflicts could spread to the detriment of national unity and development is always clear and present. This is because post-colonial Ghanaian society is not merely multi-ethnic in composition but also socially intermingled in a very complex way. The activation or mobilization of ethnicity in any particular region can spill over into other regions. For this reason, the resurgence of ethno-political or communal violence could have as far reaching a consequence as the peaceful, effective resolution or management of such conflicts.

The choice facing Ghana is one between authoritarian deterrence and the democratic management of ethnopolitical conflicts. The mode of formation of the multi-ethnic nation-state of Ghana has so far been predominantly authoritarian. However, the objectives of ethnopolitical mobilisation in the country appear to be neither radical nor revolutionary since a fundamental or major change in the territorial structure of the country is not the political demand. For many ethnically mobilised groups, the recognition of their fundamental human and democratic rights, including the effective exercise of citizenship rights in the multi-ethnic nation state, is the major focus of political action. The 1994 ethnopolitical conflict that pitched the Konkonbas against the Nanunbas is presented to illustrate this point. To begin with, why the resort to violence? As we shall show, political and ideological considerations loomed large in the dispute.

Konkonba-Dagomba Relations

The Konkonbas and Dagombas belong to two distinct ethnic groups whose members have lived closely as neighbours for centuries. The Dagomba, together with the Mamprusi, Nanumba and Mossi, belong to the majority Mole-Dagbane ethnic group whilst the Konkonba form part of the minority Gurma. The history of the relationship between these two groups is important because it defines the general context within which Konkonba relations with the Nanumba and the Gonja chiefdoms also take place. Konkonba-Dagomba relations became political in character sometime during the early 16th century (Tait, 1964:4). This was the time when the centralised state of Dagomba was known to have invaded and expelled the Konkonba from lands which later became the eastern part of the Dagomba state. These were the regions of Yendi, which became the seat of the highest paramountcy of the kingdom, and Sambu. The Konkonbas moved and settled on land to the north-east of the Dagomba. They considered the new settlement as independent of Dagomba rule. But not all the Konkonbas moved to the north-east of the Oti river that served as a demarcation line of some sort between them and the Dagomba. Some remained in the areas controlled or ruled by the Dagomba. Consequently, the Konkonbas were split between areas under Dagomba rule and those outside Dagomba rule. Indeed, the Germans who arrived in the area in 1896, prior to the British annexation of 1898, distinguished between the independent Konkonba and the conquered Konkonba (Tait, 1964).

According to Tait, the Dagomba had no administrative system or standing army with which to control those Konkonba whom they neither absorbed nor expelled. Dagomba "rule" was limited to sporadic raids to obtain the slaves needed for the annual tribute to Ashanti. But in addition, farm or agriculture products like yams, corn, and sorghum were also collected from the Konkonbas by the Dagomba chiefs. In spite of these payments, most of the Konkonba, except those in the chiefdom of Gushiegu, never admitted Dagomba rule (Tait, 1964:9). However, they were also unable to free themselves from Dagomba rule because they could not defend themselves against Dagomba raids whenever they occurred (Tait, 1964:12). The "powerlessness" of the Konkonba was often translated into violent revenge on nearby Dagomba communities. Out of this peculiar pattern of Konkonba resistance against Dagomba rule emerged a territorial gap between them. In the 1950s, as Tait suggested, the gap was closed by a westward drift of the Konkonba who began to occupy the land. The nature of

Dagomba responses to the Konkonba expansion or westward drift has not been disclosed in Tait's works. But, by inference, Tait seems to suggest that the Konkonba territorial expansion went unchallenged.

It was probably the Dagomba's fear of the Konkonba's ability to be "infinitely loyal to a fellow clansman, instantly aggressive to an outsider" (Tait, 1964:12) that prevented their direct incorporation into the Dagomba state. This, according to Tait, enabled the Konkonba to "preserve their own way of life". If this was actually the case, then one can argue that violence contributed in part to the westward drift of the hitherto independent Konkonba who lived to the east of the Oti river for centuries. But to what extent did the British annexation and imposition of indirect rule affect the hostile or violent relationship between the Konkonba and the Dagomba? Did the British colonial state stay aloof from the violent conflicts in the area, or did it act by creating an institutional framework for controlling such conflicts effectively?

Effect of British Colonial Rule

There is some evidence to support the claim that after the British formally amalgamated the Northern Territories with the rest of the Gold Coast in 1934, efforts were made to extend the spheres of jurisdiction of the Dagomba chiefs within the general context of the colonial chieftaincy ordinances of the 1930s and 1940s. These ordinances, as earlier suggested, were introduced to strengthen the power of the chiefs via-a-vis the so-called rebellious commoners who, as in Ashanti and other areas, were challenging the authority of the chiefs as functionaries of the colonial state. The British, according to Tait, ignored the historical division between the "Konkonba under Dagomba rule" and the "independent riverain Konkonba". Consequently, within the broad context of its policy of indirect rule, Britain proceeded to strengthen the power of the Dagomba chiefs over the Konkonba living under their jurisdiction. These were the eastern chiefdoms of Zabzugu, Sunson and Demon. However, by the mid-1940s through to the early 1950s, sections of the Konkonba were rebelling "against continual extortion" in these areas. In response to that violence, the British built a police station in Saboba.

In addition to the strengthening of the powers of chiefs, the British also encouraged the appointment of Konkonba sub-chiefs in the Dagomba chiefdom of Gushiegu. These sub-chiefs were, however, of very little importance/ significance to the Konkonba unless they were also Kokonba elders in their own right (Tait, 1964:10–11). The lack of legitimacy of the sub-chieftaincyship among the Konkonba underpinned the failure of the institutional framework put in place by the British for managing Dagomba-Konkonba relations at the local government level. While the attempt to create an institutional framework where one had not hitherto existed was not a bad idea *per se*, it would seem that the authoritarian character of that framework ultimately reinforced pre-colonial conflicts between the two ethnic groups.

British political amalgamation of the Northern Territories with the rest of the Gold Coast had one practical significance. It did not merely lump together the pre-colonial centralised states of the northern Dagomba kingdoms and the acephalous political traditions of the Konkonba, but also reproduced their prevailing political conflicts into the colonial and post-colonial state systems. From there on, the major question was whether the hostile relations between the two groups could be transformed into a peaceful, civil relationship within the institutional framework of the state.

Relations in the Decolonisation and Post-Colonial Eras

The violent clashes of 1994 between the Konkonba and their ethnically different neighbours were a tragic and dramatic reminder of the fact that the historically hostile relations between them have not been transformed. Tait had, in his observations in the 1950s, identified the growing trade carried on in some of the Konkonba markets as a potent instrument of change. These markets were becoming the focal points around which thriving commercial centres were organised bringing together Konkonba sellers of sheep, goats, fowl, grain and yams; Yoruba traders in cloths, beads, bicycle parts, and hoe blades; and Mossi butchers and weavers (Tait, 1964:11-12). How far Tait's "forecast" has been realised in the nearly four decades of post-colonial authoritarian state rule is yet to be empirically ascertained. There is scanty information on how the economic development or growth of Konkonba markets has affected the social structure of the Konkonba. This renders the task of explaining the role of the uneven development factor in ethnopolitical conflicts very unfeasible today.

A wide chronological gap in the systematic documentation of Konkonba-Dagomba political relations in the post-colonial era also leaves us with little factual information to inform analysis or policy-making. Tait's work ended abruptly in 1956 and was published in 1961 and 1964. What happened to the political relationship between the two ethnic groups in the period between 1957 and 1980 is yet to documented. This notwithstanding, it would not be unreasonable to conjecture that the mode of management of the conflict between the two groups in the post-colonial period has not fundamentally differed from that of the colonial era. Under Ghana's authoritarian regimes, from the CPP to the PNDC, ethnopolitical conflicts have tended to atrophy while the periods of democratisation, albeit brief, they have generally tended to resurge. Between 1952 and 1966, Nkrumah used the CPP's organisational framework to counterbalance the power of the chiefs in the regions and the districts. This policy is generally assumed to have undermined the authority of the chiefs which the colonial state had acted to strengthen in the 1930s and 1940s. It did not however alter the authoritarian essence of governance into which the CPP increasingly slid.

With the exception of the periods 1969–71, 1979–81 and since 1993, Ghana's post-1966 regimes have been predominantly military and authoritarian. This makes the absence of an institutional framework for democratic politics very conspicuous. Not surprisingly, the resurgence of ethnopolitical conflicts has tended to be violent because of the lack of an institutional-political framework facilitative of peaceful political management. In the absence of the deterrent presence of coercive force, there is often no institutional framework for civil and rational political behaviour leading to the peaceful resolution of conflict at least at local governmental levels. It is within the context of a general lack of a tried and effective institutional-political framework that the resurgence of violent conflicts between the Konkonba and their neighbours will be analysed.

The 1994 Ethnopolitical Rebellion

The war of 1994 (31 January–10 February) was essentially a resurgence of the violent conflict that occurred in 1981. Both the 1981 and 1994 conflicts occurred during transitions to democracy. But while the 1981 conflict was confined to the Konkonba and the Nanumba, the 1994 war drew in the Gonjas and the Dagombas as well. What explains the resurgence and spread of this ethnopolitical violence? It is generally assumed that the Konkonba went to war with the Nanumba and then with the Gonja and the Dagomba because of a dispute over land and paramountcy (*Daily Graphic*, 10 February 1994). A closer look at the arguments and counter-arguments on the issues does not, however, explain how the demand for land and paramountcy translated into violence. In fact the incident that ignited the infernal clashes even seems to make the link between Konkonba demands and the outbreak of war spurious. The quarrel began over the sale of a guinea fowl which sparked off a fight between the individuals involved and then escalated into an inter-ethnic war. Strange as these series of events may be, their significance would be better understood if the war is perceived as an ethnopolitical rebellion. Rebellion against whom? For what reasons and by what means?

The manner in which the war was fought suggests that the groups involved acted essentially as members of pre-colonial ethnic nations rather than as citizens of the Ghanaian state. They appeared not to be interested any more in looking to the central state to resolve their conflicts. In fact, at the point of the outbreak of violence, all the groups were looking inwardly to themselves, rather than to the state, for protection and security. There was clearly no recognition of the central state; if there was, then its presence was not felt or seriously reckoned with. In addition, I would also argue that the issues raised by the inter-ethnic conflict could not be resolved without some reform or change in political relations and the institutional framework for their conduct. It could not be done without a decisive and constructive intervention by the state. The nature of the violence indicates that either existing grievances have generally been ignored or that the institutional framework for managing ethnopolitical conflicts has not enabled the core issues to be addressed effectively. The violence drew attention to this problem but, it did so in a manner that put the central state on the spot and raised serious questions about its capacity to enhance the peaceful resolution of prevailing conflicts.

After the military intervened and effectively stopped the war in 1981, the Limann government commissioned investigations into the causes of the conflicts in the area. Similar investigations were also authorised in the mid- and late 1980s. The reports of the three different committees/commissions of enquiry have neither been published nor implemented (*Uhuru*, 2, 1994; *Daily Graphic*, 11 February 1994; *Ghanaian Times* 17 February 1994). Not publishing the reports has led to a dearth of information on the conflict and stifled a rational and factually-based public debate on how to peacefully resolve the conflict. It looks as if over the period 1981–1994, the state did not move beyond *ad hoc* security measures to contain the violence in the region. The government's indecisive attitude raises questions about why it chose not to act on the issues. More importantly, how did its failure to be decisive affect the relationship between the ethnic groups and the state? One of the issues which illustratively answers the question is the conflict over the idea of a Konkonba paramountcy.

The Case for Konkonba Paramountcy

Prior to January 1994, the Konkonba were understood to have petitioned the central government and the National House of Chiefs for the creation of a Konkonba paramountcy in the Northern Region. Whether this demand formed part of the issues that led to the war of 1981 is difficult to establish factually. However, if it is assumed that the paramountcy demand can be dated from 1981, then it can be postulated that at the time hostilities broke out in 1994, the issue had been around for about thirteen years. Not too long a time one may say, given the history of struggles for land and political power in other societies the world over. But when outstanding conflicts degenerate into war causing extensive destruction to already underdeveloped regions, the length of time ceases to be the important factor upon which to judge the perpetrators of that violence. The more interesting question is: what are the arguments for the Konkonba paramountcy and what was the nature of the state's response to them? For now, the arguments for and against the paramountcy can only be documented by putting together sketchy press articles and reports. These sources also present the case *against* the Konkonba claim in more eloquent terms than the case *for* it.

The closest one comes to capturing the fundamental issues upon which the Konkonba rest their claim is the historical account given by Tait and to which we referred earlier in this chapter. It is the assertion that the Konkonba, a traditionally acephalous group, have never recognised Dagomba rule over them but have also not been able to free themselves from the overlordship of the latter (Tait, 1964: 18). The history of their hostile relationship however defines the broader context of the 1994 war, rather than explains it. It has been suggested that the Konkonba demand was merely a reaction to "leaked" information regarding the creation of twelve new paramountcies intended to "address minority tribe concerns" in the Northern Region. The proposed distribution of the new paramountcies excluded the Konkonbas. Suspicion of their political exclusion led the Konkonba Youth Association to petition the National House of Chiefs and the government for the creation of a Konkonba Paramountcy (*Daily Graphic*, 23 February 1994). The association, which is led by learned Konkonba elites, proposed to name the paramountcy *Ukpaikpabor* (*Daily Graphic*, 23 March 1994) and argued for it on three principal grounds: representation, citizenship and land.

The Konkonba argue that they form the second largest group among the five major ethnic groups in the region. However, "they do not have any representation on the traditional council" and feel excluded from holding political offices be it at the regional or district levels of the state (*Daily Graphic*, 10 February 1994; *Uhuru*, 2, 1994:22). Underneath this problem is the apparent lack of recognition of the Konkonba both as citizens of Ghana and as original inhabitants of the land on which they live by the politically dominant ethnic groups. They are made to feel stateless and landless, despite the fact that "intermarriages" have led to a fusion of "Konkonba blood in the Dagomba paramountcy". The Konkonba have countered their opponents by citing historical references that establish their claim as original inhabitants and owners of land in what is now the Northern Region of Ghana. Much more than a claim for the restoration of ancient Konkonba land, the reference to history proves the point that they have always been part of the land that was incorporated into the Gold Coast and was retained as part of the territorial sovereign state of Ghana. Hence their assertion of a "legitimate right" to Ghanaian citizenship and a share of the land. But there is a counter view to the Konkonba argument.

The Case against Konkonba Paramountcy

The case against the paramountcy begins with an identification of land as the primary source of the conflict. It has been suggested that the creation of a Konkonba paramountcy would require taking land away from the other ethnic groups of the region (*Daily Graphic*, 11 February 1994:7). The argument is simple but powerfully expressed: "Paramountcy must rest on land which the Konkonba do not have and, therefore, they cannot have a paramountcy" (*Daily Graphic*, 23 March 1994; 11 February 1994). In support of this argument, history and culture are used conjointly. The Dagombas claim that their chiefdoms were already established in the early 15th century, prior to Konkonba settlement of those lands. The Konkonbas have since been known as immigrants and tenants, rather than owners, of the land they claim to be theirs. In addition to their alleged immigrant status, reference is made to the acephalous character of the social and political organisation of the Konkonba. In contrast to the centralised states of the Dagomba Kingdom, the Konkonba political formations were neither centralised nor hierarchically structured. Their highest officials were elders, not chiefs, and it was not until the 1930s and 1940s that Konkonba "sub-chiefs" were first appointed (Tait, 1964).

Both the immigrant origin of the Konkonba and their traditionally "state-less" form of political organisation preclude any legitimate claim from them to land and, consequently, paramountcy. Even if these arguments are considered to have been put forward essentially to undermine the basis of the Konkonba paramountcy claim, they highlight a fundamental contestation which would have to be factually addressed, if any compromise on the land issue is ever to be reached. In addition to these points, it has also been suggested that practical problems impede the creation of any Konkonba land because "the other ethnic groups have not been amenable to the idea of a Konkonba paramountcy". So long as some ethnic groups find the Konkonba aspiration "unacceptable", any government decision may result in the intensification or escalation of the violence (*Daily Graphic*, 11 February 1994:7). Essentially on these grounds, the idea of a Konkonba paramountcy is rejected.

Because the Konkonba have built their case around citizenship and the Dagomba chiefdoms reject it on the grounds of tradition and history, the two groups have been speaking across rather than to each other. There is no deny-ing that there is a potential for conflict built into their respective claims. However, it is not this conflict *per se* that is challenging but rather, how it can be managed or resolved peacefully. What are the institutional processes for addressing such conflicts? How did the groups in conflict take to these channels and how did the central state respond to them?

Institutional Relapse and Outbreak of Violence

Apart from the deterrent presence of its armed personnel, the central govern-ment has not, in the past, moved beyond military intervention to create condi-tions for the peaceful resolution of the conflict in the Northern Region. Inability to perform the latter function is evident in the institutional relapse that pre-ceded the outbreak of ethno-political rebellion. The closest linkage between the violence and the state's institutional relapse can be deduced from statements made by two members of parliament who represented the different rival groups. One suggests that the Konkonba "believe that it is only through vio-lence that their main objective of acquiring land and elevation of Konkonba chiefs to the status of paramountcy could be achieved" (Ibn Chambas, Nanumba, *Daily Graphic*, 10 February 1994). To substantiate this point, reference is made to a *procedural* flaw in the manner in which the Konkonba submitted their memorandum for paramountcy. According to the proponents of this posi-tion, it is not the absence or lack of institutional channels that led to the violence but the unwillingness of the Konkonba to pursue their paramountcy ambitions within the existing channels. The Konkonba Youth Association violated laid down procedures by addressing its memorandum to the central government and the National House of Chiefs, instead of the Regional House of Chiefs and the *Ya-Na* of Dagomba. In so doing, it did not only disregard but also probably offended the regional traditional authority vested with the power to create new paramountcies.

The Konkonba, according to another suggestion, were inadvertently encouraged to flout established procedures when the President of Ghana, during the 1992 electoral campaign, made a promise to assist them to attain the paramountcy. This might have aroused the suspicion of the *Ya-Na* of Dagomba and "neighbouring ethnic groups" regarding the motives of the government (*Daily Graphic*, 19 February 1994:7). In the circumstances, the failure of the Konkonba to conform to existing institutional procedures for processing memoranda for paramountcy resulted in their case being left unattended.

A contending point of view suggests that there was no institutional-procedural flaw in the conduct of the Konkonba. The violence, it would seem, was the result of "misrule and disrespect for other ethnic groups" in a regional or local power relationship that was "totally unacceptable, undemocratic and not practicable in Ghana" (Moses Mabenga, Konkonba, *Ghanaian Times*, 10 February 1994). Lack of confidence in (or recognition of the legitimacy of) the regional institutions, it seems, led the Konkonba to look beyond the regional authority to the central state and its institutions. At this stage, a conflict over "the rules of the game" can be deduced from the statements made by the influential members of the rival Konkonba and Nanumba groups. Here was the institutional dimension of the conflict, i.e. the issue that put the state at the centre of the resolution of the conflict. But it is not evident, from the available records, that the central government and the National House of Chiefs moved decisively to tackle the issues prior to the outbreak of violence in late January 1994. As earlier noted, the reports of various committees/commissions of enquiry submitted in the 1980s had also not been published. Whatever the reasons were, the lack of action on the part of the central state did not enhance the resolution of the conflict over "the rules of the game" at the regional level. It led to a private build up of arms in the immediate areas of conflict.

Armed Rebellion?

Press reports indicate that both the Nanumba and Konkonba had been stockpiling arms prior to the 1994 war. In fact, it has been suggested that both sides had, since 1981, accused each other of "preparing for war again" (*Daily Graphic*, 11 February 1994:7). This was probably occurring, despite the total statutory ban on the possession of arms and ammunition in the Nanumba, East Gonja and Krachi Traditional areas by Executive Instruments 1 and 15 issued, respectively, in 1981 and 1985 (NRCD 58, 1972). It is suggested that the Nanumbas believed that the police had ignored complaints that the Konkonba were stockpiling arms for a large scale offensive against them. Such complaints or warnings were also reported to have been made either directly to government officials or through the press several months before the war (*The Mirror*, 19 February 1994; *Ghanaian Chronicle*, 31 October 1993). But the government's response, whatever form it took, neither allayed the fears of the Nanumba nor assured the Dagombas of protection when the war finally began. Tension mounted over the years as a spiral of suspicion, threat, arms build-up, and inaction on the part of the state finally pushed the ethnic groups to the edge. Physical combat had become inevitable.

It began with a raid on the armoury of the Bimbila Police Station by a mob of Nanumbas who were reacting angrily to the interception and seizure of arms and ammunition being transported by road to the area. After emptying the police armoury, the police station was set on fire. According to police sources, local opinion leaders led the mob attack on the police station (*Daily Graphic*, 11 February 1994:7). The action of the Nanumba demonstrated a loss of confidence in the ability of the central state, and for that matter, the local police to protect them against a Konkonba offensive which they believed was pending. When the war finally broke out, the Nanumba relied on the police armoury they had captured, while the Konkonba used light weapons, including bows and arrows and guns. Despite the presence of the 6th Infantry Battalion of the Ghana army and a detachment of the Airborne Force in the municipality of Tamale, the Dagomba felt compelled to set up a war office and an ammunition manufacturing depot during the war (*Uhuru*, 2, 1994). Hence, the Dagombas, like the Konkonba and Nanumba, also showed a lack of confidence in the ability of the state's military garrison to protect them.

The history of slow central government response to the prevailing conflict in the Northern Region raised doubts, among the rival ethnic groups, about its ability not only to protect them but also to assist them to resolve their conflicts peacefully. Although the destruction of the police station strategically enhanced the violence that subsequently occurred, the political significance of that action needs to be clearly put in focus. In the absence of an institutional framework within which all the groups, at the local level, felt they could effectively pursue their aspirations, the police station, which was the only symbol of the presence of the modern state at the local-level, stood bare and deprived of political legitimacy. Until 1989 when local government reforms led to the creation of partly elective District Assemblies in the country, Ghana had no deliberative and representative framework at the local level. Traditional councils had existed but they had remained largely unelective and were narrowly confined to matters of customary and traditional practices. By and large, the ineffectiveness of these institutions to resolve chieftaincy disputes contributed to intra-ethnic violence at the local level (*Uhuru*, 2, 1994; *Ghanaian Times*, 14 February 1994).

Both the weakness of chieftaincy institutions and the general lack of a politically representative framework at local levels contributed to an institutional vacuum which politically robbed the police of their legitimacy and portrayed them as naked coercive instruments incapable of ensuring security and peace in the area. Consequently, war broke out in 1994 at a time when a cycle of mutual suspicion over the stockpiling of weapons and preparations for war fed on the loss of political legitimacy by the local police, the only symbol of the modern state in the local community. Apparently at that point, the central government appeared to have effectively let down all the parties to the conflict. There is no evidence that it favoured one against the other. Rather, it simply did not appear to have acted either pro-actively or decisively to allay the feeling of insecurity on each side. The cause of the war must, therefore, be traced jointly to the conduct of the state and the lack of a viable institutional-political framework within which open deliberations on the contending points of conflict could have taken place. Can the state ever respond effectively and constructively to the ethno-political challenges to its authority? It is to this question that we now turn our attention.

STATE RESPONSE TO ETHNOPOLITICAL IDEOLOGY

Why do communal groups resort to violence over issues which the state, as the central political authority of the land, can be duly expected to manage or resolve in peaceful/democratic ways? I have argued that it is partly due to the lack of an institutional-political framework for shaping the conduct of the parties to a dispute and to re-direct them into rational and democratic delibera- tions. It is the responsibility of the central state to fulfil these conditions. While Ghana's past authoritarian regimes upheld the centralised structure of the state, they failed to develop the institutional capacity that can enhance the resolution of conflicts democratically, especially at the local levels. This is also the claim of the Konkonba. For the Nanumba and, perhaps, the Dagomba the central state appeared incapable of underwriting the security of their lives and property in the face of suspicion that the rival Konkonba were building up arms for war.

The inability of successive governments since 1981 to implement commis- sioned reports on the causes of the conflict also created a situation within which rival ethnic groups appeared to be taking the law into their own hands. The case for the political management or peaceful resolution of the ethnopolitical violence in the Northern Region rests on the creation of an institutional-political framework that is more conducive to rational deliberation and negotiations leading to compromises over contending issues. But this can only be done through a statecraft that facilitates a dispassionate examination of the factual basis of the claims and counter-claims over which violent conflict occurs. Upon closer examination of the arguments for and against the Konkonba paramountcy, one would be struck by the ability of the respective proponents to reason and state their cases. If so, at what point in time did reason translate into violence and why? In my opinion, the intensity of the ideological and polit- ical factors at play made any rational deliberations between the rival groups without the intervention of the state impossible. Political intervention by the state had become necessary but there was no proof that it could be delivered. A few examples would illustrate this point.

To use the *ancient* origins and culture of any ethnic group as the basis upon which to reject their claims to citizenship rights in the modern state of the 1990s suggests a politico-ideological standpoint at variance with contemporary reality. The point is, any perception of the Konkonba as "immigrants" originating from the neighbouring Republic of Togo contradicts the reality that they are recognised by law as Ghanaians with a legitimate electoral constituency and representation in the national parliament. Otherwise, it would be justified to ask: who has violated the constitution of Ghana by conferring citizenship on the Konkonbas since 1957 when Ghana acquired its sovereign state status? Was it the colonial state or Nkrumah or the post-Nkrumah regimes which, of course, include the PNDC and the NDC government? The Konkonbas are, incontrovertibly, citizens of Ghana and therefore Ghanaians. It would require not only a reversal of the sovereign status of Ghana but also the undoing of the colonial annexation of the land on which they had lived for centuries and, prior to 1934, to de-nationalise them as citizens of Ghana.

On the other hand, it can similarly be argued that since the traditional political organisation of the Konkonba was acephalous and never centralised like the states of the Dagomba chiefdoms, the demand for paramountcy in the late twentieth century lacks legitimacy whether on grounds of tradition or citizenship. Chiefs in Ghana, including the paramountcies, derive their legitimacy primarily from tradition and history and only, secondarily, from the modern state. Citizenship alone may be sufficient a qualification for holding national political office but not adequate for holding a traditional office in the indigenous ethnic community, whether at regional, district or local levels. This is why the justification of Konkonba "legitimate right" to paramountcy on grounds of citizenship alone is flawed. Any attempt to ignore this fact instantly creates major political problems. What would be the relationship between the Konkonba Paramountcy and the principal Dagomba Paramountcy held by the *Ya-Na*? Is it political parity with the traditional Dagomba paramountcy that the Konkonbas are seeking? Or is their demand also an admission of Dagomba rule over them after centuries of resistance and assertion of Konkonba autonomy?

If the Konkonba demand is interpreted as a solid shift in their political and ideological position in favour of accepting Dagomba rule under the *Ya-Na*, then one of the major obstacles to peaceful political relations between the groups may be disappearing. However, if the claim of Konkonba paramountcy is aimed at creating political parity with the traditional Dagomba paramountcy, then there arises a very difficult problem which might never be solved. Both tradition and history do not appear to support the position that the Konkonba have a "legitimate right" to a chiefly paramountcy; one had never existed. How can such a claim be effectively dealt with by the state? Is a peaceful resolution of the conflict possible? The two examples show the nature of the ideological and political issues at stake and indicate that the problem cannot be resolved without bringing the state back into the arena. What forms of state intervention can enhance the prospects for a peaceful conflict resolution?

In Search of Credible State Intervention?

A number of issues have so far been identified which require state intervention. Those bordering on the ideological and the political cannot be resolved without state intervention. But what form of intervention is necessary? The clearest statement of the state's policy regarding the land question was made by the NDC government official responsible for chieftaincy affairs. He was reported to have stated that the government "will thoroughly investigate all land and boundary problems in order to restore peace in the country" (*Ghanaian Times*, 14 February 1994). Government intervention through the setting up of committees of investigation has so far been ineffective due to the apparent inability of successive governments to publish and/or implement the proposals contained in the reports submitted. It is the one area where neither governmental threats nor promises have been credibly followed through in the past. It is, therefore, not the sort of intervention that would enhance the peaceful resolution of conflicts. Lack of state action has not only disappointed rival groups, but also ultimately led to violence and constrained the peaceful resolution of conflicts.

The only sphere where effective state intervention has been evident is the imposition of security measures through the peace-keeping roles of army and special police task forces. The government has, in response to the 1994 rebellion, moved beyond the security operations to the procedural question and its institutional requirements. For example, the Konkonba Youth Association's memorandum for the paramountcy has now been formally submitted to the Regional House of Chiefs. The second movement has occurred at the institutional level where a Permanent Negotiating Team has also been established to work towards an effective resolution of the conflict. Its work is complemented by the presence of the army and police Special Task Force. It is clear from these measures that the government has moved beyond the law and order enforcement function to the legal-rational or administrative sphere. Evidently, a negotiating team would simply not act as a fact-finding committee. So, by implication, the state itself has moved, somewhat, beyond the committee/commission stage of conflict resolution. Yet there is a huge deficit of public confidence in the ability of government to implement reports or agreements, given the record of its past performance.

Although state intervention of any kind that prevents ethnopolitical violence is important and commendable, short-term solutions are also clearly understood not to be adequate substitutes for long-term ones unless they serve as incremental steps towards a lasting solution. This task requires another type of state intervention, perhaps a more difficult and challenging one. It is the creation of conditions within which conflict over "the rules of the game" could be managed and resolved through reform or a re-definition of existing rules via negotiations. The need for an institutional-political or political-rational sphere in which representation by elites and participation by the mobilised masses in democratic deliberations over issues in dispute can be encouraged, can hardly be overemphasised. The ideological and political issues that underpin competing ethnicities cannot all be resolved through negotiations with only the elites of the different groups. The wider public sphere consisting of the villages, districts and region where the war took place have to be brought into the politics of rational and democratic deliberations to resolve these issues. What framework exists for this function?

The political parties have a role to play. But so too should the various youth associations and occupational groups. The challenge lies in how to create an institutional framework which, while accommodating the plurality of groups also facilitates their political integration. Such a framework would at worst increase the institutional options for the peaceful resolution of conflicts. At best, it will cloth the existing regional administrative and chieftaincy institutions with the political legitimacy they lack today but which they also urgently require for any effective performance. This is the one area where action is vitally required and public debate could generate ideas to inform the decisions of the negotiating machineries.

If the points raised so far centre on the argument that a different type of state intervention is required, there are also a number of areas where the law enforcement functions of the state need to be reinforced. In other words, a distinction is being drawn between two types of state intervention. The first consists of building public confidence in the capacity of the state to promote the peaceful resolution of conflicts through negotiated pacts and democratic institution-building. The second involves law enforcement functions which have to be strengthened in order to restore public confidence in the state's ability to exercise its sovereign power. In the case of the latter, a few examples will be instructive. First of all, the legitimacy of the citizenship of the Konkonba is a matter on which decisive action from the state is required. The identity of its citizens cannot be dealt with by any other authority within the territorial confines of the state except the central government. Prompt action on this question, i.e. a political re-affirmation of the Konkonba as Ghanaians, would enhance the work of the negotiating team by removing one of the major contentious issues in the conflict.

Resolving the citizenship issue should facilitate the resolution of the land question. If the state can juridically defend or protect the citizenship of the Konkonba, then it should also be prepared to act decisively to resolve the land issue. Land can certainly not be taken away by force from citizens organised as specific ethnic groups and given to citizens from other ethnic groups. In the highly complex situation that prevails in the Northern Region, it would require enormous resources, including army and police presence, to protect the land that will be created for the Konkonba. However, a re-distribution of land which is based on the state underwriting the *quid pro quo* may be more popular than the confiscation of land. It could take the form of compensation through increased development project funding in the areas where land is ceded to enhance peaceful relations. Whatever the modalities agreed upon to resolve the land question, the state must be able to exercise its powers to enforce agreements and to deter violations.

On the issue of the relationship between a future Konkonba paramountcy and the *Ya-Na* of Dagomba, it is essentially a matter for negotiation, compromise and agreement between the parties to the conflict. This is one of the important areas where diplomatic statecraft can deal with an historically troublesome, if not intractable problem, i.e. the political relationship between the Konkonba and the Dagomba. However, the facts speak for themselves. The status of the paramountcy of the *Ya-Na* cannot be challenged at will by any group without the risk of a violent conflict. The state must decisively remove this issue from the arena of contestation. Either it formulates a clear policy on the political status of the paramountcies or it re-defines the basis of their authority and power relationships with different paramountcies as well as the state.

In the long-run, a political solution may not only be less expensive in economic and human terms, but also provide the basis for a peaceful and incremental solution of historically-rooted conflicts like that between the Konkonba and the Dagomba chiefdoms. Uneven socio-economic development may ultimately explain why the north has become the most volatile conflict region of the Ghanaian nation-state. It is possible that the relatively underdeveloped state of the region explains the strength of the intensity of the ethnic or cultural distinctiveness of the Konkonba, the Gonjas, and Dagombas. In an era of multi-party politics, these subjective identities can be manipulated for various purposes. Ironically, the members of parliament of the warring factions belong to the same party. The solution to the conflict is not simply a matter of development resources and projects. It is also a question of political power, reason and democratic politics.

CONCLUSION: THE DEMOCRATIC ROUTE TO THE INTEGRATION
OF THE NATION AND STATE

The history of the recent ethnopolitical rebellion in Ghana's Northern Region can be taken as clear evidence of the existence of conflicts that predate the creation and growth of the modern multi-ethnic nation state. It has been shown that Ghana's authoritarian regimes have largely presided over the degeneration of these conflicts into ethnopolitical rebellions, unable to deal with their causes and to resolve them democratically/peacefully. Thus, during transitions to democracy when authoritarian rule is reformed and liberal democratic constitutions are installed, ethnopolitical conflicts, including violence, resurge especially at local levels. I have argued that it is not the open expression of these conflicts that constitutes the challenge to the multi-ethnic nation-state but rather their democratic management or resolution. It essentially requires the creation or reform of existing institutional structures to facilitate rational and democratic deliberations. It is the lack of such a framework plus the legacy of authoritarianism that explain the resurgence of ethnopolitical violence during transitions to democracy.

The ethnopolitical challenge to the nation-state is, in that regard, a claim for *politics* in which social groups can autonomously organise to participate democratically in national and local decision-making, in arenas that affect their interests and capacity to act. What form the framework being advocated would take remains an empirical question. However, the liberal democratic constitutional framework has essentially defined the broad context within which local institutions can be created or reformed to enable democratic representation. The function of such representative institutions is not to replace the existing district and regional bureaucracies of the state. It can complement their functions by accrediting them with political legitimacy.

The experiences of the 1950s show that ethnopolitical protests can be effectively managed within the framework of a liberal democratic constitution. The NLM federalist claim and the Togoland question were dealt with effectively through elections and constitutional reforms in 1956 and 1957. Violence only erupted when the CPP government broke the seal of the democratic agreement on the creation of elective regional assemblies in the late 1950s. Violence has also attended party politics because of intolerance among political and opinion leaders and their refusal to recognise the right of opposing groups to exist within the state. But ethnopolitical rebellion essentially draws attention to the lack of institutions for rational and democratic deliberations in conflict resolution especially at the local level. Thus, it challenges the central state either to create conditions for their peaceful resolution or undermine its own political legitimacy and survival.

BIBLIOGRAPHY

Austin, D., 1964, *Politics in Ghana 1946–60*, Oxford University Press, Oxford.

Beckman, B., 1992, "Whose Democracy? Bourgeois versus Popular Democracy", in L. Rudebeck (ed.), *When Democracy Makes Sense*, AKUT, Uppsala.

Bendix, Richard, 1964, *Nation-Building and Citizenship*, John Wiley and Sons, New York.

Chazan, N., 1983, *An Anatomy of Ghanaian Politics: Managing Political Recession 1969-82*, Westview, Boulder, Colorado.

Davidson, B., 1992, *The Black Man's Burden*, James Cury, London.

Gurr, T., 1993, *Minorities at Risk: A Global View of Ethnopolitical Conflicts*, United States Institute of Peace Press, Washington, D.C.

Hettne, Björn, 1990, *Development Theory and the Three Worlds*, John Wiley and Sons, N. Y.

Huntington, S.P., 1968, *Political Order in Changing Societies*, Yale U. P., New Haven.

Hydén, G., 1984, "Ethnicity and State Coherence in Africa", *Ethnic Studies Report*, Vol. II, No. 1, January.

Hydén, G., 1988, "State and Nation under Stress", in Swedish Ministry of Foreign Affairs, *Recovery in Africa: A Challenge for Development Cooperation in the 90s*, Swedish Ministry of Foreign Affairs, Stockholm.

Krasner, S.D., 1984, "Approaches to the State: Alternative Conceptions and Historical Dynamics", *Comparative Politics*, Vol. 19, No. 29.

Lema, A., 1993, *Africa Divided: The Creation of "Ethnic Groups"*, Lund U. P., Lund.

Lindqvist, S., 1974, *Linkages between Domestic and Foreign Policy: The Record of Ghana, 1957-1966*, Studentlitteratur, Lund.

Nzongola-Ntalaja, Georges, 1993, *Nation-Building and State-Building in Africa*, SAPES Trust Occasional Paper Series No. 3, Harare.

Ray, D.I., 1986, *Ghana: Politics, Economy and Society*, Francis Pinter, London.

Rooney, David, 1988, *Kwame Nkrumah: The Political Kingdom in the Third World*, I.B. Tauris and Co. Ltd., London.

Rothchild, D. and R.L. Curry, 1978, *Scarcity, Choice and Public Policy in Middle Africa*, University of California Press, Berkeley.

Sandbrook, R., 1985, *The Politics of Africa's Economic Stagnation*, Cambridge University Press, Cambridge.

Shivji, Issa G. (ed.), 1986, *The State and the Working People in Tanzania*, CODESRIA Books.

Shivji, Issa G., 1992, *Fight My Beloved Continent: New Democracy in Africa*, SAPES Trust, 1992.

Stavenhagen, R., 1986, *Ethnopolitical: A Neglected Dimension in Development Thinking*, in R. Anthorpe and Kráhl A., Development Studies: Critique and Renewal, Leiden.

Tait, David, 1964, *The Konkonba of Northern Ghana*, Oxford University Press, Oxford, second reprint.

Taylor, C., 1979/1993, "Why Do Nations Have to Become States", in G. Laforest (ed.), *Reconciling the Solitudes: Essays on Canadian Federalism and Nationalism*, McGill-Queens University Press, Montreal and Kingston.

Toulmin, Stephen, 1992, *Cosmopolis: The Hidden Agenda of Modernity*, University of Chicago Press, Chicago.

NEWSPAPERS AND PERIODICALS

Daily Graphic
Ghanaian Chronicle
Ghanaian Times
The Mirror
Uhuru.

Chapter 6

The Nation-State Project and Conflict in Zimbabwe

Lloyd M. Sachikonye

INTRODUCTION

The post-independence government of Zimbabwe, like other governments in developing societies, has placed a great deal of emphasis on the concept of national unity. This is a reflection of the realization that national consciousness still rests on a fragile basis and that other forms of consciousness and identity continue to co-exist, albeit in modified forms, alongside this emergent national consciousness. While the existence of other forms of consciousness may not, by itself, constitute a problem, it becomes one when their existence contradicts or obstructs the implementation of the nation-state project. The post-independence government of Zimbabwe views the inculcation of national consciousness and the dilution of ethnic or regional particularism as a major challenge in its project of nation-building. Part of the challenge relates to the eradication of residual forms of institutional racism which was a distinctive feature of the white-settler colonial state. This chapter surveys the attempts made by the government to execute this unitary project and the pitfalls which the pursuit of the project has encountered. It examines the social and ideological basis of the project and the continuing political pressures on it.

We begin the chapter by outlining the *problématique* of the nation-state in contemporary Africa. We then trace the origins of the unitary project in the social basis, ideology and objectives of the nationalist movement. Specific measures to consolidate the nation-state after independence are analyzed in relation to the reconciliation and coalition-building policies espoused by the ruling ZANU-PF party. The setbacks to the unitary project between 1982 and 1987 are assessed with reference to the collapse of the initial post-independence attempt at a government of national unity and the civil conflict that subsequently erupted in the Matabeleland provinces. Finally, the chapter examines the continued pressures which, potentially, could have divisive outcomes for the ruling elite grouped around ZANU-PF and adverse consequences for the quest for national economic reform and ethnic and racial reconciliation.

THE PROBLÉMATIQUE OF THE NATION-STATE IN AFRICA

In the African context, the nation-state, with a few exceptions, derives a great deal of its territorial integrity from colonial boundaries carved out arbitrarily in the 19th century. Those boundaries often took little account of existing political, economic and cultural relationships in African societies with the consequence that whole societies and polities were disrupted by the creation of new territorial boundaries. The challenge of fashioning out modern nation-states from the resultant artificial territorial entities became infinitely more difficult after independence. To return to pre-colonial boundaries, however, would have opened a Pandora's box and hence the decision of the Organization of African Unity tacitly to recognise the territorial integrity of nation-states based on the boundaries inherited from colonialism. The gigantic task facing post-independence governments has been to weld the disparate ethnic entities or nationalities together in a non-coercive manner and thereby promote political and economic stability.

A number of social scientists have questioned the acquiescence of African nationalists to the colonially-derived nation-state. Some have argued that:

> the concept of the nation became attached to the territorial entities of the colonial partition, not as a matter of necessity in the organization of the anti-colonial struggle ... but as a result of the interplay of imperialist and African petit bourgeois interests (Nzongola–Ntalaja, 1988).

To others, the very conception of the nation as the colonially-created nation:

> to be built on the basis of (the) consolidation, rather than (the) creative destruction of the colonial legacy, is itself indicative of a neo-colonial commitment reflecting a class alliance. It is not surprising, then, to see that most of the theories of building new nations out of arbitrarily created colonial territories, find supporting echoes, if not inspiration from organic intellectuals of imperialism—modernization theoreticians especially (Wamba, 1991).

A few other perceptive activists were aware that the acceptance of the post-colonial nation-state meant the acceptance of the legacy of the colonial partition and of the moral and political practices of colonial rule in its institutional dimension. The embrace of colonially-created boundaries was, therefore, bound to be a major handicap (Davidson, 1992). To these analysts:

> ... the colonial partition had inserted the continent into a framework of purely artificial and often positively harmful frontiers. There were others who perceived that a petty-bourgeois nationalism was bound to remain a nationalism subordinate to external powers organized on a capital-owning and capital-commanding basis (Davidson, 1992).

These analysts are sensitive to the clear limitations of contemporary nation-state projects in Africa. They have argued that creative approaches are required to handle the diverse problems which these projects encounter. A re-drawing of boundaries at this stage is not, however, a feasible proposition; in any case, the artificially constructed nation-states have acquired a life of their own, including their own nationalist expression. Zimbabwe is one such state grappling with an inherited, unwieldy legacy of ethnic, regional and racial particularisms and the sharp inequalities inherited from its white-settler colonial past. Although it is a relatively small country of about 10.5 million people and has only two domi-nant ethnic groups—the Ndebele and Shona—it has experienced major conflicts and pressures derived from those legacies.

THE NATIONALIST MOVEMENT AND THE UNITARY PROJECT IN ZIMBABWE

The first phase of the development of the Zimbabwean nationalist movement (from the 1940s to 1950s) shared common characteristics with the independence movements in other African countries. It was a broadly united movement with a minimalist agenda centring on a peaceful and constitutional transfer of power to the black majority. A major feature of the early forms of Zimbabwean nation-alism was the fusion of urban- and rural-based struggles. The anti-colonial movement during this phase drew upon common grievances concerning land expropriation, livestock de-stocking, poor working conditions and the general social oppression faced by the peasant and working classes to press the case for independence. It was an awareness of the potential strength and radicalism of the worker-peasant demands and the possibility of a class alliance between them that led the colonial state to seek to co-opt rural traditional chiefs and repress the trade union movement. The popular base of such labour organisa-tions as the Reformed Industrial Commercial Union and the African Workers Voice Association, organized by well-known nationalists such as Masotsha Ndlovu, Charles Mzingeli and Benjamin Burombo, testified to the resonance of the urban-rural protest movements.

In the latter phase of the development of the nationalist movement, its pre-viously strong urban-rural dimension began to weaken as it became largely dominated by a petit-bourgeois leadership based in the towns. Thus, from having been a broadly integrative social movement, nationalism became increasingly centralised within an elite recruited from the petit-bourgeoisie. The extensive mobilization that occurred during the phase of the armed national liberation struggle from the mid-1960s to 1979 did not fundamentally alter the character of the nationalist movement itself. In fact, the movement became more centralised and the ambition of its leadership was to co-opt potentially autonomous organizations, such as trade union, youth and women's organiza-tions and cooperatives, which could provide a basis for alternative centres of power to emerge.

The popular social base of the nationalist movement was, therefore, fractured as a consequence of the strong desire by the movement's petit-bourgeois leadership to monopolise political power and decision-making. The potentially integrative force of nationalism was thus forfeited as were the pan-ethnic and urban-rural solidarities that had been salient to the character and strength of an earlier phase of the nationalist movement. As the different fractions of the petit-bourgeoisie contended openly and earnestly for power, splits symbolized their narrow ambitions. In those power struggles, ethnic and regional particularisms were often mobilised and utilized. The nationalist movement, previously led by a pan-ethnic leadership in the 1950s, was to be riven into Ndebele and Shona factions under ZAPU and ZANU respectively in the 1960s. A third rump of the movement emerged in the 1970s under such well-known figures as Ndabaningi Sithole, Abel Muzorewa and James Chikerema, a rump which was prepared to cut a deal with the white minority regime.

It is our contention here that although the nationalist movement operated in a colonial context of "divide and rule", of disparate ethnic groups, and of other social forces with a diversity of interests and objectives, it squandered the potential which existed in the popular opposition to the colonial nation-state to build a strong pan-ethnic secular and democratic national liberation movement. That popular basis of nationalism should have been harnessed in a more concerted and innovative manner to develop a consciousness impervious to the negative ethnic and racial manipulations which became common place follow-ing Zimbabwe's independence in 1980.

Like similar nationalist movements in much of Africa, the Zimbabwean movement was characterised by an ideological ambiguity which genuflections to socialism could not obscure—for too long. It did not seek so much a funda-mental reorganization of society based on equity and justice as the acquisition of state power and the levers of accumulation. Yet initially, it had drawn on popularly-based yearnings and aspirations for a more just society. Different social forces had been united in their struggle for such a more equitable and just society and attempts at social distribution immediately after independence were geared towards this direction. The peasantry had a stake in land redistri-bution, workers in improved employment security, and the emergent bourgeoisie in upward mobility within the public sector and a respectable share in the opportunities for accumulation that existed in the private sector.

Land and wage reforms and the policy of Africanization in the public service reflected an attempt to mould a "social contract" between the different social movements which constituted the nationalist coalition. But the reform policies were limited and, soon after independence, quickly encountered struc-tural limitations. With the exception of these limited attempts at social redistri-bution, the inherited property relations were more or less preserved intact. Growing social contradictions towards the end of the decade of the 1980s were soon to set the post-colonial government on a collision course with such popular social groups as labour, students and consumer groups. Attempts at demobilizing or co-opting these social forces characterized the government's *ad hoc* response to those sharpening contradictions.

The point in all of the foregoing is not to argue that the nationalist movement did not view a unitary project as crucial, if not indispensable, to the task of maintaining the territorial integrity and sovereignty of the newly-independent Zimbabwean state. In fact, there was little doubt that the core of the movement would not tolerate anything that remotely threatened or appeared to threaten the dismemberment of the country. The point which we have been driving at is that the unitary project was, from the outset, already a diluted one as a consequence of the dissipation of energies on inter-party and leadership rivalries which exploited ethnic and regional sentiments. This dilution was reinforced by the diminution of a popular social base for the government and the ruling party following the demobilization and/or alienation of key social movements. Rhetorical espousal of national unity can occur simultaneously with subterranean attempts to concentrate power within certain power blocs or ethnic alliances in a way which undermines the very quest for unity. The legacy of divisions based on intra-elite struggles for power was a fully-fledged conflict which burst out within three years of Zimbabwe's independence. However, before we explore the dimensions of that conflict, let us consider how the post-independence government in Zimbabwe defined its unitary project and what the main components of the project were.

THE POST-INDEPENDENCE GOVERNMENT AND THE UNITARY PROJECT

The new post-independence government acceded to power amidst the constraints of the Lancaster House Constitution and the geopolitical/military threat from the then apartheid regime in South Africa. Its room for manoeuvre was generally limited. Further, ZANU-PF, which won the highest number of seats at independence (57 out of 100), was short of the important two-thirds majority necessary for major constitutional amendments. This was the immediate context within which the imperative of national unity was enunciated. As the architect of the post-independence government explained:

> ... by its multi-faceted character and effect, national political unity not only enhances the national spirit, but in so doing creates a conducive atmosphere for the reconciliation of divergent and sometimes antagonistic political and social outlooks and philosophies. By its ennobling and elevating effect, national unity destroys petty and divisive loyalties based upon tribe, region, race, sex and religions and in their place creates and nurtures a national ethos. It has the capacity and power to sublimate these inferior and divisive energies into a superior and transcendent spirit (Mugabe, 1989).

In the first year of independence, there was, therefore, a conscious attempt to create an atmosphere of national unity and stability. In that respect, the policy of reconciliation between the erstwhile warring parties and among the races was conceived. It was a policy hailed for its pragmatism; its outcome was the pre-empting of a white exodus such as had occurred in neighbouring Mozambique. The economy and the machinery of the government did not, therefore, collapse.

Some analysts have interpreted the policy of reconciliation as a bargain with the 100,000 or so whites who stayed on after 1980. The bargain, according to Herbst, was that:

> ... the whites can stay, continue to operate with their businesses and farms, and lead the "colonial life style" that they are accustomed to for the rest of their lives. How-ever, their children are discouraged from staying. ... The racial bargain implies that Zimbabwe will not have to Africanize the economy by force because in a generation or so the white population will have dwindled into insignificance (Herbst, 1990).

However, as Herbst himself acknowledges, this reconciliation policy rested on a fragile basis at the best of times. There had been "a reconciliation of interests" but not of attitudes: the significant electoral victory in 1985 of Ian Smith's party (which won 15 of 20 seats specially reserved for whites) over a more liberal-minded group of white candidates demonstrated this embarrassingly to the Mugabe government.

It is questionable whether it is even helpful to view the reconciliation policy as one which achieved "a reconciliation of interests" especially in view of the growing antagonism among blacks towards the policy in the 1990s. But this is not to assert that in those first few years of independence, the policy did not enhance the credibility and international respectability of the Mugabe govern-ment. It is difficult to think of what an alternative policy towards the whites should have been in the aftermath of the liberation struggle and in the context of the belligerent destabilization strategy of the neighbouring racist regime in South Africa. In our view, in spite of its obvious limitations, the reconciliation policy was a component of the "national unity" project as defined by Mugabe and the ruling ZANU-PF. The "racial bargain", for what it was worth, has since come unstuck but while it lasted, racial tolerance was an important feature of the stability which prevailed in the post-independence period.

Of course, the most important component of the unitary project related to internal unity within the nationalist movement whose two main fractions were ZANU-PF and PF-ZAPU. We have already observed that such a unitary project as was conceived by the nationalist movement was neither coherent nor cohe-sive. Power struggles had resulted in the formation of those fractions which drew their support from ethnic bases in Mashonaland and Matabeleland respectively. The Patriotic Front formed in 1976, and prior to it, the African National Council, represented attempts to unify the different tendencies within the nationalist movement. As it was candidly admitted:

> the tribal character of both ZANU and ZAPU could be explained only in terms of loyalties emanating from old feudal social formations, which revolved around the authority of the tribal king. The fact that the leader of ZANU was Shona and that of

ZAPU was Ndebele, played into these feudal loyalties with the result that the Shonas tended to drift to ZANU while the Ndebele tended to drift to ZAPU (Mugabe, 1989).

The unitary project was tenuous even after the formation of the Patriotic Front. It was so weak in concept and practice that the two fractions fought the independence elections separately. Subsequent attempts to establish a government of national unity initially succeeded (but only partially) with the appointment of several ZAPU ministers in that government. ZAPU's leader, Joshua Nkomo, refused the constitutional Presidency, preferring a cabinet position in which he could wield substantial power. Tensions, exacerbated by the discovery of arms caches on ZAPU-owned properties, provided the immediate context for the collapse of that fragile government of national unity in 1982. In the next section we will explore the consequences of that collapse and the subsequent gradual movement towards a compromise between ZANU-PF and PF-ZAPU.

There were other elements in the amorphous unitary project pursued by the Mugabe government at independence. The pursuit of state constitutionalism in mediating conflicts between various social interests was one method utilised to enhance the new government's credibility. At least for the period 1980-87, the Lancaster House constitutional provisions were not tampered with. Provisions concerning property relations and minority interests were not assailed. While this provided a semblance of stability, it also blocked opportunities for reform, especially that pertaining to the land question. The principal element in an indecisive land policy was the resettlement of land-hungry peasants but in the end only a third of the projected 160,000 families were allocated land by 1990. Although popular but disorganized pressure existed for substantial agrarian reform, the stalling of the reform process by the government was viewed in some quarters as reflecting the ruling elites' acquiescence with the basic structure of property relations pertaining to land. Revelations in 1994 which pointed to the predominance of this elite (consisting of politicians, senior bureaucrats, military officers, and other notables) in the ownership both of state tenant farms and private farms confirmed some suspicions regarding the government's weak commitment to a substantive agrarian reform programme.

Finally, the unitary project was often conceptualized in somewhat narrow terms from a party political perspective. We have discussed elsewhere the elements of what we loosely termed the ZANU-PF's "hegemonic project" which was primarily centred on the subordination to itself of the major civil society institutions ranging from organizations of black entrepreneurs to women and youth groups and the mass media (Sachikonye, 1994). At the heart of the unitary project was the goal of achieving the ascendancy of the ZANU-PF vis-a-vis other political groups. One expression of this desire was the stated goal, from the mid-1980s onwards, to establish a one-party state. The one-party state would represent the fruition of the unitary project. It was forcefully argued that:

> Zimbabweans realised that there would never be permanent peace, development, democracy and social justice in Zimbabwe for as long as there existed two political

parties based upon regional or tribal consideration. What was needed was one political party to which everybody would owe allegiance and be a member, irrespective of tribe, religion or race (Mugabe, 1989).

While there may be some basis for the assertion that regionalism and "tribalism" can, in certain circumstances, militate against stability, it does not follow that the existence of only one party can guarantee such stability. Yet, increasingly, this line was articulated by ZANU-PF. There were references to a "one-party participatory democracy" which it would be ZANU-PF's vocation to construct. There were scathing pronouncements about the role of opposition parties:

> national unity under ZANU-PF discourages the formation of opposition parties by exposing their bankruptcy in political and ideological direction. Indeed, against the background of the existence of a united, mass democratic, socialist-oriented national party, what political programme and ideological direction can an opposition party give to the people as an alternative? (Mugabe, 1989).

Clearly, as the 1980s wore on, the project of national unity was increasingly reduced by ZANU-PF to the issue of single-party rule. This was hardly original as much of Africa in the 1980s was still wedded, with a few exceptions, to the orthodoxy of single-party rule. The debates surrounding the one-party state and the subsequent climb-down of ZANU-PF have been dealt with at greater length elsewhere (Mandaza and Sachikonye, 1991). The only caveat we would add here is that even so, ZANU-PF was not monolithic and especially after the Unity Accord with PF-ZAPU in 1987, there were different currents of opinion within it on the one-party state question. In the next section, we examine the collapse of the unitary project and its eventual resuscitation.

THE COLLAPSE OF THE UNITARY PROJECT AND ITS RESUSCITATION: 1982–87

As we have already observed, although it was a powerful force in the struggle against white-settler colonialism, the nationalist movement itself was riven with divisions. Nevertheless, those divisions, compounded as they were by ethnic tendencies, were not capable of displacing the overall objective of the movement to dislodge the settler regime and seize state power. Squabbles between the petit-bourgeois leadership of the two nationalist fractions, ZANU-PF and PF-ZAPU, did not extend to disputes over the territorial integrity of the existing state. There were no debates on or threats of secession despite those squabbles. However, the collapse of the government of national unity in 1982 created a much more volatile atmosphere in the newly-independent state. Not only were PF-ZAPU cabinet ministers sacked, a civil war of a low-intensity nature also erupted in Matabeleland and raged intermittently between 1982 and 1987.

Thousands of casualties resulted from the armed clashes which occurred between the Zimbabwean military forces and the so-called "dissidents" or "bandits" (who were ex-combatants from PF-ZAPU's liberation army). Civilians constituted the majority of the casualties as the military sought to flush out the "dissidents" who were basically engaged in a guerrilla war. Property estimated in millions of dollars was destroyed, and by 1984, about 500,000 acres of commercial farmland had been abandoned by farmers in Matabeleland (Ncube, 1989). Clearly, there existed amongst the Ndebele peasantry some disaffection over access to land and this would have been thoroughly exploited by the "dissidents" who depended on the succour and security intelligence supplied by the rural populace.

The economic and human cost of that civil conflict has still not been fully evaluated. It was certainly enormous. Development projects could not be implemented under conditions of low-intensity guerrilla warfare. The size of the "dissident" army may have run into several hundreds but it received substantial material and intelligence support from a sympathetic civilian population. The army, which included both ex-combatants and deserters from the newly-constituted Zimbabwe National Army (ZNA), was never really short of arms. However, as the conflict widened to include the third province of Midlands, there were allegations of collusion between the "dissidents" and South African agents. A group of "dissidents" which called itself "Super ZAPU" was reportedly receiving assistance from the South African military. This was interpreted as a case of the articulation in Zimbabwe of the latter's destabilization strategy in the Southern African region.

The presumed support for the "dissidents" by the racist South Africans provided the Mugabe government with another pretext for intensifying military operations in Matabeleland and inflicting punishment on the civilian population. Curfews such as had been enforced during the liberation struggle were imposed; the food weapon was used as a method of coercion against civilians during the drought years of 1981–83. As one observer recalled:

> the suffering of the people arising from the security situation was exacerbated by a drought, which had resulted in an almost total crop failure. In May 1982, Government instituted a drought relief programme for the region. The delivery of relief supplies, however, was very inconsistent. The food situation was further exacerbated by the fact that store owners were unable to transport goods to their stores during this period, and as no buses were running neither the people nor food commodities could be transported between rural and urban centres (Auret, 1992).

The deployment of a North Korean-trained army brigade to the affected provinces raised the level of reported brutalities; the alienation of the civilian peasant population from the army and government became more noticeable.

This account of the context and progression of the civil conflict in the Matabeleland and Midlands provinces is not meant merely to describe the disastrous consequences of the collapse of the nationalist coalition in 1982. It also suggests an all-too familiar scenario in Africa of how a nation-state gradually but inexorably slides into a bloody conflict which, over time, becomes more complex and difficult to resolve. Similar conflicts, but on a grander scale, were underway in neighbouring Angola and Mozambique. However, the Zimbabwean conflict was more unjustified precisely because it was primarily the outcome, not of inherent ethnically-based differences, but of power-struggles within the leadership of the nationalist coalition. The conflicts in Angola and Mozambique were, of course, fuelled by the more explicit and aggressive intervention of South Africa, but if they represented negative lessons for the new Zimbabwe government, the lessons were not thoroughly digested. The "iron-fist" policy employed against the "bandits"—such was the nomenclature also used in Mozambique—had been expected to quell the dissident problem once and for all, and marginalize PF-ZAPU politically. It failed woefully between 1982–87. PF-ZAPU won handsomely in general and local elections in 1985. At the same time, the ethnic bitterness generated by the conflict became more hardened.

The limitations of the military approach to the "dissident" problem were to become quite clear as the fighting dragged on but their repercussions were far-reaching:

> ... many lives were lost, property robbed, or burnt and thousands fled their homes. Development programmes came to a near standstill. Going side by side with this, there were accusations and counter-accusations traded between ZANU-PF and PF-ZAPU with each party blaming the other for the state of terror in western Zimbabwe. While there was little or no development in Matabeleland and part of the Midlands, development went ahead in the provinces of Mashonaland, Manica-land and most parts of Masvingo and the Midlands. The country was thus divided into two parts of unequal development. The government's policy of regional equity in development had been compromised (Mugabe, 1989).

This candour was possible with the benefit of hindsight but these eventualities would, in any case, have been inevitable once brazenly coercive measures, rather than political means, were employed in tackling the crisis. We shall return to the long-term effects of the civil conflict, especially in relation to the heightening of ethnic consciousness, in the next section.

Let us now examine briefly how the nationalist coalition was resuscitated in the late 1980s and how that affected the civil conflict. Protracted negotiations for unity between PF-ZAPU and ZANU-PF began in earnest in 1985. The pressure for reconciliation between these two fractions of the nationalist movement increased because of the economic, human and political cost of the conflict in Matabeleland and parts of the Midlands. Neither of the two fractions was reaping political dividends from it, nor were either of them fully in control of their forces or supporters on the ground. In its proposals, PF-ZAPU suggested the merger of the two political parties with Mugabe serving as the president of the united party. It also suggested that the united party should have two vice-presidents, one from ZAPU and one from ZANU respectively. PF-ZAPU also proposed that the name of the new party should be "ZANU-ZAPU". ZANU countered by urging PF-ZAPU negotiators to drop the name of their party, disband and join ZANU (Chiwewe, 1989).

The haggling between the two parties involved six meetings of the Unity Committee (drawn from the two parties) and nine meetings between Robert Mugabe and Joshua Nkomo. Intensive discussions centred on the sharing of positions of influence and power in the merged party, and of portfolios in the cabinet. The terms of the agreement, otherwise known as the Unity Accord and signed in December 1987, were quite significant in that they were underpinned by a conscious realisation that "the two parties jointly command the over-whelming majority of the people of Zimbabwe as evidenced by the general election results of 1980 and 1985 respectively" (Chiwewe, 1989). At the same time, the leadership of PF-ZAPU pledged "to take immediate vigorous steps to eliminate and end the insecurity and violence prevalent in Matabeleland". More disconcertingly, inserted into the agreement was also a stipulated intention to establish a one-party state in Zimbabwe. From ZANU-PF's perspective, with the PF-ZAPU's agreement to merge, no credible opposition existed any longer to act as an obstacle to its long-held objective to establish a one-party state. But what was nevertheless surprising was PF-ZAPU's acquiescence with this clause in the agreement.

The five years between 1982 and 1987 marked a phase in which ZANU-PF's hegemonic project, such as it was, was under the severest strain. Although PF-ZAPU did not proclaim any intention to separate the Matabeleland provinces from the rest of the country, it had generated a great deal of ethnic support during the civil conflict. The ethnic sentiments sharpened as casualties mounted and development lagged. This was the severest test of the unitary project. As we will show in the next section, the awakened ethnic sentiments in Matabele-land, articulated in the form of hatred towards the Shona-dominated ZANU-PF, would continue to simmer after the 1987 Unity Accord. Following the Accord, there was a restructuring of the two parties with the merging of their cell, branch, district, provincial and national executive structures. At the formal level at least, the fusion of the structures of the two parties signified a new era in post-independence politics in Zimbabwe. The political symbolism which was reflected in the spectacle of the erstwhile "warring parties" mobilizing jointly and their top leaders addressing rallies in Ndebele and Shona heartlands also signified this new era.

Clearly, following the Unity Accord, the unitary project in post-indepen-dence Zimbabwe had been resuscitated but on a more assured basis than at the occasion of the formation of the Patriotic Front in 1976 and the government of national unity in 1980. In this new phase, following the fratricidal "trial of strength" between ZANU-PF and PF-ZAPU, there were substantial personal and group material interests at stake to ensure that the Accord was given a chance to succeed by its authors. For the PF-ZAPU elite in particular, some of whose assets consisting of farms and other property had been expropriated at the height of the dissident campaign, the Unity Accord provided a basis for the resumption of their participation in the capitalist accumulation process. This was presumably more crucial for some individual leaders than the creation of propitious conditions for democratization as against lending support to the one-party state concept. This attitude among the PF-ZAPU elite was one which many in the Zimbabwe democratic and human rights movement were to find both disappointing and despiriting.

CONTINUED PRESSURES ON THE UNITARY PROJECT

Several sets of pressures currently beset the project of national unity and could undermine ZANU-PF's efforts in the post-Unity Accord period. The first relates to the overt switch to orthodox, market-based economic liberalization following indecisive attempts at socialist-oriented redistribution measures and at implementing a Leadership Code to curb more rapacious forms of accumulation by the political leadership. Economic liberalization has been effected through a structural adjustment programme (SAP) whose first phase ran from 1990 to 1994. Its chief objectives were the opening up of the economy to market forces through trade and monetary policy liberalization, the deregulation of industrial relations, the reduction of the budget deficit, the withdrawal of subsidies, and the promotion of an outward orientation in a hitherto inward-looking economy. There was a great deal of contestation of the terms of the adjustment programme by certain sectors of the business community, labour unions, and consumer associations which had been marginalized in the original design of the programme. The introduction of the austerity package which included considerable cuts in social sector spending also slashed the incomes of the middle and lower income groups. The removal of subsidies on basic commodities (especially food) and services created the basis for popular alienation, especially among the working poor.

While the adjustment programme drew favourable financial and political support from international financial institutions such as the World Bank and the International Monetary Fund and from the leading Western donor countries, the shift in economic policy, as represented by these developments, underscored a more explicit ideological shift from a populist-oriented outlook to advocacy of an explicitly capitalist path to development. In the process, the fragile "social contract" between an initially weak labour movement and the state collapsed during this period. In the 1990 elections, the bulk of the opposition vote was drawn from the urban-based working-class. Thus, although the adjustment programme has not, by itself, provided the full conditions for the crystallization of a stronger opposition challenge to the incumbent government, it has created sufficient conditions for widespread discontent, especially amongst low-income groups and consumer associations. Its objective of accelerated growth of five per cent annually between 1990 and 1995 fell short of being achieved (Gibbon, 1995). Social pressures emanating from the continued increase in unemployment (of up to 40 per cent) could provide a basis for a political tinder-box.

More generally, the adoption of adjustment measures suggested that the government had become increasingly distant from its erstwhile grassroots constituency but closer to wealthier sections of society and the international financial institutions (IFIs). Although the tensions generated by these pressures do not appear, as such, to threaten national unity directly or immediately, they chip away at the hegemony and legitimacy of the ruling ZANU-PF party. Of wider significance are the stresses and strains which have been created by shrinkage of resources, especially public resources, available to different regions and "party clients"; this has caused dissension within ZAPU-PF as we will see later in this chapter.

Intra-party dissensions could potentially undermine the unitary project in a more serious manner. This is because they could threaten the broad cohesion of the reconstituted nationalist coalition of ZANU-PF and force the break-away of some fractions. For, in spite of the triumphalism which attended the Unity Accord in 1987 and the subsequent party congresses, fault-lines exist in the edifice of ZANU-PF. Those divisions require expert handling. We will allude only to several of those fault-lines which, although papered over in the past few years, could deepen with negative outcomes for the party. One of the most critical fault-lines in this regard relates to the renewed power struggles within the party leadership at the provincial level. This is presumably inevitable given the crucial significance of the provincial base as a launching pad for leadership bids in such party institutions as the Central Committee and Politburo. Some analysts have commented on this phenomenon of provincial barons:

> the tendency for these barons with their local base to compete with each other at the national level posed several kinds of difficulties within the party. First, the sustaining of their local base and the furthering of their national standing determined their tactical calculations rather than the furtherance of any coherent strategy. They had to be opportunist and acquisitive to gain the spoils to be able to pass them on, and there were thus in-built tendencies, apart from their own personal interests, to corruption and to nepotism (Cliffe and Stoneman, 1989).

Provincial level competition among the party elite, based as it was on the ability of the competitors to mobilise local support, has stirred up a factionalism with ethnic connotations even within the groups which constitute the Shona. The recent power struggles in the Masvingo and Harare provinces reflected some of these tendencies. First, there were clashes of interest between the top party leadership and the provincial leadership over how the power structure at the provincial level should be constructed in the run-up to the 1995 elections. In Masvingo, the scramble for political leadership was between the well-known heavy weight, Eddison Zvogbo, and Vice-President Simon Muzenda each of whom backed surrogates, namely Stan Mudenge and Dzikamai Mavhaire, for the provincial chair of the party. It was a scramble which became characterised by bitter recriminations between the two party factions ranged behind the two contesters for provincial chairmanship. The recriminations degenerated to the level where Zvogbo publicly questioned the nationalist and liberation struggle credentials of his opponents. The cohesion of the provincial party structures became threatened as the two factions sought to woo rural supporters behind them. It required mediation and several visits to the province by the party's Vice-President Nkomo, National Chairman Msika and Political Commissar Mahachi for calm to be restored. Even the Speaker of Parliament was moved to denounce the factional struggles in these terms:

> Such malicious manipulations by some unscrupulous individuals to further their own political agendas should be condemned in the strongest of terms. ... Politicians should expend their energies towards accountability and transparency, and more importantly towards the development of the economy (Speaker Makombe as quoted in the *Daily Gazette*, 14 May 1994).

In essence these struggles centred on control of party and governmental leadership positions at the provincial level; there was no ideological dimension to them. The same could be said about the acrimony between the top national leadership of the party and the provincial leadership in Harare. The dispute between them was related to the authority to select candidates to stand in local bye-elections; the provincial leadership under the mercurial Herbert Ushewokunze sought to assert its autonomy and safeguard its base of patronage. Although the resultant crisis never reached the level in Masvingo, it illustrated the tenuousness of the relationship between the party centre and the provinces. The provincial dimension easily incorporates ethnic sentiments which feed on feelings of popular alienation and grassroots revulsion against the top party leadership and government policies. This became explicit in the Matabeleland provinces in 1992–94. The immediate context for the verbal flare-up between Ndebele leaders and ZANU-PF's top leadership was the SAP-related shrinkage in available public resources due to substantial cutbacks in governmental spending but this factor was also reinforced by the general perception in Matabeleland that the bulk of development expenditure was being directed to other provinces.

The resources in question ranged from public investment to student quotas at tertiary institutions of learning (including teachers' colleges). In the opinion of Ndebele leaders, their region was being discriminated against in the allocation of national resources. As we have observed elsewhere:

> Such prominent politicians as Mabhena (a provincial governor); Lesabe ; (a government minister); Malinga (the mayor of Bulawayo) and Malunga (the late respected parliamentarian) ruefully observed that Matabeleland was not being allocated a fair proportion of those resources. To worsen matters, Shona students from outside the region allegedly dominated enrolment in colleges. The census figures (of 1992) for the province's population had been allegedly "doctored" to show only a marginal increase, so as to limit the amount of resources which Matabeleland deserved, it was further argued (Sachikonye, 1994).

There certainly existed a basis for the widely-shared sentiment that the Matabeleland provinces were more economically backward than others (and Mugabe himself admitted this as quoted in a previous section of this chapter) although there is disagreement about whether there was a conscious policy by ZANU-PF to perpetrate underdevelopment in the area.

A criticism often laid at the door of Ndebele politicians (by grassroots constituents and opposition spokesmen) was that they had not pursued the development of their province as vigorously as other politicians. According to this critique, the Unity Accord might have conferred certain benefits in terms of power and wealth to individual PF-ZAPU elites, but these had not trickled down to the masses of the Ndebele people. In that context, regional discrimination becomes a popular explanation for the social and economic difficulties experienced. This would explain such frequent calls as that the Ndebele should take to the streets in their thousands and stage demonstrations against perceived Shona domination and that non-Ndebele speakers should not be awarded jobs in Matabeleland. Further, a festering sore remains, the government's refusal to award compensation to the civilian victims of the 1982–87 civil conflict or to provide humanitarian assistance to the widows and children of these victims. If the procrastination of the government in resolving the water question in the drought-prone region is added to these complaints, then we have a checklist of grievances on which ethnic sentiments can be easily focused and have increasingly been focused in spite of the Unity Accord.

The manipulation of these grievances to play the ethnic card has been termed "cheap politicking" not only by the top ZANU-PF leadership itself but also by the press. As one newspaper put it in forthright terms:

> the problem (of tribalism) remains one which is fuelled by small-minded politicians. The Shona and Ndebele have not fought each other since the "kneeless" ones invaded the country. What we have had are attempts by diverse politicians to set them at each other's throats again (*Daily Gazette*, 13 December 1994).

The element of manipulation can be potentially strong because of the existence of grievances, no matter how poorly conceptualized or misleadingly explained. In the present conjuncture, what has prevented the situation from getting out of hand and unravelling the unitary project has been the commitment of the former leadership of the defunct PF-ZAPU (principally Joshua Nkomo, Cephas Msika and Dumiso Dabengwa) to the Unity Accord and cohesion within ZANU-PF. To that extent, the eight-year old compromise symbolized by that Accord has acted as a brake on potentially more militant demands for the renegotiation of the terms on which the present nation-state was constituted. Post-Nkomo, Msika, and Dabengwa, it is not unlikely that the Accord will come under some strain unless concerted and credible attempts are made to address the concerns of the Ndebele people.

Finally, let us consider how another factor, that of the race question, increasingly impinges on the unitary project in a broad sense. The question of race has become, in the 1990s, much more explosive than at any period since independence. Briefly, the question relates to the terms and consequences of the reconciliation policy which we discussed in a previous section. While the policy may have worked, for a while at least, in promoting some stability in race relations, blacks have increasingly viewed it as an obstruction to their economic advancement. Black business groups (or "indigenous" business groups as they often prefer to call themselves) have become exasperated and are restive over the snail-like pace at which their advancement is occurring. Increasingly, they blame the institutions of the relatively wealthy white community for blocking that advancement through restrictive lending practices (by the largely white-owned financial institutions), unfair competition (through the monopolistic/oligopolistic activities of the mainly white-controlled monopolies), and insensitive treatment of indebted businessmen (through repossession of their residential property).

There has also been a groundswell, within the context of the adjustment programme, of opposition to what have been perceived as the continued racial privileges and superior advantages in the economy enjoyed by the white minority. Ironically, the phase of economic liberalization has unleashed a burst of black entrepreneurship but also stringent conditions for them due to astronomical interest rates. A notable number of black-owned small and medium-sized enterprises have gone bust. Such groups as the Indigenous Business Centre (IBDC) and the Zimbabwe National Chambers of Commerce (ZNCC) have bitterly complained about the effects of adjustment on the borrowing or debt-servicing capacity of the business interests they represent. They view the financial sector, consisting of commercial banks, building societies, insurance corporations and pension funds, as ranged against them. Further, the challenge to the greater powers acquired by the state through the Land Acquisition Act—to identify commercial farm-land for purchase and redistribution—by the white-dominated Commercial Farmers Union (CFU) has been interpreted in racial terms. The whites are seen as monopolizing "ill-gotten" fruits from the era of the "colonial conquest" while being utterly oblivious of the pressures being generated within the peasantry for land redistribution.

The sense of anger among black business interests towards the "privileged" white sector has been given vent in statements by certain political figures, notably Joshua Nkomo (who has considerable business interests himself), by the business groups themselves, but also by the student leadership and sections of the press. Demonstrations were organized in 1994 and January 1995 specifically against "white racism" and "privileges" by university students, the IBDC, the bank workers' union and various other interest groups. These have been mounted to act as a mobilizing vehicle and a source of public pressure on the Mugabe government to institute financial reforms more favourable to black business groups. The present economic liberalization programme has, therefore, had the unintended effect of squeezing the fledgling black entrepreneurial sector and, in so doing, sharpening grievances against whites generally and the reconciliation policy in particular. The situation is still too fluid to enable us to gauge whether both the government and the white business community will review their policies with a constructive response. If they do not, national unity will suffer a setback with an increase in racial intolerance.

SUMMARY AND CONCLUSION

This chapter has traced the attempts to create a durable basis for national unity within the existing territorial entity carved out during colonization. After show-ing that the concept of the post-colonial nation-state continues to be a problem-atic one—given the often artificial basis of that state and the contestation of the terms on which it was constituted—the chapter surveyed how the nationalist movement appropriated and defined the concept during the independence struggle. As elsewhere in Africa, the nationalist movement came to be domi-nated by a petit-bourgeois leadership which increasingly viewed the nation-state as an arena for the exercise of power as well as a basis for accumulation. The popular and unifying character of the movement which had originally been signified by a strong participation by such movements as those of labour, the youth and women, amongst others, was weakened by the demobilization or marginalization of these movements at independence. It was argued that within the Zimbabwean context, the unitary project after an early phase of popularity which also had a unifying character, became fragmented with the division in the nationalist movement into ZAPU and ZANU.

The legacy of disunity between the two fractions has haunted the post-inde-pendence movement, as we showed. It was observed that there were no strong ideological differences between the two fractions although ZAPU received much of its external assistance from the then Soviet Union and ZANU from China. The contest between the two fractions essentially became a power struggle between the two sets of petit-bourgeois leadership for national power. In the process, ethnic sentiments and support bases were drawn upon by both ZANU and ZAPU. The chapter then showed how the unitary project was weakened at independence and how miscalculations and the legacy of division undermined the government of national unity that was initially set up. The uni-fying potential of the reconciliation policy and a constitutionalist approach to reform was not sufficient to mitigate the slide into a civil conflict in 1982–87. The chapter observed that this was the strongest challenge to the unitary project even though ZAPU did not actively seek the dismemberment of the existing nation-state. As it became more obvious that the "trial of strength" between the two fractions would get more and more expensive in political and human terms, the stage was set for a Unity Accord in 1987 which eventually provided a stronger foundation for the unitary project.

As some analysts have observed:

> ... although most past regimes in Africa have brought some combinations of class and ethnic interests together into positions of political power at the centre, they have often tended to under-represent one interest group or another, at a great potential cost in terms of civil tension or strife (Rothchild and Foley, 1988).

By co-opting leading class and ethnic representatives into the ruling elite, it is possible to reduce the scale and intensity of their demands and to maintain the political system, albeit at a possible cost in terms of economic efficiency

(Rothchild and Foley, 1988). We showed in this chapter that such a compromise can create a stronger basis for national unity even though pressures for regional equity and democratization continue to accumulate. In the Zimbabwean context, the legacy of racial polarization further complicates the terms on which that unitary project could proceed. In any case, the consolidation of the nation-state will be a long-drawn out process. This exercise might thrive better in conditions of peace and stability; it will certainly founder under conditions of political authoritarianism and the monopoly of power.

BIBLIOGRAPHY

Auret, D., 1992, *Reaching for Justice*, Mambo Press and Catholic Commission for Justice and Peace, Gweru.

Banana, C. (ed.), 1989, *Turmoil and Tenacity*, College Press, Harare.

Chiwewe, W.A., 1989, "Unity Negotiations", in C. Banana (ed.) *Turmoil and Tenacity*, College Press, Harare.

Cliffe, L. and C. Stoneman, 1989, *Zimbabwe: Politics, Economics and Society*, Pinter Publications, London and New York.

Davidson, B., 1992, *The Black Man's Burden*, James Currey, London.

Gibbon, P. (ed.), 1995, *Structural Adjustment and the Working Poor in Zimbabwe*, Nordiska Afrikainstitutet, Uppsala.

Herbst, J., 1990, *State Politics in Zimbabwe*, University of Zimbabwe Publications, Harare.

Mandaza, I. and L.M. Sachikonye (eds.), 1991, *The One-Party State and Democracy*, SAPES, Harare.

Mugabe, R., 1989, "The Unity Accord: Its Promise for the Future", in C. Banana (ed.), *Turmoil and Tenacity*, College Press, Harare.

Ncube, W., 1989, "The Post-Unity Period: Development, Benefits and Problems", in C. Banana (ed.) *Turmoil and Tenacity*, College Press, Harare.

Nzongola-Ntalaja, G., 1988, "Nation Building and State Building in Africa", (mimeo), Harare.

Rothchild, D. and M.W. Foley, 1988, "African States and Politics of Inclusive Coalitions", in D. Rothchild and N. Chazan (eds.), *The Precarious Balance: State and Society in Africa*, Westview Press, Boulder, Colorado.

Sachikonye, L.M., 1994, "Popular Movements, State and Ideology in Zimbabwe", (mimeo), Kampala.

Shivji, I.G. (ed.), 1991, *State and Constitutionalism: An African Debate on Democracy*, SAPES, Harare.

Wamba-dia-Wamba, E., 1991, "Discourse on the National Question", in I.G. Shivji (ed.) *State and Constitutionalism: An African Debate on Democracy*, SAPES, Harare.

Chapter 7

The National Question in Zaire: Challenges to the Nation-State Project

Ernest Wamba-dia-Wamba

INTRODUCTION

The National Question refers to how the global form of social existence, characterizing the relationship of society to its environment, is historically or politically arrived at. Who is or is not a member of that society? Who is an outsider? How has the social membership changed? Does every member enjoy the same rights as those of every other member? How are these rights recognized and protected? Is there an "interest" ("national", for example) common to all? How is this commonalty founded? Solutions aimed at addressing the National Question deal with those questions. There are two sides or aspects to the Question: an objective side where the nation-state refers to the complete subordination of the National Question to the state, i.e. the state as creator and organizer of the nation, and a subjective aspect involving a subjective capacity in which the common people (*les gens*), independently of the state, constitute a national subjectivity or national community serving as a reference for political solidarity and action.

It is possible to distinguish two processes by which the nation-states in the former colonies of Africa were constituted. The first is related to the attempt to create a nation-state on the basis of the colonial conquest while the second centres on the formation of a national community on the basis of common cultural origins or a people's mass struggle of resistance against domination or the threat of domination by foreign invaders. In the case of the former, the formation of the nation is done from the top, by the colonial state for example, while in the case of the latter, it is achieved through people's self-determination at the bottom.

The emphasis in the colonially-created or -inspired nation-state project is placed heavily on the state and its (coercive) apparatuses: the construction of the nation is confused with the development (growth) of the state. In the case of a state formed by conquest, militarism determines the shape and character of national institutions. The state, erected through conquest, gives priority to the pursuit of the objectives of "territorial integrity" or "national unity" at the expense of mass organizations. Social categories incarnating the state appara- tuses, and who conceive of themselves as being national, think of national self- determination as simply entailing a reform of the colonial state through the Africanization of its institutions (i.e. getting rid of/replacing colonialists). The self-determination of local communities is viewed as secession by the "state nationalists". These constitute a category of elites who use the state apparatuses to "defend the nation".

The second tendency in the nation-state formation process departs from the first precisely because it refers to the process of self-determination by local communities based on common origins, historical experiences of struggles, common life, etc. through which profound aspirations have been formed. It calls for a real transformation of the colonial state to make it democratic/ representative and capable of empowering people against foreign domination. The challenge, in Africa, has, very briefly, centred on the difficulty of satis- factorily articulating those two opposite tendencies in the quest for national unity.

In the case of Zaire, despite the changes which have occurred, its global form of social existence, in terms of recognized rights and differences has, until very recently, remained essentially colonial. There has not been a fundamental change in the social membership of the country in spite of the apparent transi- tion from the Belgian Congo to Zaire. The only thing that appeared to have changed was the departure of colonialists. The contradictory, dependent, and hierarchical "tribal" (ethnic) structure created by the colonial state did not change fundamentally. The Belgian nationality group which was the ruling elite of the colonial period acted and spoke in the name of "civilization" and "devel- opment" which it claimed to incarnate. This group aimed at creating, through the colonial state, a "territorial nation" dependent on Belgium in particular and the West more generally. At some point, members of the group even dreamed of making the Belgian Congo another province of Belgium.

The Zairean *national tribaliste* (Lumuna-Sando, 1978) group which took over the reins of state power after the departure of the Belgian colonialists has tried to rule in the name of an "abstract state unity" (premised on a colonially- created territorial unity) incarnated by the legacy of the colonial state and a programme of "nation-building" from above. This group seeks either to Africanize or nationalize the colonial legacy as an authentic project of the nation-state. Until about 1990, contradictions within the *national tribaliste* ruling group were resolved through the identification of the "abstract national state unity" with the "father of the nation" in the person of President and Founder of the party, Mouvement Populaire de la Revolution (MPR). Struggles aimed at preserving the legacy of the colonial state when it was seriously threatened— respectively by Lumumbist and Mulelist nationalists, for example—took the form, in some cases, of pro-colonial secessions or *coups d'état*.

Under the conditions created by colonialism and the post-colonial *national tribaliste* ruling elites, resort to constitutionalism has , in essence, been a way of justifying a one-sided, unilateral approach to tackling the National Question: a national minority-based state, incarnated in one person, oppressing the majority of the people on the basis of class, ethnicity, or nationality. The rights enjoyed by a Pygmy, a Muyaka, a Kongo, an Ngbandi, a Lunda, a worker, a peasant, etc. are, effectively, not the same. The constitution, in spelling out only the rights of the President/Founder who is also seen as being above the constitution, simultaneously subordinates the rights of all groups to his own.

It would seem that the correct resolution of the National Question in the context of a multi-national or multi-ethnic Zaire requires a federalist conception of "multi-national unity" in a manner consistent with the demands of democratic governance. Positions articulated at the Zairean National Sovereign Conference opposing state/national sovereignty to the sovereignty of the people or demands for a democratic prescription on the basis of which the state should rest seem to go against popular yearnings for the establishment of an enduring, democratic nation-state project in the country. It would seem then that the National Question in Zaire is one which will be with us for some time to come. What we seek to do in this chapter is to provide a few historical points of reference that might enable us to properly appraise the challenges faced by the nation-state project in Zaire. The hope is that we would be able to move a step closer towards the goal of founding the project on a democratic basis that is representative of the aspirations of the majority of the peoples of Zaire.

THE FORMATION OF ZAIRE

The "territorial shell" (Schatzberg, 1988:139) known as Zaire was formed and gradually and forcibly "unified" as an outcome of colonialism and the post-colonial centralization of power on the basis of an external dependence. The territory still bears the marks of the brutalities of the Red Rubber rule of the Congo Free State (1874–1908), the extreme arbitrariness of Belgian colonial rule and its associated "civilising mission" (1908–1960) which was based on the tri-partite alliance of the church, the administrative bureaucracy, and the corporations as derived from the *Charte Coloniale*, the anti-Lumumba secessions (1960–1963) that were supported—if not initiated—by the leading Western powers and their monopolies, the anti-neo-colonial armed mass insurrections that occurred over the period 1961 to 1968, and the "oppressive dialectics" (Schatzberg, 1988) of the so-called Mobutiste state. Central to this process of formation and deformation has been what C.K. Lumuna-Sando (1978) referred to as the "colonialist Congolization" process: a process which involved the disintegration of pre-existing local political communities (e.g. kingdoms) and their subsequent integration into a bureaucratic and absolutist-totalitarian colonial state which organized and protected a process of plunder and exploitation in favour of outside capitalist interests.

To achieve that objective, a double strategy was used. The first centred around the physico-politico-ideological dismantling of organized political formations which rested on distinct nationalities and which offered resistance to the imposition of colonial rule (the Kongo, Kuba, Lulua, Yaka, Luba, etc.). The second revolved around a reliance on collaborators and/or the conscious creation of "de-tribalized" ethnic groups (Bangala, Bakusu, Luba, Lokele, etc.). These groups were linked to the colonial state (as represented by the church, the administration and the corporations) and were created through incorporation into the colonial army of occupation (*Force Publique*), colonial labour camps, and the *centres extra-coutumiers* (including the missions). The legitimizing ideologies of the Congolization process were simple: white supremacist, anti-slavery, anti-paganist, salvationist, civilizationist, and developmentalist. The Congolese nation-state was supposed to have been born out of this process.

THE NATIONAL QUESTION IN ZAIRE

The adjective "Belgian" in references to the Belgian colony of the Congo should be taken seriously. Although formally a dependent appendage of the Belgian metropolitan state—functionally, the case for the relative autonomy of the Belgian colonial state could be made—the Belgian colony was not without its own ethnic underpinnings (Young and Turner, 1984). The global form of social existence of the colony, organized by a colonial state serving as an instrument of Belgian class domination over all the native peoples (in their multiple or contradictory composition which the colonizers exploited to the fullest) for Belgian-rooted international capitalist interests, was one in which a racial national foreign group oppressed and exploited a colonized, culturally (even racially) pluralist majority whose national rights were denied. The colonized non-white majority was organized on the basis of white supremacist practices and ideology. This gave rise to a racist and paternalist tribal hierarchization of the native African society. New ethnic or "tribal" identities or mentalities were forged: warlike tribes were discovered and opposed to docile ones. The mutual and consistent recognition of each other's ethnically, racially or nationally based differences and group rights became impossible.

Some native elements (Lumuna-Sando's *national tribalistes*, for example) became fully integrated into the colonial state. Their consciousness was determined by the French language, the Christian religion, Western education, and compradorial socio-economic interests. The *immatriculation* practice reinforced their consciousness of submission to colonial authority. The only "native" languages they could speak were the standardized and bastardized variants recognized by the colonial state: Kikongo ya Leta, Lingala, Swahili and Ciluba which were later on declared "national languages". These "native" elements—

seen as *interlocuteurs valables* by the colonial authorities—were vested with the task of "nation-building" after independence. Their "évolue" consciousness was a consciousness of submission to "Western civilization"; "nation-building" became more of a process of consolidation of the colonial legacy rather than of its destruction. It became a process working for the continuation of "Congolization".

Attempts by Lumumbist nationalists to interrupt the reproduction of the "Congolization" process failed. To curtail those attempts, local opponents of Lumumba and international capitalist interests provoked the secessions of Kasai and Katanga from the rest of the country. Lumumbist nationalists tried to use the apparatuses inherited from the colonial state to bring back, by force, the provinces that were attempting to secede. In the process, they tended to consolidate the colonial legacy built on centralization and the forced integration of the local political communities. Their "national tribalist" form of consciousness was not yet sufficiently revolutionized by their active involvement in struggles for national independence. They still viewed "national unity" or "national integration" in the same forcible, centralized manner as the former colonialists.

The *national tribaliste* group which replaced the Belgian national minority in the state, was not unified nationality-wise. It was thus open to all kinds of divisive solicitations in the context of an inherited colonialist structure that was based on an uneven hierarchy of cultural and ethnic differences. Any conception of "national unity" through a federation or confederation appeared to the Lumumbist nationalists as a form of territorial balkanization that had to be resisted. D. Fogel (1982:13–14) was basically right when he wrote that:

> Lumumba's state centralist program, while superficially progressive as against the tribalist and secessionist strivings of Tshombe, Kalondji, and Kasa-Vubu, was in fact a non-solution to the tribal problem. Lumumba's Congolese nationalism was devoid of revolutionary social content, because it attempted to base itself on idealized state governmental institutions, rather than on the social programme of workers and peasants revolution. Such a program would not attempt to impose Congolese state "unity" through force of arms—least of all through the armed forces of the existing, (neo) colonial state—but would systematically mobilize the exploited masses of the people against their exploiters, both imperialist and local. It would uphold democratic local self-government as well as the free development of tribal languages and the positive aspects of tribal culture. Lumumba, by placing abstract Congolese state "unity" at the centre of his political programme, found himself in the ironical position of taking over the reins of the Belgian colonial state. Even after that state spurted wildly out from under him, it was a simple matter of time for the tribal secessionist demagogues to portray Lumumba as the continuer of the oppressive colonial regime in Leopoldville.

This long and important quotation had to be reproduced here because in it, Fogel put his finger right on the "wound" at the heart of the National Question in Zaire: the view that there is an abstract state or "national unity" upholding a common national interest common to all classes and ethnic or nationality groups. Behind this claim lies an attempt at consolidating the legacy of the colonial state thereby making it difficult to correctly take up the resolution of both the national and social questions. It is questionable, though, to put at the same level, Tshombe's, Kalondji's and Kasa-Vubu's so-called secessionist strivings. In a context in which the independent political organization of workers and peasants was not possible—divided as they were by the colonial state's *national tribalisme*—the call by Kasa-Vubu's party for a federation was the closest to a possible program for upholding "democratic local self-government". This was consistent with the historical origins of the Alliance de Bakongo (ABAKO) which initially agitated for the renaissance of the colonially dismantled Kongo civilization and culture.

The idea of creating ABAKO came from the colonially-neglected rural enclave of Manyanga. In the hands of "civilized" (*évolues* or *national tribalistes*) Kongolese elements, ABAKO's original project was abandoned. The party became oriented towards integration into the abstract project of Congolese state "unity". In a sense, the programme of Lumumba's Mouvement National Congolais (MNC), appears, on the other hand, to have been partially realized by the Mobutiste state i.e. the project of building a one-party centralized state. Until very recently, the National Question in Zaire remained essentially organized around the neo-colonial question. Imperialist domination still operated through the dynamics of the consolidation of the legacy of the colonial state in the hands of a minority which benefited from it. The Zairean people are still struggling for a genuine national independence. This leaves open the possible transformation of the essentially colonially-organized global form of social existence of society characterizing its specific relationship to its environment.

SECESSIONS AND THREATS OF SECESSION

Secessionist tendencies constitute a major challenge to a nation-state project. A rich scientific literature exists analysing the Katanga (now Shaba) and South Kasai (now Kasai Oriental) secessions (Nzongola-Ntalaja 1987, 1988; Ilunga Kabongo 1973; Libois 1963; Chome 1966; M'Bokolo 1978, 1983, 1985). It is clearly shown in this literature that, in both cases, mere cultural pluralism was not enough to provoke secessions. The dynamics of political struggles over the preservation/dissolution of power relations that were essentially colonial in origin offers a more useful explanation of the secessions. Those struggles were triggered off by the orientation which Lumumbist nationalists attempted to give to independence, an orientation which, in the perception of some forces, appeared to threaten those power relations. Nzongola-Ntalaja (1987:55) wrote:

> It is true that the Lunda and other ethnic groups of southern Katanga (now Shaba) were resentful of their lower socio-economic status in comparison to the predominantly Luba-Kasai settlers of the urban and mining centres. In defining these settlers as "strangers" who ought to be sent home, the "authentic Katangans" were hoping to eliminate them from the field of inter-ethnic competition for jobs, social welfare and political power. However, the secession itself was clearly a case of internal settlement, the work of European settlers who had since 1958 determined that the only realistic way to advance their interests was to have

Africans assimilate their secessionist views and defend them as their own. The party of secession, Moise Tshombe's *Confédération des Associations Tribales du Katanga* (CONAKAT), was the auxiliary arm of white settler politics and its voice through African intermediaries.

The "internal settlement" was colonially-derived and was forged through the dynamic inter-relationship between the state, class and race as well as ethnic hierarchization and conflict. The dynamics of the "internal settlement" determined the forces which were favourable to the continuation of the "Congolization" process of imperialist plunder and economic exploitation and those who were opposed to it. The "settlement" operated through regional forces and circumstances and used ethnic claims to destabilize nationalists based on the national arena whose outlook and programmes threatened the prospects for the continuation or consolidation of the colonial legacy. Recently, the Mobutiste *mouvance présidentielle* used the same tactic to destabilize the rising pro-federalist national tendency that was threatening Mobutu's power.

Unlike the secessionist attempts in Katanga, those in South Kasai were, in a sense, entirely the work of Congolese themselves and as such appeared to have a different set of dynamics. An analysis of the position of the Luba-Kasai in relation to the colonial state shows them to be "co-colonizers with the Belgians" i.e., a social extension of the colonial state. From this point of view, secessionist attempts in South Kasai could be seen as a form of political struggle to preserve the essential dynamics of the colonial state in order to guarantee the position of the Luba-Kasai as "co-colonizers". The Lumumbist conception of independence was, therefore, perceived as a threat to the survival of the Luba-Kasai as a group. Ilunga Mbiye Kabongo (1973:220 as cited in Nzongola-Ntalaja, 1988) explained the situation as follows:

> As Belgian colonization expanded in Kasai and Katanga, the Luba became the best agents of the colonizers, who used them as catechists, teachers, clerks and manual workers. Their language, Tshiluba, was even imposed upon the entire Kasai Province, becoming one of the four "national" languages of the Congo.

This ethnic nationalism was a petty bourgeois ideological expression of an interest claimed to be common to all Luba-Kasai classes.

Political struggles over the control of state power, its consolidation, conservation or destruction and transformation, led Congo-Zaire, in the 1960s, to be divided in three zones of influence. The Lumumbist nationalist forces had their stronghold around Stanleyville (now Kisangani). The neo-colonial forces based in the "national arena" and wielding a *coup d'état* as their main weapon, had control of Leopoldville (Kinshasa). Political forces allied to the big mining companies and the European settlers held Elisabethville (Lubumbashi) and Bakwanga (Mbuji-Mayi). Secessions, thus, appear not as demands for or attempts at promoting the emergence of local political communities favourable to democratic local self-government, but as conjectural forms of struggles for the continuation of the colonial legacy. They were opposed to any correct resolution of the National Question requiring the destruction of the colonial state legacy *per se*. "Internal settlement" Katanga and "co-colonizer" Luba-Kasai secessionist attempts could not have led to the recognition, on the basis of equality, of cultural or ethnic differences for a truly democratic and decentralized state.

CONSTITUTIONALISM AND THE NATION-STATE PROJECT

It would appear that in a multi-national or multi-ethnic country, a correct resolution of the National Question requires that the various nationalities or ethnic groups should have their specific rights constitutionally recognized. The decrees enacted by King Leopold II to establish, legalize and legitimize his brutish Red Rubber rule of naked force in the eyes of the Berlin Conference and the international community did not recognize those rights. The *Charte Colonial*, like the royal decrees and the *Loi Fondamentale* (the first post-colonial constitution) as well as the various Mobutiste constitutions (1967–1991) were based on a constitutionalism conceived and organized outside the large masses of people in whose name the constitutions were supposedly enacted in the first place. The Luluabourg Constitution of 1964, which was put to a referendum, was never implemented; as it was suspended by Mobutu's 1965 *coup d'état*. Constitutional exercises have, therefore, tended systematically to uphold and "legitimize" arbitrariness. At no time since independence have critical considerations relating to ethnic differences, along the lines suggested by Guillaume Pambou Tchivounda (1982), been taken into account in the constitution-making process. The attempt by the National Sovereign Conference to address ethnic or regional considerations led to "geopolitical" or "tribal" and regionalist degenerations that frustrated the process.

The experience of the Congo Free State has been thoroughly exposed, especially by the anti-Red Rubber movement (Morel, 1910). The *Charte Coloniale* was based on a white, Western supremacist justification of imperial domination, oppression, despotism, hegemony over, and exploitation of, colonized populations. The racist notions that underpinned the *Charte* were fed first to children and then to their young brothers and sisters. It organized a manichean dichotomy separating the "civilized" whites from the "savage natives", whites who were "human" from less human blacks, and a body of "superior modern" laws for whites from "inferior customary" law for the "natives". In that context, not only "the rights of the first occupant" (Kasa-Vubu's speech, 1946) were ignored, but also those of the various cultural, racial or nationality "minorities"—unevenly developed as they were—in the country. The rights of the people and of nationalities were not constitutionally recognized. Pragmatic considerations alone led, after the First World War, to the recognition of some colonially-determined rights favourable, in the last instance, to the continuation of colonialism.

Colonial society was erected on the systematic violation of the national rights of colonized people. As such, it was the very opposite of an egalitarian and democratic society. The implementation of the *Charte Coloniale* met with rebellions and resistance from the colonized peoples. In a bid to accommodate the limited victories emanating from the colonized people's sustained struggles for reforms, the colonial state was forced to introduce modifications in the implementation of the *Charte*. Clearly, anti-state mass rebellions are the motive force for the transformation of the state either in the direction of reform or greater repression. A study of the modifications to the naked brutality sanctioned by the *Charte* would help us to deepen a comparison between pre-colonial Leopoldian and post-colonial Mobutiste authoritarianism. The "decolonization phase" of the colonial state (Young and Turner, 1984), characterised as it was by a growing intensification of the activities of the national independence movement, witnessed the reluctant recognition by the colonial authorities of limited political rights (e.g. the right of association, including the right to form political parties). It is interesting to note that it was the *national tribalistes* or *évolues* who, in the *Manifeste de la Conscience Congolaise*, used the distinction *évolues* and *bush people* (civilized and savage) to defend their limited rights and interests and to position themselves as *interlocuteurs valables*.

The *Loi Fondamentale*, the first constitutional law of the independent Congo, although discussed at the Round Table Conference that ran from 20 January to 20 February 1960, was, for all intents and purposes, a Belgian creation. The Belgian government intended to pattern the new nation on the Belgian model, a model that has not been successful even in handling the Belgian National Question. As Thomas Kanza (1977:89) put it:

> The *Loi Fondamentale* had juridical implications exactly like those of the Belgian monarchical constitution: a head of state who "rules" but does not govern; a government supervised and able to be dismissed by the head of state; an over-large and relatively powerless parliament consisting of a Chamber of Representatives and a Senate.

The elaboration of the *Loi Fondamentale* was based on Belgian hopes that King Baudouin would be chosen as Head of State of the Congo (Young, 1965:51). The limitations and flaws of the *Loi* have been extensively studied and are well documented. It was targeted more towards shaping the Congo as a Belgian duplicate rather than as an expression of the recognition of Congolese specificities. Not only did the *Loi Fondamentale* fail to prevent or help resolve the "Congo crisis", it, in fact, triggered it off and exacerbated it. It is said that Herman Cohen, the former United States Assistant Secretary of State for Africa, has suggested (1992) a similar arrangement as a mechanism for "power sharing": "Mobutu remains, rules but does not govern". And the "Zaire crisis" goes on.

The practice of elaborating constitutional texts that bear no relationship whatsoever to local realities and which are do not incorporate people's active participation which began with the *Loi Fondamentale* became institutionalized in the principles and practice of post-colonial politics and constitution-making.

The texts, thus, became nothing more than decorative constitutional icons. The National Sovereign Conference tried to change this situation but its decisions have been systematically blocked and set aside as required by the dynamics and manoeuvres necessary for the continuation of Mobutu's rule.

Under the "absolutist" (Callaghy, 1984) Mobutiste state, constitutionalism, especially since 1974, has been based on one fundamental principle, namely that the President/Founder of the State Party, the *Mouvement Populaire de la Révolution*, the core of the constitution, is above the constitutional law. This is clearly indicated in the *Texte de la Loi Portant Revision de la Constitution du 24 Juin 1967*, especially *Titre VIII: Dispositions Speciales*. This has facilitated the institutionalization of an authoritarian, arbitrary, and personalized rule. It has also meant the complete political demobilization of the people of Zaire. This is openly recognized by the party slogan: "whether one wants it or not, every native of Zaire is automatically a member of the State Party". Party membership, to say nothing about party adherence, is made compulsory. Citizenship, nationality and party membership are equated. Mobutism, claimed to be the basis of the constitution, is defined as the "set of acts and thoughts of the President/ Founder". Presidential arbitrariness is thus legitimized and made free from the juridical restrictions implied by the rest of the constitution. People's participation in constitution-making, in all its phases, has been absent. The resulting text itself basically glossed over basic problems of the global form of social existence of the Zairean society.

The 1974 constitution, like the previous ones, cannot be said to have been enacted by the people. Instead of the usual opening phrase of a constitution "we the people...do ordain and establish this constitution...", we have in the 1974 text, "We the Zairean people, united inside the *Mouvement Populaire de la Révolution* guided by Mobutism..." In other words, the state party proclaims its constitution in the name of the Zairean people whose political will and active participation are made irrelevant. This type of constitutionalism removes any chance for the regimes in power to marshal sufficient legitimacy to govern the people. Those regimes are thus increasingly isolated and unpopular, relying only on repressive state apparatuses. This makes the democratization process impossible and with it the possibility of correctly resolving the National Question, i.e. the constitutional recognition of various types of democratic rights. The leaders of those regimes govern by unleashing sustained repression on the masses of people.

The usual procedure for ensuring that a people makes its own constitution is to subject the constitutional draft to public debate after which it is either adopted by a constituent assembly of deputies freely elected by the people for that purpose or endorsed by a referendum. The use of a regular legislature is not preferred because this is a regular organ of the state which has its interests to protect. The violation of this procedure, respected only in the case of the 1964 constitution, is very serious in the case of Zaire where the centralization of power has gone, at least formally, from a *statization* of society to a *personalization* or *privatization* of the *statization* process itself.

The defence of public liberty (*liberté publique*) and the "moralization" of the state, as Saint-Just recognized long ago (Lazarus, 1988), depend on the existence of civil political institutions independent of the state and rooted in the large masses of the people. The state cannot self-moralize nor defend public liberty *per se*. A process of decentralization of power, which allows civil political institutions and the empowerment of local political communities (local self-determination), is a prerequisite for a type of constitutionalism which would enhance the prospects for the correct resolution of the National Question. Unity in diversity and not unity incarnated by a "father of the nation" (a nation has no father) rooted in an abstract state organ will be the basis for solving the National Question. A federalist conception of national unity recognizing cultural, ethnic and linguistic pluralism will be a positive framework for such a resolution. The democratization process will, however, require more than the mere federalist framework. It will require a democratic prescription on the federal state itself.

DEMOCRATIC PRESCRIPTION ON THE FEDERAL STATE

Brief comments on this important issue are in order here; a fuller treatment of the question would, of course, require another paper altogether. Democracy must be organized around the category, *gens de partout* (people of all walks of life). The democratic prescription may be formulated this way: *il n'ya d'État démocratique que l'État des gens de Partout* (the only democratic state is a state of the people of all walks of life). An authentic state must rest on the multiplicity and diversity of the people: old, young, peasants, workers, people of diverse national or ethnic origins, merchants, intellectuals, professionals, women, men, atheists, believers, etc. But a democratic state must not rest exclusively or narrowly on one religious or ethnic identity. The key must be the *multiplicity* and *diversity* of the entire society *per se*. Furthermore, the state must not be a simple composition or expression (reflection) of this multiplicity ; it must transcend it with new categories. These must not be derived from the social being which may be cultural, linguistic, religious, professional, etc. These conditions are required to prevent differences from becoming discriminations. I think that the non-racial and non-sexist democratic state conception in South Africa is close to this prescription. Concepts such as "citizen" (unfortunately devalued by phenomena such as Mobutist *Authenticity*) and *ndugu* are examples of abstract terms necessary to transcend the multiplicity.

A state which does not transcend the multiplicity and diversity of the peoples on which it rests is open to becoming racist and/or fundamentalist, ethnically discriminatory as well as criminal. The crucial element of democratic prescription is *des gens de partout*. It guarantees civil peace. A democratic state is a state of civil peace. A state which rests on ethnic or "community" (region, clan) or religious characteristics is a state of civil tensions and wars. No peace will come to the Middle East, for example, as long as the states rest on narrow or exclusive religious or ethnic foundations. An authentic Palestinian State must include Israelis, Arabs, Jews, Palestinians, women, men, workers, etc., and rest on the multiplicity and diversity of its people. The same holds for ex-Yugoslavia and many African countries. To be possible, a democratic state requires thus new categories such as "the country", *des gens de partout*, "the state", etc. not as forming a formalized juridical system, but as objects of political prescription.

The category, "the country", understood strictly in the sense of the people who live or want to live in it, is essential to a democratic state. The de-racialization, de-ethnization or de-religionisation of the category is required by the democratic prescription. The category, "the state", seen as having both objective and subjective aspects is necessary. From the point of view of rational knowledge, the state in its historical evolution and functioning, opens up, under limited conditions—it is true—a field of *possible* actions. The subjective aspect of the state determines which possible action is claimed (or viewed) as the *necessary* action. A state decision is a particular response to a general necessity; the general necessity does not automatically dictate that particular response: alternative particular responses are always possible. The particular response originates from a political prescription through a mode of politics. That is why the subjective aspect of the state is attached to the objective one but not in a dialectical relationship (L'Organisation Politique, 1995). The state, politics and economy must be studied on a face-to-face basis. Neither can or should be deduced from the other. They can all be, politically, objects of prescriptions. There is no state decision which is not an outcome of a political prescription.

The federal state, to be democratic, must satisfy some of the requirements briefly discussed above. The category "region" or "federal province" or "state" must be understood as composed of people who live or want to live there and not rest on an exclusive or a discriminatory ethnic composition, for example. *Des gens de partout* have the right to organize themselves in a region, any region of their choice or liking—this is the democratic meaning of self-determination at all levels.

The draft of the Constitution of the Federal Republic of the Congo, elaborated by the National Sovereign Conference, is supposed to be a constitutional expression of a democratic prescription on a federal state. A close analysis of this draft would be necessary to see whether or not it fulfils the requirements of a democratic prescription. We do not have enough space here to do so. Suffice it to note that there are some strong points in the draft fulfilling the requirements but it also contains some obstacles as well. The latter includes the category "Congolese citizenship" which is not in line with *des gens de partout* but incarnates and expresses ethnic origins. And the region is often viewed in terms of cultural-cum-ethnic origins that have a potential to be exclusivist and discriminatory.

From the preamble of the draft constitution, obstacles to democratization are castigated: individualism, nepotism, clanism, tribalism and regionalism; and supporting elements to democratization are underlined: freedom (including freedom of the individual), equality, justice, work and solidarity. Article 4 asserts that the Congolese people incarnate national sovereignty and no individual or fraction of the people may usurp that popular sovereignty. Articles 3 and 6 clarify the modalities of political pluralism and make the institutionalization of a single party a treasonable crime. Articles 7 and 8 prescribe people's right to rebel against an individual or group of individuals who seize power or stay in power by force in contradiction to the specifications of the constitution. The articles fall short of prescribing the people's right of recall over their elected representatives at any time.

The obligation of the individual to refuse to carry out a manifestly illegal order is asserted in the draft constitution. Freedom is first of all the freedom of the one who dissents. These are some of the strong points. The possibility of achieving a break with a submissive, accommodating consciousness—which is the anchor of emancipatory politics—is affirmed. It would take too long to do the required political analysis of the constitutional draft here. Of course, in Africa, most often, the constitution is not respected—due, in part, to what I call a "submissive culture". That is, constitutions are not expressions of political prescriptions on the state emanating from independent politics rooted in the organizations based on the category des gens de partout.

CONCLUSION

The above are but a few short reflections on the important question of the nation-state project in Zaire. I tried to show that there is a close link between the historicity of the National Question, secessions and anti-people constitutionalism in Zaire. The collapse of what has often been presented as a nation-state project is due to the failure to correctly address the National Question. Of course, the authoritarian nation-state scheme cannot be the solution to the Question. What is needed is a democratic state. We will have occasions in the future to elaborate on this democratic requirement in the quest for a resolution of the crisis of the post-colonial nation-state in Africa generally and Zaire in particular.

BIBLIOGRAPHY

Amselle, Jean-Loup and Elikia M'bokolo (eds.), 1985, *Au Coeur de l'Ethnie: Ethnies, Tribalisme et État en Afrique*, Editions la Decouverte/Textes a l'Appui, Paris.

Callaghy, Thomas M., 1984, *The State-Society Struggle: Zaire in Comparative Perspective*, Columbia University Press, New York.

Chome, Jules, 1966, *Le Drame de Luluabourg*, Editions de Remerques Congolaises, Bruxelles.

Comité Zaire, 1978, *Zaire le Dossier de la Recolonisation*, Editions de l'Harmattan, Paris.

Coquery-Vidrovitch, C., Alain Forest, and Herbert Weiss (eds.), 1987, *Rebellions–Révolution au Zaire: 1963-1965*, Editions de l'Harmattan, Paris.

Fogel, D., 1982, *Africa in Struggle*, Ism Press Inc., Seattle.

Galle, Hubert and Yannis Thanassekos, 1983, *Le Congo: De la Decourverte a l'Independance*, Editions J.N. Collet, Bruxelles.

Libois, Gérard, 1963, *Secession au Katanga*, Bruxelles.

Jewsiewicki, B., 1986, *Images et Pratiques de l'Identité Ethnique au Congo Belge: La Construction d'une Culture Politique de la "Modernisation". Réflexions à Partir de l'Exemple Luba*, Unpublished manuscript.

Kanza, Thomas, 1977, *The Rise and Fall of Patrice Lumumba: Conflict in the Congo*, Schenkman Publishing Co., Cambridge, Mass.

Lazarus, Sylvain, 1988, *La Catégorie de Révolution dans la Révolution Française*, Les Conferences du Perroquet, No. 15, March, Paris.

L'Organisation Politique, 1995, *La Distance Politique*, No. 11, January, Paris.

Lumuna-Sando, C.K., 1978, *Nationalisme? Tribalisme? La Question Nationale au Congo (Zaire)*, Cahier A.F.R.I.C.A, Bruxelles.

M'Bokolo, Elikia, 1978, "Ethnicité, Régionalisme et Nationalisme au Shaba", *Le Monde Diplomatique*, July.

M'Bokolo, Elikia, 1983, "Historicité et Pouvoir d'État en Afrique Noir: Réflexions Sur les Pratiques d'Etat et les Ideologies Dominantes", *Relations Internationales*, No. 34.

M'Bokolo, Elikia, 1985, "Le Séparatisme Katangais", in Jean-Loup Amselle and Elikia M'Bokolo, *Au Coeur de l'Ethnie: Ethnies, Tribalisme et l'Etat en Afrique*, Editions de la Découverte, Paris.

Morel, E.D., 1906, *The Red Rubber*, Nassau Print, New York.

Nzongola-Ntalaja, G., 1987, *Revolution and Counter-Revolution in Africa*, Institute for African Alternatives & Zed Books Ltd, London and New Jersey.

Nzongola-Ntalaja, G., 1988, "Nation-Building and State-Building in Africa", (mimeo).

Obenga, Theophile, 1977, *Le Zaire: Civilisations Traditionnelles et Culture Moderne*, Presences Africaine, Paris.

Pambou Tchivounda, Guillaume, 1982, *Essai sur l'État Africain Postcolonial*, Librairie Generale de Droit et de Jurisprudence, Paris.

Schatzberg, Michael G., 1988, *The Dialectics of Oppression in Zaire*, Indiana University Press, Bloomington and Indianapolis.

Tshimanga, wa Tshibangu, 1976, *Histoire du Zaire*, Editions du CERURI, Bukavu.

Wamba-dia-Wamba, E., 1988, "Notes on Theoretical Problems of the National Question in Africa", (mimeo), Dar es Salaam.

Wamba-dia-Wamba, E., 1991, "Discourse on the National Question", in Issa G. Shivji (ed.), *State and Constitutionalism: An African Debate on Democracy*, SAPES Books, Harare. .

Young, C., 1965, *Politics in the Congo*, Princeton University Press, Princeton, NJ.

Young, C. and Thomas Turner, 1984, *The Rise and Decline of the Zairean State*, The University of Wisconsin Press, Madison, Wisc. and London.

Chapter 8

Christianity and Islam Contending for the Throne on the Tanzanian Mainland

Nestor N. Luanda

INTRODUCTION

In recent times, religion has re-emerged as a major issue in Tanzanian national politics. This is as true of politics on the mainland as it is in Zanzibar. It has also become a factor in the relationship between the mainland and Zanzibar, feeding, on the one hand, into the demands for a separate Tanganyika government that is gathering pace on the mainland and, on the other hand, into the growing feeling of disaffection, in certain Zanzibar circles, about the union with Tanganyika that resulted in the birth of Tanzania. At the heart of the re-emergence of religion as an important factor in Tanzanian politics is the struggle between the Muslim and Christian establishments for pre-eminence in national affairs. This struggle has entailed competition between them for control of the secular nation-state which Chama Cha Mapinduzi, the single party that ruled the country until the multi-party reforms of the 1990s, strove to build as part of its national unity project.

This chapter is concerned with analysing the religious challenges which have been posed to the Tanzanian nation-state by the resurgence of religious politics in the country. Particular attention is paid to the period leading up to and following the re-introduction, in the early 1990s, of a multi-party political system in the country. An attempt is also made to review the responses of the state to the religious challenges confronting it and the constitutional problems raised by the challenges. The focus of our analysis will be on developments on the Tanzanian mainland. Thus although references are made in the chapter to developments in Zanzibar, these are only for the purpose of clarifying the context and consequence of the politics of religion on the mainland and the challenges which are posed to the post-colonial nation-state project.

THE POLITICS OF RELIGION IN TANZANIA:
SOME BACKGROUND ISSUES

Historically, the Christian church (especially the Roman catholic church), has had and, to some extent, still maintains very special bonds with key members of the political elite in Tanzania (Sivalon, 1990:94). It has been able to forge these bonds through the mission education system (which the Roman catholic church dominated), the contributions of the church to the independence struggle, its role in leadership training, and the pastoral/sacramental links which it has had with many members of the governing elite. The privileged access to the officials of the post-colonial state that flowed from these bonds have enabled the catholic church to carve out a special niche for itself in the political affairs of Tanzania. Using its influence among state officials and in the wider society, the church has argued strenuously for the state not only to foster religion as a matter of duty, but in so doing, to also develop and maintain close contact with the representatives of the various religious groups in the country. At the same time, church leaders have taken the view that the state should not have any rights over the convictions of the citizenry. It has been suggested by some commentators that this "secularised religiosity" on the part of the church represents a direct infringement on Section 19 of the Constitution of the United Republic of Tanzania which affirms the right of individual citizens to freedom of religion but insists that the conduct and management of religious communities shall not be part of the functions of the state (URT, 1990; Omari, 1987).

The Roman catholic church gave priority importance to encouraging practising African Catholics to take an active part in the activities of the sole ruling party, Chama Cha Mapinduzi (CCM), which dominated Tanzanian political life until the early 1990s. For the hierarchy of the church, this was the surest way of keeping African nationalists and the governing elite in particular from falling under the influence of "undesirable" agents, particularly the communists. In this connection, the Lay Apostolate Department was charged with the task of nurturing the governing elite along the path of "secularised religiosity". Its operations were carried out in two sectors: the spiritual lay apostolate (which includes various devotional societies) and the social lay apostolate (which encompasses Catholic Action, Young Christian Workers and a variety of social guilds, among others). The operations of the social lay apostolate sector are not specifically religious but are rather social in orientation although premised on catholic principles. Professionals, business people, nurses, teachers and union leaders form the main targets of the social lay apostolate. "If they are going to be local leaders any way, they might as well be with us for if we do not include them they may be against us" (Sivalon, 1990:94).

Sivalon surmises that a pervasive characteristic of the social ministry of Catholicism in Tanzania from the early 1950s to the mid-1960s was the protection of the place of the institutional church in society. Indeed, over the years, Catholicism became another institution and possibly the only one capable of matching, even challenging Chama Cha Mapinduzi. "Secular religiosity" as defined and operationalised by the catholic church was primarily geared towards combating Marxism which was seen as the primary threat to the church. However, from 1960 to 1966, another element emerged that reinforced the self-protective/-perpetuating character of the catholic establishment: the fear of Islam. Sivalon captures this fear when he states that:

> Islam becomes more and more a problem. The Muslims succeeded to have a very big influence in policy making in Tanzania, trying to supplant our influence with their own and to profit to the utmost from our social services without accepting the principle of collaboration in a pluralist way as laid down by the state (Sivalon, 1990:124).

The Tanzanian catholic establishment feared the rapid growth of the Muslim influence in the country. The Christian churches in general believed that they had been making every effort to live in harmony and cooperation with other religions in the context of a pluralist society, respecting the freedom of conscience of individuals and, more controversially, the separation of church and state. They did not think that the Muslim establishment was prepared to reciprocate their gesture in this regard. Instead, according to the catholic hierarchy, Muslims were intent on furthering their own interests, both religiously and politically, using political pressure to weaken the Christian position. The catholic church "fears that the Muslims are interested in establishing a Muslim state" (Omari, 1987: 65). This fear has been reinforced by the fact that in certain North African states, the Muslim Brotherhood "strongly emphasises the supranational character of Islam. To Muslim Brotherhood, all Muslims form a single "nation"... The ultimate goal of Muslim Brotherhood is the creation of an Islamic state encompassing all Muslims" (Westerlund, 1982).

Tanzania is, constitutionally, a secular nation-state. It is important in discussing the religious challenges to the secular nation-state project to make a distinction between mainstream Muslims and those that espouse extremist positions. The generality of Tanzanian Muslims have not advanced any demands for the creation of a Muslim nation-state. Rather, it is those Muslims who can be characterised as fundamentalists who have demanded the creation of an Islamic nation-state in Tanzania. As can be expected, this has generated a great deal of concern and controversy. It should not be surprising, therefore, that during the 1990s, Islam became a focal point for some of the social and political disputes and conflicts that rocked the country. In February 1993, in his first public comment on religious controversies, President Ali Hassan Mwinyi confessed: "Religious (Islamic) fanaticism is now vivid. This we must admit". (*The Express*, January 28, 1993; February 3, 1993).

The Roman catholic church fears that if the Muslim influence in the country grows, it would lose its dominant position in society and its privileged access to the state. This fear has tended to fuel controversies between the leaders of the Christian and Muslim religions, with the Muslims insisting that Tanzania is, in fact, a leading Muslim country in the East Africa region given the number of self-confessed Muslims in the country's total population. According to Muslim leaders, followers of Islam constitute the majority of Tanzania's population. When reference is made to the country's census figures which show the contrary, Muslim leaders often insist that the numbers have been "doctored for political reasons to show Muslims are trailing behind Christians in numerical strength" (Said, 1993:2). In 1986, of the estimated 22 million inhabitants in Tanzania, 44 per cent were officially classified as Christian, 32.5 per cent Muslim, and 22.8 per cent traditionalists (Said, 1993:4).

There have been attempts to underline the role which Muslims have played in the construction of the modern Tanzanian state as a counter-balance to the role which the church and mission-educated politicians claim to have played. Thus, references have been made in the growing debate on religion in Tanzania to the role which Muslims played in the struggle for national self-determination. According to Kaniki, both the struggle for independence and nationalist politics in Tanganyika had a very strong Muslim input (Kaniki, 1980). It is also claimed that the first uprising against British colonial rule in 1939 occurred in predominantly Muslim areas. The Dockworkers' Union and its strike of 1947 were led by Muslims. Furthermore, Muslims enjoyed a preponderance over Christians in the Tanzanian African National Union (TANU) in terms of membership figures. The Elders Council, a vanguard committee of Muslims within TANU, did, in fact, challenge the Christian hegemony over the party. The Elders Council was known for its unrelenting demands for equal representation between Muslims and Christians in the government. In 1963 the Elders Council was dissolved allegedly for mixing politics with religion.

It is, of course important to stress that although the partisan revisionism occasioned by the controversies of the 1990s might suggest otherwise, Muslims in the CCM did not organise and act as a specific Muslim/Islamic bloc. In fact, it can be categorically asserted that Muslims did not constitute a bloc within the CCM by acting as an Islamic interest group on religious, political, or any other issues. The closest that Tanzania came to experiencing an organized Muslim opposition/challenge to the *status quo* before the 1990s was the formation of the All Muslim National Union of Tanganyika (AMNUT). This organization, apart from its religious functions, was politically opposed to TANU. It is on record that AMNUT wanted a delay of independence for Tanganyika in order, as it claimed, to gain time to educate the majority of Muslims who were "overwhelmed" by Christians. The British government was strongly urged to stay longer until the "uneducated" Muslims could gain "proper" education so as to have their rightful share of state offices and national resources when independence came. It is AMNUT which had all along been pushing the idea that Muslims formed a majority in Tanzania.

Furthermore, AMNUT believed that the secularization of TANU was a euphemism for Christian domination over the Muslims. It also criticized TANU for not supporting Muslim/Islamic education in Tanzania. AMNUT was one organization which took a stand against TANU's decision to introduce a one party state. It declared itself to be in favour of a multi-party system. When AMNUT and other opposition parties/organizations were banned in 1964, Sheikh Yahya Hussein who was one of AMNUT's front-line leaders, founded the Nationalist Enterprise Party. Chief Abdala Fundikira (related to Sheikh Yahya Hussein by marriage) was named the leader of the ill-fated Nationalist Enterprise Party. Many AMNUT leaders believed that the Christians who were at the head of state institutions were using state power against Islam and the interests of Muslims.

1968 witnessed the outbreak of the "Muslim crisis" in Tanzania when the East African Muslim Welfare Society was banned. The Society was established in 1945 at Mombasa by the Aga Khan who also became its Patron. Its objective was to promote Islam in East Africa and to raise the standard of living of the African Muslims in the area. In leadership and finance, the Asian Shia Muslims, in particular the Ismailis, were the guiding force in the Society. In a sense, the Society was a pan-Islamic brotherhood. In 1961, its headquarters were moved from Mombasa to Dar es Salaam and Chief Abdala Fundikira became President of the Society. While TANU, the leading nationalist movement, was striving for national unity, the East African Muslim Welfare Society was striving for pan-Islamic unity. The Society became a religious interest group that threatened TANU's declared goal of striving for a secular basis for Tanzanian unity.

The two top leaders of the East African Muslim Welfare Society in Tanzania were Tewa Saidi Towa (President) and Bibi Titi Mohammed (Vice-President). They were both African Muslims, former ministers, and members of parliament. They were both important politicians who were well known within TANU and who, by 1968, had reason to side with the anti-TANU Muslims in the Society against the party. In 1968, hard-core nationalists within TANU argued that the Society's constitution had become totally antiquated. They argued for the Africanisation of the offices of Secretary General and Education Secretary in the Society and demanded that its Patron should be a Tanzanian African elected by Tanzanian Muslims. These hard-line elements openly canvassed the position that those who were against TANU and the government should not be allowed to be the leaders of Muslims in Tanzania. They also castigated the Society as an instrument of the big bourgeoisie for exploiting the common people. Their views against the Society eventually prevailed and in 1968, it was banned.

Tanzanian Muslims broke away from the East African Muslim Welfare Society and formed the National Muslim Council (*Baraza Kuu la Waislamu Tanzania*—BAKWATA) in December 1968. But many saw BAKWATA as an organ of the ruling party while others treated it as an organ of the state. As a consequence, some Muslims decided to organize themselves independently of BAKWATA. There were, as of 1994, over one hundred Muslim organizations in mainland Tanzania. Muslims in general feel that "CCM is weak, it no longer commands the respect it did before because it has been de-islamized" (Said, 1993:4). Muslims perceive both Christianity and the state as fellow collaborators against Islam. The massive resurgence of a Muslim identity in Tanzania is clear testimony to the failure, or at least limited achievement of the repressive approach which the state and the ruling CCM took to autonomous forms of organization among Muslims.

CHRISTIANITY AND ISLAM DURING THE PERIOD OF POLITICAL LIBERALIZATION

We have observed elsewhere that during the course of the 1980s, the credibility and legitimacy of the state in Tanzania began seriously to be eroded. This credibility/legitimacy deficit has been reinforced by the social and ideological vacuum that has characterized the 1990s. The opposition groups that emerged in the 1990s have, on the whole, been unable to articulate a broad national alternative that could stem the diminishing legitimacy of the state and the increasing ideological vacuum that is felt in the country. In the context of the deepening social crisis in the country, ethnic tensions, regional parochialism, narrow and petty nationalistic tendencies, and religious tensions have increasingly become the order of the day in Tanzania (Luanda, 1993:67). Let us now elaborate a bit more on the religious forms of identity and mobilisation that have been witnessed in Tanzania since the early 1990s and the ways in which they have called Tanzania's secular constitutional foundation into question.

The Muslim Challenge to the Secular Nation-State Project

In March 1991, Chief Abdala Fundikira, a former Minister of Justice in the first independence government, currently Chairman of the Union for Multi-Party Democracy, defender of chiefly institutions and "above all, together with Sheikh Yahaya Hussein, (one of) the most prominent Muslim opponents of TANU, the predecessor of CCM" (Westerlund, 1977:94), challenged religious leaders to participate in the debate for multiparty democracy in Tanzania. Referring specifically to the Koranic Reading Development Council (Baraza La Ukuzaji Kurani Tanzania—BALUKTA), Chief Fundikira emphasized that Muslim leaders had an important role to play in the political liberalization process. He surmised: "BALUKTA has the social and religious responsibility to serve the Muslim and general community at large. One such important responsibility is to educate the Muslim masses and others about their political and legal rights" (*Family Mirror*, April, 1991).

It is significant, though not all together surprising, that Chief Fundikira addressed his concerns to BALUKTA rather than BAKWATA, the legally constituted/recognised Muslim organ in Tanzania. BAKWATA is the brainchild of CCM and for Fundikira, that was enough reason not to have anything to do with it given his own antagonism towards the CCM. BAKWATA's organizational structure is virtually a carbon copy of the CCM's structure and its leadership is dominated by Muslims who are also CCM leaders. Many Muslims pay no attention to BAKWATA which they see as a Muslim branch of CCM. Apart from the fact that Chief Fundikira holds a prominent position among the Muslims of Tanzania, in the 1960s he was president of the East African Muslim Welfare Society which, as we noted earlier, was declared illegal by the government and banned (Westerlund, 1977:94).

In addressing himself to the BALUKTA, Chief Fundikara did so in the settled knowledge that in Sheikh Kassim bin Jumaa bin Hamis (Kwa Mtoro mosque), a founding member of both the East African Muslim Welfare Society and Baraza Kuu la Waislamu, he had an ally. Kassim bin Jumaa bin Hamis came to prominence in 1983 when he publicly denounced BAKWATA for not defending the rights of Muslims and castigated its leadership for being ineffective. BALUKTA, formed in 1987 in opposition to BAKWATA, is the brainchild of Sheikh Kassim bin Jumaa bin Hamis. Unlike BAKWATA which was legally registered with the Ministry of Home Affairs (as the only organ for Muslims in Tanzania), BALUKTA was registered at the Office of the Administrator-General of Trustees where Sheikh Kassim bin Jumaa bin Hamis (conveniently) worked (in charge of Muslim affairs). BALUKTA was registered as a public trustee for the Muslim community. Within a very short space of time, BALUKTA usurped all the tasks, duties and rites—Muslim inheritance law, divorce, *fata*, etc.—hitherto performed by BAKWATA.

In the view of many on the Tanzanian mainland, the first major issue that signalled the onset of direct Muslim challenges to the unitary secular state during the 1990s was the unilateral decision by Zanzibar to join the Organization of Islamic Conference (OIC). Towards the end of December 1992 the local news media, especially the newly established newspapers, were literally filled with sensational stories about the Islamization of Tanzania which Zanzibar's OIC membership portended. The emerging opposition seized on the concern which the OIC affair generated among many on the mainland and called on the President and the Minister for Foreign Affairs to resign their offices with immediate effect. There were also discordant voices within the government itself. But the President, a Zanzibari and a self-proclaimed devout Muslim, defended Zanzibar's admission to the Jeddah-based OIC saying that it was economically motivated and had no religious connotations. According to him:

> It is true that Zanzibar has joined the OIC but purely for social and economic gains not religious. But we all know that Zanzibar does not need a religious certificate to know that most of its citizens are Muslims. They have been so since the seventh century... My fellow Tanzanians, Zanzibar is in a hopeless economic situation and it is simply trying to seek old and new donors and the OIC is a religious body by name but it has economic endeavours Zanzibar stands to gain development assistance from the OIC which owns an Islamic bank. We are not going to allow ourselves into religious relations (*Mfanyakazi*, January 28–February 3, 1993; Nyerere, 1994).

The divisions in Tanzanian society brought about by the OIC controversy took distinct religious forms. In general, Muslims applauded Zanzibar's action. No doubt, part of the Muslim response was in reaction to the widespread Muslim-bashing that was perpetrated by the local press (*Daily News*, July 23, 1993). Muslims argued that all through its history, Tanzania had been joining various international organizations. In all of these dealings, the question of the violation of the country's constitution was never once raised. Tanzania is a member of the Red Cross, Christian Refugees Services, Catholic Old Boy's Association, and Social Guild. All of these are international Christian organizations. Muslims further alleged that there is a document entitled "Memorandum of Understanding" between Tanzania and certain European nations about assisting Christian organizations with educational and medical facilities (*Mfanyakazi*, January 27, 1993).

The objectives of the OIC, according to the Muslims who supported Zanzibar's decision to join it, are not narrowly based on the quest for religious advantage. They include the protection of the right of every nation to self-determination, non-interference in the internal affairs of member-states, respect for and protection of the internationally-recognized borders of members nations, the enhancement and furtherance of international co-operation in social, cultural and scientific matters, and the provision of interest-free loans for development in member-nations (*Mizani*, July 2, l993; *Mizani*, April 29, 1994). For these Muslims, the claim that there is a conspiracy to islamize Tanzania is pure fantasy (*Mizani*, January 15, 1994). If there was any challenge to the secularity of the Tanzanian nation-state, it arose more from the fact that the union government had paid only lip service to the goal of building a non-sectarian nation-state where all citizens could feel equal.

Aboud Jumbe, a former president of Zanzibar, added his voice to the growing chorus of Muslim criticism of the one-sided secularity of the Tanzanian post-colonial nation-state project when he publicly stated that the CCM had, by commission or omission, tended to marginalise and under-represent Muslims in the organs of government. Jumbe argued that since independence, Tanzanians in general and Muslims in particular had been led to believe that their country is genuinely a secular unitary nation-state. For slightly over thirty years, Tanzanians sang "freedom and unity", and "freedom and work"—songs which became the mainstay of Tanzania's post-colonial mythologies. These mythologies, buttressed by "national icons" like *Mwenge*—the Torch—planted at the top of Mount Kilimanjaro at independence, supposedly came to symbolize Tanzania and its spirit. Citizens believed in the Tanzania project and felt proud of being Tanzanians. But in reality, all these were, according to Jumbe, sweet dreams; Tanzanians were living in wonderland.

By the 1990s, the sweet dreams had become shattered: tribalism, regionalism, religious, racial and sexual discrimination, absolute poverty and other social ills had become the lot of Tanzanians. Many came to realise that the secularity of the unitary nation-state is a huge lie. Jumbe expanded on his view by pointing to the lop-sidedness of Muslim and Christian representation in the organs of power. Thus, although, in the CCM, Muslims form a majority at the annual conference and, in the government, Muslims are a majority in the parliament, in executive organs like the National Executive Committee of the CCM and the cabinet, Muslims are in a minority in absolute terms. What Muslims were demanding, according to Jumbe, were freedom, equality, justice, equal representation in organs of power and governance, and equal opportunities in socio-economic development (*Mwananchi*, March 22–28, 1993). The outcry against Zanzibar's membership of the OIC was little more than a "subterfuge" (perpetrated by Christians) to remove President Ali Hassan Mwinyi from power (*Mizani*, January 15, 1993).

The Tanzanian unitary secular nation-state project has certainly been seriously undermined by the OIC controversy. In addition to putting the union between the mainland and Zanzibar under a severe strain, it has significantly altered the political, constitutional, and religious landscape of Tanzania. Most ordinary Muslims in Tanzania defended Zanzibar's (unilateral) action to join the OIC. In doing this, many of them challenged the principle of the unitary secular nation-state. However, the most serious challenge came from mujahidin elements within BALUKTA organised around its chairman, Sheikh Yahya Hussein and the firebrand Sheikh Kassim bin Jumaa. Kwa Mtoro Mosque, situated along Livingstone Street in Dar es Salaam, served as the command post of mujahidin. At the height of the mujahidin's activities, around April 1993, the state authorities claimed to have come across circumstantial evidence that the mujahidin (through the BALUKTA leadership) had contacts with Iran, the Islamic Party of Kenya and a Muslim university in Egypt (*Family Mirror*, April 1993).

The nature of challenges posed by BALUKTA to the secular state may be similar, in broad terms, to those that emanated from the generality of the Muslim community. However, the method by which BALUKTA challenged the unitary secular nation-state is markedly different. BALUKTA called for an end to the oppression of Muslims. It argued that it is blasphemy for Muslims to be ruled by Christians and, therefore, demanded the creation of an Islamic state. In this regard, Muslims were exhorted not to vote for "kaffirs" or Christians. BALUKTA singled out certain key cabinet ministers for removal from the government: John Malecela (Prime Minister) because the ceremony occasioning the signing of the document for restoring ownership of schools to Christian organizations from which they were expropriated in the first place took place in his office; Edward Lowassa (Minister of State in the Prime Minister's Office) because he was responsible for actually signing the aforementioned document; Damian Lubuva (Attorney General) allegedly because he stole the document containing proposals for constitutional changes made by the former Zanzibar President Aboud Jumbe; Dr. William Shija (Minister of Information and Broadcasting) because he banned the newspapers *Cheka* and *Michapo* but did not outlaw *Motomoto* which revealed the OIC scandal; and Pius Msekwa (Speaker of the National Assembly) because he was one of the key players in the drafting of the Union Constitution for Tanganyika and Zanzibar (*Baraza*, April 1993; *Wasaa*, June 1993; *Mizani*, July 2, 1993).

In place of the "kaffirs" whom it targeted for direct attack, BALUKTA (which firmly believes that Muslims form the majority of the electorate) put up a list of eight Muslim names (all of them serving ministers) from which the next president and cabinet of the country should be chosen. The names in question are: Kighoma Malima (Minister for Finance) for President; Ahmed Diria (Minister of Labour); Jakaya Kikwete (Minister for Energy and Minerals), Amran Mayagila (Minister for Health), Fatma Said Ali (Manpower), and Abdulrahman Kinana (Minister, President's Office with responsibility for Defence and National Service). Significantly, many out of these were later to be moved by President Mwinyi to key posts in the December 1994 cabinet reshuffle (*Family Mirror*, December, 1994). BALUKTA also demanded the abolition of BAKWATA which it claimed had betrayed Muslims. Like many ordinary Muslims, BALUKTA demanded equal representation for Muslims in all state organs. But more than that, it also wanted the state to allow the formation of Islamic political parties. Deriving from that demand, certain key Muslim figures have formed a Muslim political party, the National Emancipation and Mass Advancement NEMA. NEMA has been registered by the authorities.

Initially, the BALUKTA's challenges were confined to the mosques in the form of "mihadhara" (sermons). Kwa Mtoro Mosque in Dar es Salaam was the epicentre for this activity although other mosques in Morogoro, Mwanza and Arusha also played their part. Within a short period of time however, the "mihadhara" became street assemblies. Commuter bus services—called "daladala" in Dar es Salaam provided another forum for "mihadhara" transmitted through recorded cassettes. The high point of BALUKTA's challenges to the secular unitary nation-state was the attack on pork butcheries on 9 April 1994 (which was a Good Friday). It is claimed that some five hundred Muslim youths had been registered at Kwa Mtoro Mosque in Dar es Salaam to serve in the Islamic army being formed to fight in the *jihad* (holy war) declared by the BALUKTA mujahidin against the state to protest the marginalization of Muslims by Christians. In April 1993 newspapers featured stories about containers of arms intercepted by customs officials at the port of Dar es Salaam (*Sunday News*, April 11, 1993; *Mwananchi*, April 12–18, 1993). It was alleged that Iran, to which several BALUKTA leaders are allied, was the main supplier of arms for the *jihad*. There were also stories about home-made bombs being unearthed at certain Muslim homes in Dar es Salaam.

Plans to attack pork butcheries (and poison beer at Tanzania Breweries, burn groceries, bars, guest houses and disrupt Easter celebrations) were hatched at Kwa Mtoro Mosque. The staging posts for the attacks were established by the imams of Makuti, Kagera, Mwembe-Chai, Tandale and Sisikwa Sisi mosques in the Magomeni–Manzese area. Prior to the attacks, the imams of these mosques wrote to the authorities demanding the closure of pork butcheries. On 6 April 1994 the Minister for Internal Affairs, Augustine Mrema, met the imams and told them that the pork butcheries are legally licensed to transact business. Sheikh Abubakr Mwaipopo (Kwa Ntoro Mosque) is alleged to have incited the

Kwa Mtoro Mosque congregation on 9 April 1993 to defy government orders prohibiting attacks on pork butcheries. Some time in the afternoon of Good Friday, hundreds of Muslims marched along Morogoro Road in the Magomeni area. As they approached Mbotomu Pork Centre and Argentina Pork Butchery, they formed an extended line, one of them blew a whistle and the mujahidin went on the offensive amidst chants of *Allah Akbar!* (God is Great). They destroyed property and went away with weighing machines and other equipment (*Mwananchi*, April 12–18, 1993; *Uhuru*, April 14, 1993). Thirty eight members of the mujahidin alleged to have taken part in attacking the pork butcheries were arrested and prosecuted. None of the BALUKTA leaders was on the scene. The thirty eight mujahidin were taken to court on 12 April 1993 and charged with conspiring to disturb the peace, destroy property, and steal. They were also charged with demonstrating contrary to the law (*Uhuru*, April 14, 1993).

On the same day, Muslims from Kwa Mtoro Mosque marched in a procession to the Central Police Station to demand the release of the arrested mujahidin. The marchers carried red and white flags with banners which read: "Muslims are ready to die in defence of their fellow Muslims" (*Daily News*, April 13, 1993). The demonstration was broken up by the police and thirteen of the marchers were arrested. Sheikh Yahya Hussein, Chairman of BALUKTA was arrested on 15 April 1993 and formally charged with fanning the wave of Islamic fundamentalism in Tanzania. After a few appearances in court, Sheikh Kassim bin Jumaa fled to Kenya. Sheikh Yahya Hussein admitted in court that the Muslims who mounted the attack on pork shops were his followers and the "mihadhara" in the cassettes were his (*Uhuru*, April 17, 1993; *Motomoto*, April 17, 1993). He also admitted to having instigated the attack on pork shops in order to pressurize the government and the ruling party to grant Muslims their rights. He said: "Ni Kweli mimi nimewahiziza walalamike dhidi ya CCM... Wabaneni watu wa CCM ili mpatiwe haki zenu... Ni kweli CCM inafanya makosa. Nitawadhibiti ... lakini sitazuia kudai haki zao" (*Uhuru*, April 14, 1993).

The case dragged on for almost the whole of 1993. In September 1993, Sheikh Kassim bin Jumaa recanted his militancy and expelled the mujahidin from Kwa Mtoro Mosque. He said he no longer believed in fundamentalism. He vowed to work with the government and the CCM in building a peaceful country (*Shaba*, September 14–20, 1993). Sheikh Kassim bin Jumaa became afflicted with an incurable disease and passed away at Mikocheni Hospital. To many a Muslim, Sheikh Kassim bin Jumaa was a hero, a defender of and fighter for the democratic rights of Muslims (*Baraza*, January 17–23, 1994). Sheikh Yahya Hussein, once described by Nyerere as a hooligan on whom he had "impeccable" evidence relating to his false identity (*Rai*, January 27, 1994) does not seem to entertain any fundamentalist views any longer. Only minor skirmishes have been reported in Morogoro, Mwanza and Arusha involving the fundamentalists. Those Muslim fundamentalists who still had any appetite left for fight resorted to returning their CCM cards and renouncing their membership of the party which they claim had betrayed them (*Mfanyakazi*, May 26, 1993). Appeals to Muslim identity thus continue to play a role in the political life of the country.

The Christian Challenge to the Secular Nation-State

If 1993 was dominated by Muslim challenges to the secular unitary nation-state project in Tanzania, 1994 marked the onset of direct challenges by the Christian churches both to the state and the CCM. The challenges that emanated from the Christian churches were championed by established Christian organizations, namely, the Christian Council of Tanzania, the Tanzania Episcopal Conference, and the Church of the Province of Tanzania. The activism on the part of these established churches was triggered by the OIC controversy.

In February 1993, President Ali Hassan Mwinyi summoned Christian bishops (Tanzania Episcopal Conference, Evangelical Lutheran Church and the Church of the Province of Tanzania) to State House. The meeting was prompted by a stern statement (which included an ultimatum) from the catholic church whose bishops had lambasted the government over its alleged inaction when mujahidin groups (operating under BALUKTA) were openly "preaching contempt, slanders and blasphemies against the Christian faith". The catholic bishops' statement was issued on 28 February 1993. In part, the statement said:

> We have been maintaining a low profile yet we are not asleep. We have made the rough investigations; we have analyzed; we have prayed and been closely follow-ing up the events taking place in the country. This is the right time. With this statement we set to work... We are fed up with the government stance for not taking measures to stop them (*Family Mirror*, March, 1993).

In May 1993, the Catholic bishops issued a pastoral letter saying that most of the country's top leaders lacked self-respect, were liars and cared too much for personal material and bodily pleasures than for the country and humanity. The letter went on to say that "the political arena was full of hypocrisy, lies, tricks and laxity. As a result, leadership is unstable, the nation has lost political direc-tion and gets easily swayed by external forces" (*Heko*, June 24–30, 1993). How-ever, it was the OIC affair that brought about the bitterest attacks against the government from the Christian churches. A meeting of Bishops of the Christian Council of Tanzania, held from 9 to 10 June 1993 at Dodoma, resolved to ask President Ali Hassan Mwinyi to prevail upon Zanzibar to remove itself from the OIC. Further, the resolution blamed the National Assembly for failing to prevent Zanzibar from joining an international islamic organization. Zanzibar's action, according to them, grossly violated the Union Constitution. On the question of the Union, the Christian Council of Tanzania recommended a federal structure involving three governments, one Zanzibari, one mainland, and one union. They also urged that the citizenry should be allowed to partici-pate fully in deciding the question of the country's structure of governance (*Family Mirror*, May, 1993).

Similarly, the Evangelical Lutheran Church of Tanzania (ELCT) came out strongly in opposition to Zanzibar's decision to join the OIC. It called for all those responsible for Zanzibar's action to be brought to book. This was because Zanzibar's action had very grave consequences for Tanzania's secular constitution. It would entail and involve Tanzania subscribing to Sharia law. According to the ELCT,

> Christian churches believe and recognize Tanzania as a secular unitary nation-state and so are the political parties. However, Tanzanians believe in God. According to the Tanzanian constitution, the government is duty bound to protect the freedom of conscience of all its citizens without discrimination (*Mfanyakazi*, August 25, 1993).

The ELCT pointed out that amongst other things, the objectives of the OIC are: to further and develop Islamic solidarity among member-nations; secure, maintain and protect Islamic Holy Shrines (sites); support the struggles of the peoples of Pakistan and to assist them in the liberation of their country; and to further the struggles of all Muslims in protecting their honour, freedom, and rights.

These objectives, according to the ELCT, are religious and fundamentally Islamic. Tanzania should not join the OIC or any other religious (Islamic) organizations. In allowing Zanzibar membership of the OIC, the top national leadership has blatantly violated the constitution. The ELCT statement finished by calling for the resignation of leaders who were implicated in the violation of the constitution (*Family Mirror*, September, 1993 and December, 1993). There are many other serious issues and accusations directed by the Christian churches against the state: economic mismanagement, embezzlement, misuse of public funds, grants, donations and loans, greed on the part of top national leaders, and mismanagement of the country's natural resources.

By the beginning of 1994, the challenges from the Christian churches to the state literally resembled those of a party in opposition. The Episcopal Lutheran Church of Tanzania and the Tanzania Episcopal Conference were the most vocal and probably the most effective. The Christian churches demanded transparency in government, the rule of law, responsible government, human rights and constitutionality. They took it upon themselves to directly disseminate educational material in support of democracy (*Mfanyakazi*, March 23, 1994). In the words of Amani Mwenegoha, the General Secretary of the Evangelical Lutheran Church:

> The present CCM government has lost direction; and has no ability to govern. It hardly listens to the people. The government does not command respect from the governed. However, the CCM government has earned a notorious reputation for greed, self-aggrandizement by a few leaders at top, and embezzlement. The CCM government should step down to make way for a transitional government of national unity. We must educate the whole society about the rotten political situation, their rights and obligations. Our leaders have betrayed the nation in every conceivable way. The citizens were not involved in the making of the present Constitution. The very leaders who made this Constitution blatantly violate it. Repression has become rampant. Sons and daughters of peasants and workers are denied

the right to good quality education. Those of the wealthy are sent abroad to Kenya and Britain by the wealth created by the poor (*Kiongozi*, December 1–15, 1994).

Clearly, by the end of 1994, the front-line role of the church as a critic of the government had become firmly established in the Tanzanian political land-scape. The churches' statements of criticism fed into the popular quest for new forms of politics in the country and helped to focus opposition to the CCM's way of running the country.

CONCLUSION

For a country which prided itself on its record of ethnic harmony and religious tolerance, the events which have unfolded in Tanzania since the early 1990s suggest a growing loss of faith in the post-colonial nation-state project. If for Muslims, this loss of faith has taken the form of a direct questioning of the secu-lar basis of the project, among Christians, it has taken the form of open scepti-cism about the state's ability to maintain and defend a secular constitution. The response of the state to the growth in religious identities has, on the whole, been intolerant, even repressive. Yet, if the experience of the 1960s is anything to go by, it is certain that repression will fail to establish a basis for a lasting solution to the increasing incidence of intolerance associated with the resurgence of religious identities. Ultimately, questions of state legitimacy and the increasing social polarization in the country, as evidenced by the growing gap between the rich and the poor, will have to be tackled as part and parcel of efforts at tackling both Christian and Muslim political and religious extremism. The challenge before Tanzania therefore is not merely the adoption of multi-party politics but, perhaps more importantly, a democratic frame of governance that emphasises accountability to the governed by the governors and restores faith in the country.

BIBLIOGRAPHY

Kaniki, M.Y. (ed.), 1980, *Tanzania under German Colonial Rule*, Longman Group Ltd., London.

Luanda, Nestor N., 1993, "Democratization and the Politics of the Opposition in Tanzania", (mimeo), Dar Es Salaam.

Nyerere, J. K., 1994, *Uongozi na Hatima ya Tanzania*, Zimbabwe Publishing House, Harare.

Omari, C.K., 1987, "Christian–Muslim Relations in Tanzania", in *Report of a Seminar Sponsored by the Lutheran World Federation and the Project for Christian Muslim Relations in Africa*, 28 May, Nairobi.

Said, Mohamed, 1993, "Islam and Politics in Tanzania", (mimeo), Nairobi.

Sivalon, J.C., 1990, *Roman Catholicism and the Defining of Tanzanian Socialism, 1953–1985: An Analysis of the Social Ministry of the Roman Catholic Church in Tanzania*, PhD Thesis, University of St. Michel's College, Canada.

The United Republic of Tanzania, 1990, *The Constitution of the United Republic of Tanzania*, Government Printer, Dar es Salaam.

Westerlund D., 1982 , *From Socialism to Islam? Notes on Islam as a Political Factor in Contemporary Africa*, Scandinavian Institute of African Studies, Research Report, No. 61, Uppsala.

Westerlund, D., 1977 , *Ujamaa na Dini: A Study of Some Aspects of Society and Religion in Tanzania, 1961–1977*, Acta Universitas Stockholmiensis, Stockholm Studies in Comparative Religion.

NEWSPAPERS AND PERIODICALS

Baraza.
Business Times.
Daily News.
Family Mirror.
Heko.
Kiongozi.
Majira.
Mfanyakazi.
Mizani.
Motomoto.
Mwanachi.
Rai.
Shaba.
Sunday News.
The Express.

Chapter 9

Resuscitating the *Majimbo* Project: The Politics of Deconstructing the Unitary State in Kenya

Mutahi Ngunyi

INTRODUCTION:
THE CRISIS OF THE NATION-STATE PROJECT IN KENYA

The post-colonial nation-state project in Africa is in crisis. The union between "
... the "nation" in the sense of an ethnic coalition and the "state" as the principal
source of political authority is (increasingly) coming under pressure ... (and)
(t)he question is less whether the nation-state can be rescued, than how long
and painful this transition to new forms of federation and political community
will be" (*Africa Confidential*, January 1995:1). The unitary approach to the nation-
state project was the choice of the state nationalists who led Africa to independence. This choice tended to consolidate the colonial state's top-down "nation-
building" programme whose primary concern was to integrate the diversified
ethnic nationalities who constituted the state under one centralized authority.
This was not only seen as desirable, it was also seen as a *conditio sine qua non* if
Africa was to avoid civil war and foster rapid development. Hence, the integration project was pursued using all means available to the state—including
armed force.

Under the post-colonial unitary project, the contract binding the nationalities
to the state was cast in terms that were non-negotiable and total. The devolution of power to the nationalities was left to the discretion of the national
leader who did it through a highly subjective process of "geographical
balancing" and "discrete inclusiveness". The totality of this arrangement not
only led to the ethnicisation of resource allocation favouring the ethnic coalitions in power, it also subsequently saw the emergence of political monolithism
and its logical "horse rider", the maximum leader. At the normative level, this
led to the entrenchment of *presidentialism* at the expense of *constitutionalism*. But
three decades after most African countries attained their independence, this
political arrangement is experiencing a serious crisis of political legitimacy.

The legitimacy crisis of the state, which is so closely tied to the overall unravelling of the post-colonial secular nation-state project, largely derives from the developmental problems that are contingent on the state's dwindling resources and its increasing loss of economic hegemony to diverse forces in civil society. It is, of course, highly debatable if these forces are independent of the state. Whatever the case, what seems to result from this development in many African countries is a precarious balance between polarised power centres. On the one hand, we have " ... the authority of the state, compromised politically and economically ... (while on the other hand, we have) ... a political periphery formed from an alliance of (forces) marginalised by the state but unable, as yet, to force the centre to devolve power" (*Africa Confidential*, January 1995:3). The struggles associated with this polarisation have either taken on an ethno-regional form or, to a lesser extent, an ethno-religious character as is the case with the Islamic Party of Kenya (IPK).

The process of establishing a democratic order in Africa has taken place in the context of the constraints posed by diminished state legitimacy and increasing social fragmentation. The forces articulating popular claims in society have tended to become ethnicised as the process of democratisation matures. Similarly, the hitherto "pure" ethnic formations in society have become increasingly politicised in the face of the post-developmentalist reformulation of the state and the subsequent change in perception among some nationalities about the post-colonial unitary project. Social discourse has tended to view these "new" forms of ethnicity not as pathologies in the typical/usual sense, but as *bona fide* expressions of the desire of social forces to fight the monolithic structures of the state and the exercise of unaccountable power.

It follows from the foregoing that ethnicity should not simply or automatically be viewed as an inherently "bad thing" by and of itself but as one possible social response to political repression. In some instances, it can, in fact, be a potentially democratic force. This view that ethnicity might promote a process of democratisation by, for example, compelling the provision of a political framework within which repressed ethnicities can re-negotiate their position in the unitary project, has raised numerous questions in the discourse on the crisis of the nation-state in Africa. The first and most pertinent of these is whether the post-developmentalist "nation" can be subsumed under one centralized/unitary "state" by all means available, including force. Related to this is the sub-question of whether the state has the capacity to provide a negotiated political environment that is accommodative of competing ethnicities.

In the event that the centralized/unitary nation-state cannot hold, the second question has to do with the nature of the alternative that is available—the *federal project*. The federal alternative throws up two sub-questions. First, given the fact that the main preoccupation of the African state has been the establishment of its hegemony and right to rule, " ... we must ask what it means to balance federal and regional strength in the context of a "soft" state" (Wooley and Keller, 1994:421). Second, the question of the democratic potential of the federal project must also be critically addressed. In particular, there is the concern that a federal system of government created as a specific response to the demands of different ethnic nationalities is likely to lead to the creation of new majorities and minorities/new dominant and dominated forces within the new *jimbos*.

The third question has to do with the "ownership" of the federal project or of even a "reconditioned" nation-state project. The issue emerging in the discourse on the nation-state in this regard has to do with the intricate relationship between the federal project, its "ownership" and its democratic potential. Undoubtedly, the consolidation of the nation-state at independence was a class project. Similarly, the federal project, in most cases, is largely driven by the excluded political elite. It could, therefore, be low in popular content and its democratic potential might be more apparent than real unless popular forces make democracy a central element in the federal project. On the whole, at least insofar as the broad African experience suggests, the discourse on the federal project is concerned more with "distributional politics" and less with decentralization and power sharing as an exercise in democratic politics.

BACKGROUND CONTEXT TO THE *MAJIMBO* PROJECT IN KENYA

Unlike most African states where repressed ethnic groups are the ones at the forefront of the struggle for the devolution of state power and the creation of a federal system of government, in Kenya, the deconstruction of the unitary state is a state project. It is also a class project which is yet to go through the motions of popularisation in the "tribe". It must be mentioned, however, that at certain moments, it is cast as an "ethnic project".

The *majimbo* (regionalist/federalist) project in Kenya has its roots in the independence struggle of the country. Two constituencies dominated that struggle. On the one hand, there were the unitarists led by Jomo Kenyatta and the Kenya African National Union (KANU). The unitarists had the support of the majority ethnic communities in the country. On the other hand, there were the colonial forces and their Kenyan allies/surrogates. These congregated in the Kenya African Democratic Union (KADU). Their agenda was regionalism under the *majimbo* project. From the onset, the two positions were to be canvassed constitutionally but where no accommodation was reached, a violent alternative was threatened. In the recurring crisis of the nation-state project in Kenya, the revival of either of the two positions has been the most salient mode of articulating and championing the claims of contesting ethnic groups.

The central interests of the two opposing constituencies involved in the discourse on the nature of the Kenyan state have to do with the symbiosis between the process of accumulation and the question of political succession. Before every succession in the history of Kenya, the incumbent elite has been known to want to alter the political system with the aim of either aborting the succession and hence perpetuating its stay in power, or expanding the political space to allow it room for negotiation with the emerging "successor group". This has either been done through constitutional means or by the threat of violence. Historical evidence has shown that at the heart of this manoeuvring, is the need to protect a system of accumulation dominated by the incumbent elite.

The reason why the colonial state and its allies among the political elite entered into an alliance with KADU in fighting for the *majimbo* project was primarily for the protection of resources which they had already accumulated and the system that sustained this accumulation. Similarly, the period preceding the transition from Kenyatta to Moi witnessed a major constitutional crisis precipitated by the Change the Constitution Movement (CCM) which was spearheaded by the then powerful ethnic coalition known as the Gikuyu, Embu and Meru Association (GEMA) in 1976. This project aimed at having the constitution changed so that in the event that the president was unable to execute the duties of his office or died, the vice-president would not automatically assume power for ninety days pending an election as stipulated by the constitution.

What followed the launching of CCM were huge rallies all over the GEMA areas similar in nature to the *majimbo* rallies of September 1991 in the Rift Valley. These were later complemented by oath-taking sessions binding the Gikuyu to a cause that would ensure that the presidency never left the "House of Mumbi". The primary concern of the CCM was to protect Kikuyu capital by ensuring that the presidency did not go outside the "House of Mumbi". The revival of the *majimbo* project in 1991 is all about a Moi succession and how the dominant political elite connected to and profiting from the Moi presidency perceives its interests in relation to a "successor group".

While all of these processes of political engineering have been elite-generated and -guided, the place of the ordinary citizen has been marginal. This is also essentially true of the new *majimbo* project even though its revival has coincided with the popular quest for democratisation and the associated need to popularise political actions. The popularisation of political actions has remained elite-guided and is tailored to serve narrow interests. Where pressures for political change have emanated from forces in civil society, their popular content has been low and the campaigning structures that are built have tended to be dominated by the excluded elite. What is however different about the civil society-based attempts at pressurising for political change is that despite their domination by the political elite, they have tended to treat "popularisation" as a *sine qua non* for successful mobilisation. As to whether this is genuine or not, only an empirical investigation can tell.

It must be noted that although the nation-state project in Kenya is in crisis and the ethno-regions are demanding participation in the running of the political system, no empirical inquiries have been conducted so far to determine the extent to which the ethnic nationalities that comprise the state support federalism as envisaged by the *majimbo* project. We will however attempt to show in this chapter that the quest for the deconstruction of the unitary state through the resuscitation of the *majimbo* project is the project of an ethno-regional elite threatened with exclusion in the event that a new government comes to power (primarily through an election) in place of the Moi government. The project may have gone through certain motions of popularisation, but its rationale and sustainability have been put into question by several works (*Africa Watch*, 1993; Kuria, 1994).

AGRARIAN SOURCES OF *MAJIMBO*

Land expropriation under the colonial regime was concentrated in two areas in Kenya. These were the better-watered upland areas of Central Kenya and the fertile highlands of the Rift Valley. The upland areas were basically chosen because of their fertility, proximity to Nairobi, and prior interaction with European explorers. They were also situated along the newly completed Uganda railway. According to the colonial administration, although the railway was primarily used for purposes of extracting agricultural surplus from the hinterlands," ... a line with two ends and no middle—and thus no feeder traffic—would hardly pay" (Sorrenson, 1967:15). Central Kenya was therefore earmarked as the region to provide "feeder traffic", among other things.

The Rift Valley highlands were also traversed by the Uganda railway, but unlike central Kenya, they were not densely populated and were, therefore, easy to expropriate. Besides, the inhabitants of the highlands were " ... either shifting agriculturists or semi-nomadic pastoralists ... (and) ... their subsistence economy produced little that was worth exporting to the coast" (Sorrenson, 1967:15). Using this rationale and the "disappointing" fact that the colony did not have minerals, the European settlers were expected to make do with these highlands, probably transforming them in order to endow the colony with a vibrant economy.

The net effect of land expropriation in these two regions was the creation of two agricultural corridors which later developed incongruent forms of ethno-regional nationalisms. The first corridor is situated in Central Kenya and it brings the Kikuyus together with the Meru, Embu and Luo people. These groups formed the political coalition that founded the original Kenya African National Union (KANU). The second corridor is in the Rift Valley and brings, among others, the Kalenjins, Masai, Samburu, and Turkana together with the Luhya people of western Kenya. These groups founded the Kenya African Democratic Union (KADU). The post-independence rivalry between the two corridors derives from the manner in which their inhabitants interacted with settler agrarian capital. This rivalry also accounts for the rationale behind the initial *majimbo* project and the on-going campaign for the deconstruction of the unitary state. We shall demonstrate this later in this chapter.

In the two corridors, three types of settlements were created. The first type consisted of the Native Reserve Units. This process was legalised under the

Crown Land Ordinance of 1915. By the 1920s, organised opinion in the over-crowded Central Kenya reserves was beginning to threaten a peasant uprising. Although this was contained early enough, the colonial administration began to think of alternatives to the reserves. These were to materialise in the second quarter of 1900 as native settlement schemes. But the question of unrest in the Central Kenya reserves was also to be resolved, at least temporarily, with the migration of peasant farmers into the Rift Valley highlands as casual labourers and squatters. This migratory process marked the beginning of rivalry between the indigenous communities of the Rift Valley and the Gikuyu.

Having dealt with the native question, the second order of business was to contain the Indian peasants doing thriving business in urban centres situated along the railway. Although they could have been settled in the highland town-ships because of their business acumen, settler suspicion of Indian peasants as possible competitors resulted in their being confined to the lower country of the lake basin and the coast (Sorrenson, 1967:16). It was argued that by settling them in the hinterlands, they would open up trade with the Africans, largely because they had traded long enough with the African peasants and, therefore, understood their needs fully. Despite their role as agents for the settlers and their interaction with the African peasants, their relations with both groups were the least politicised in the colony. They were known to "straddle" when serious political issues were at stake.

The third type of settlements consisted of the White Highlands. These were finally established on the model of the colonies in Central and South Africa from where Sir Charles Eliot, the colonial governor, obtained most of his settlers. These were both Boer and British South Africans and they constituted the majority of the settlers in the Highlands. The South Africans saw themselves as pioneers "creating" a new country, but it was to be a white man's country founded in the image of a racially divided South Africa with no "nonsense about equal rights for blacks and whites". Their farming methods, their control of labour, their political techniques and objectives were all founded on South African precedents (Sorrenson, 1967:67–68).

Once fully established, the highlands impacted on the two corridors differ-ently. Given the agricultural nature of the Kikuyu in Central Kenya, they saw their proximity to settler capital as an opportunity to make their rudimentary commercial agricultural activities a veritable site for accumulation. They would, for instance, provide plantation workers with foodstuffs and "pirate" settler farming techniques in order to raise the productivity of their small farms. This was unlike their Kalenjin, Masai, Turkana and Samburu (KAMATUSA) counterparts who continued to seek paths for accumulation through pastoral activities, traversing the Great Rift Valley in search of grazing grounds and finding little to borrow from settler farming activities. In the period just before independence, these differentiated relations to settler agrarian capital became a source for the gradual ethnicisation of relations between the two corridors.

But if the gains derived from interacting with settler capital did not immediately create open rivalry between the two corridors, the migration of Kikuyus into the Rift Valley ultimately did. The expulsion of this community from the Rift Valley was to become an issue in the political processes that preceded the writing of the independence constitution at Lancaster House in London. As a response to this threat, the Kikuyu peasants in the Rift Valley formed the *Land Freedom Army* (LFA) which was later countered by the formation of the *Kenya Liaison* by certain European settler Farmers. The *Kenya Liaison* sought to expel all Kikuyu labourers from European farms in the Rift Valley should the *majimbo* constitution which it favoured not be accepted by the majority of the delegates to the Lancaster House negotiations.

While in the initial *majimbo* project, the expulsion of Kikuyus from the Rift Valley was only one of many items on the agenda, the neo-*majimbo* project tacitly views it as a *sine qua non*. But unlike the original project, the current one seeks to expel from the Rift Valley, not just the Kikuyus but all the ethnic communities supporting the political opposition. These communities include the Luos, the Abagusii, and the Luhya. In total, together with the Kikuyus, they comprise up to 46 per cent of the total population in the Rift Valley. Their migration into the Rift Valley took place in two broad phases. It is important that we delineate them because each phase accounts for a different aspect of the ethnicisation of the relationship between the two corridors. Certain political processes in each also account for the present character of the neo-*majimbo* project and could also explain the initial design of the project.

We use the Swynerton Plan of 1954 in the periodisation of the migration into the Rift Valley. This plan is significant in the sense that it either deliberately or by default fortified the growing tensions between the two corridors by (in a discriminatory, one-sided manner) legitimising African commercial agriculture and, in particular, the growing of cash crops. The plan also marks settler acceptance of the possibility that land would have to be relinquished to black Africans. The migrations that followed the plan saw the African peasant move to the Rift Valley not as a labourer or a squatter but as a land owner through the purchase of sub-divided European farms.

Pre-Swynerton Migrations

These can be traced to the second quarter of the 1900s. In this period, there developed a growing need for casual labourers to support burgeoning settler farming activities. This coincided with the massive and desperate recruitment of African peasants into the Royal African Army's Carrier Corps. Prompted by the overcrowded nature of their "reserves" and the need to avoid military service, most Kikuyu peasants opted to work as casual labourers in the settler farms (Ferudi, 1976; Zwanenberg, 1975). This move received the support of the colonial administration which wanted to forestall a peasant uprising in the overcrowded Central Kenya "reserves". The result was a phenomenal migra-tion of Kikuyu peasants into the Rift Valley Province as casual labourers on settler farms. By 1923, there were 16,000 Kikuyu peasants in Naivasha alone (Ferudi, 1976:189), while by 1934, there were 110,000 Kikuyus living outside their "reserve" (Sorrenson, 1967:80). Like in Central Kenya, the overcrowded nature of Kavirondo Province, housing the Luo and the Abagusii, saw a large migration of Luo labourers into the Rift Valley.

Between 1923 and 1943, the Kikuyus accounted for about one-third of the total labour force in the colony. What is interesting is that the Luo provided close to 40 per cent of the labour force in this same period. This fact led to the development of a "fraternity" in labour between the Kikuyus and the Luos, a "fraternity" which was strengthened by the involvement of workers drawn from both ethnic groups in the Harry Thuku Uprising of 1922 in Nairobi. That uprising is generally regarded as the earliest expression of anti-colonial nation-alism in Kenya and as an embryonic trade union activity. It also provided the earliest form of political co-operation between the two communities (Zwanenberg, 1975:221). But insofar as relations with the KAMATUSA were concerned, the Luo were not perceived by the local communities as a threat in the way the Kikuyus were perceived. And this is primarily because after the squatter system of labour was introduced, the Kikuyus became squatters in very large numbers while the workers from Kavirondo, principally Luo in composition, expressed their unwillingness to squat on European settlements for, as yet, empirically unexplored reasons. The Luo preferred to retain their role as casual labourers, a decision that probably explains their conspicuous absence in the Rift Valley settlements. Interestingly, Luo migrant labour is still abundant in most regions of the Rift Valley, especially in the tea plantations. These workers have been a target in the recent land clashes in Kericho district.

From Kavirondo, those who migrated to the Rift Valley as squatters were primarily the Maragolis, Tiriki, and Nyangori Bunyores. From as early as 1920, they had migrated to Trans Nzoia and Uasin Gishu District as squatters. During the early years however, historical evidence indicates that they usually stayed for only three years and then migrated back to Kavirondo. There are however those who stayed on, even after independence. It should however be noted that these communities, who later formed the Luhya nation in the diaspora, worked in concert with the KAMATUSA in the initial *majimbo* project. Their main representative was Masinde Muliro while Martin Shikuku represented the Luhyas in the "reserves". The oppositionist position taken by these personalities and their communities during the re-birth of multi-party politics in Kenya in the early 1990s saw a tentative break in the Luhya-Kalenjin alliance. Interestingly, it was around this time that the ethnic clashes between the Kalenjin and the Luhyas in Trans Nzoia and Uasin Gishu began (Republic of Kenya [Kiliku Report] 1992).

Second to the Kikuyu, the Kalenjin had the next largest number of squatters in the Rift Valley. By 1934 for instance, one quarter of the entire Nandi tribe had moved on to farms in Uasin Gishu, Trans Nzoia and Kisumu as squatters (Zwanenberg, 1975:231). The reasons for this migration were two fold. First, the bulk of the land that was left for them after expropriation was not sufficient for grazing. They needed to move their herds over " ... larger tracts of country, partly in order to obtain fresh grazing and partly as a prophylactic against disease" (Zwanenberg, 1975:231). Hence, they even took a 25 per cent wage cut as labourers on the Uasin Gishu railway line in order to retain their squatter status and have their herds graze in the fertile White Highlands. Their migration was, therefore, purely for green grass for their herds. Second, but more among the Kipsigis than the Elgeyo or Nandi, they squatted in the highlands with a view to recovering their lost lands should independence ever come. It is noteworthy that most of the clashes in the Kalenjin country since 1991 have primarily taken place in the Kipsigis areas.

Unlike the Kalenjin who primarily became squatters in search of pastures for their herd or the Kavirondo who were looking for a temporary solution to their economic problems, the Kikuyus migrated into the Rift Valley as squatters in search of permanent settlements. They wanted land that they could till and probably ultimately buy. According to Canon Harry Leakey, close to 90 per cent of these squatters were merely floating populations who had no space " ... because their own families did not possess enough to satisfy their needs and other families refused to let them settle permanently on their land" (Zwanenberg, 1975:226). Initially, they argued that it was better to " ... live on virgin land owned by a European farmer with permission to cultivate it ... " rather than live in reserves that had no future (Zwanenberg, 1995). Hence, their migration into the Rift Valley was driven by a search for a future and like the Kipsigis, they also had an eye on the highlands should an independent government ever be established. Before the Swynerton Plan, one out of every two squatters in the Rift Valley was a Kikuyu (Zwanenberg, 1975).

The squatter system was however short-lived. By the late 1930s, cattle farming had become more lucrative than the cultivation of cash crops. The settler farmers increasingly began to need more grazing land for their cattle. Through numerous legal amendments, the settlers began moving the squatters from their estates. According to Zwanenberg (1975), surplus land on the estates became of greater exchange value than the cheapness of squatter labour and inevitably, profitability had to take precedence over all else.

The eviction of squatters necessitated the creation of native settlement schemes to forestall a political crisis. Among the most contentious of these was the Olenguruone scheme situated in the remote areas of the Rift Valley high-lands. The squatters settled under this scheme were basically of Kikuyu origin who had found a temporary home at Mellili, in Masailand, after eviction by the settlers. The politicisation of their relations with the colonial government began soon after they settled down at Olenguruone and was occasioned by the ques-tion of ownership rights in the scheme. This was further aggravated by their growing suspicion of and resistance to the colonial administration following their eviction from the highlands. What resulted after a while was the adminis-tration of a secret mass oath among the squatters " ... to create the discipline and will for sustained resistance in the face of great hardships" (Roseberg and Nottingham, 1966:243). These oathings spread to the reserves and were meant to cement the unity of the "House of Mumbi", and to " ... resolve problems of organisation, to raise the commitment of the ... (sons of Mumbi) and to bind them together in a common struggle" (Zwanenberg, 1975:243).

The relationship between the colonial regime and the squatters in Olenguruone continued to deteriorate and in October 1949, the settlement was closed down and the squatters evicted by police to southern Kiambu and Yatta B. This experience traumatised the Kikuyu not only in the diaspora but also in the Kikuyu Native Units in Central Kenya. It also accounted in part for the Mau Mau uprising of the early 1950s and the subsequent colonial-led agrarian reforms of 1954 under the Swynerton Plan. It is worth mentioning at this point that most of these squatters were later resettled in Olenguruone in 1970 through numerous land buying companies. Also worthy of mention is the fact that Olenguruone has had among the most protracted ethnic clashes since 1991. These have been reportedly between the Kikuyus and the "resident" Kalenjin. Until recently, this place was a "Security Operations Zone" on account of the ethnic clashes witnessed in the area.

Post-Swynerton Migrations

The Swynerton Plan was adopted by the colonial administration as a response to growing political unrest in Kenya and in order to ensure that the restoration of law and order in the emergency period was effective. Two components of the plan tended to aggravate ethnic acrimony between the two corridors and to deliberately generate inequalities on the basis of which future ethnicisation of political processes would advance (Roseberg and Nottingham, 1966:304–6). These were the policies of *land consolidation* and the *Commodity Production Pro-gramme*. Both deliberately favoured Central Kenya, a move that polarised rela-tions between Central Kenya and the rest of the regions in the period before independence.

Under the new policy of land consolidation, traditional Kikuyu land tenure rules, under which a landlord was traditionally allowed to have squatters or tenants, were nullified. This meant that the existing tenants were, under the law, displaced persons. It also in effect meant creating landed and landless classes. The creation of the landless class and the repatriation of Kikuyu peasants from squatter farms in the Rift Valley back to Kikuyu Native Units in Central Kenya during the Emergency period was apparently meant to create desperation among the Kikuyu. This, in turn, would ensure that the White Highlands scheduled for sale would be disposed of to these peasants at a price dictated by the settlers. In this way, it was argued, the agricultural settler would give up his land in exchange for a commensurate measure of capital. For the Kikuyu peasants, this presented an opportunity for them to be "land owners" (something they had long craved for) but this time not under the squatter system.

A substantial number of Kikuyu peasants moved into the Rift Valley under this arrangement, occupying sub-divided farms in Laikipia, Nakuru, Nyahuru, and Rumuruti, all originally "owned" by the KAMATUSA communities. One important effect of this plan was that it placed " ... Central Province, the Kikuyu homeland, in a favoured position vis-à-vis other regions and peoples ... (by making it) ... the primary beneficiary of a major pre-independence agrarian revolution" (Harbeson, 1973:36). Historical evidence indicates that most of the other communities, especially in Nyanza and Western, ardently resisted incorporation into commercial agriculture under the plan. Other communities, like those in the coastal areas, could not benefit from the plan because the " ... confused inheritance patterns of land tenure had not been sorted out" (Harbeson, 1973:36).

Under the Commodity Production Programme of the plan, cash crop production, much coveted by the local population, was finally legalised. This was restricted to specific areas for a start and Kikuyu land was one of the areas earmarked for the development of cash crop production. This was primarily to contain the Mau Mau "rebellion" which was rapidly gaining ground in Central Kenya and to engage the unemployed youths returning home from the newly British mandated colony of Tanganyika.

The Commodity Production Programme basically promoted small-scale cash crop production in Central Kenya. As a result, between 1954 and 1959, African coffee planting increased from 4,000 to 26,000 acres and African coffee farmers rose to 89,000 in number (Roseberg and Nottingham, 1966:304). The value of coffee output rose from USD 0.4 million in 1954 to USD 15 million in 1964 (Harbeson, 1973:39). In other words, for every USD 1 worth of coffee produced in 1954, there was USD 36 produced in 1964. Similarly, by 1963, smallholder coffee production as a percentage of total production had risen to 30 per cent, up from 9 per cent in 1954 (Harbeson, 1973: 39). A substantial percentage of this was accounted for by Kikuyu farmers.

One consequence of this phenomenal growth in indigenous commercial agriculture in some areas of the country was the widespread consolidation of a pattern of regional inequalities. This was later to account for the ethnicisation of the nationalist movement and the subsequent political arrangement introduced in the post-independence period. If the colonial regime facilitated regional inequalities by default or otherwise, the Kenyatta regime fortified the same by consolidating GEMA domination of the country's economy, a process that further ethnicised political relations between the Kikuyu and the other groups. Given the position of advantage in which the GEMA ethnic groups found themselves, most of the credit made available to commercial farmers and industrialists under the colonial and post-colonial regimes went to GEMA concerns. By 1966, they enjoyed up to 64 per cent of industrial loans and 44 per cent of commercial loans (Harbeson, 1973:39). This economic differentiation resulted in ethnic rivalry, especially as political competition heightened. In a way, it is also one of the broader concerns of the *majimbo* exponents and was meant to be addressed by one of their initial development blueprints, the so-called District Focus for Rural Development Strategy.

During the post-independence period, most migrations came under the One Million Acre Scheme in which co-operatives and land-buying companies bought large sub-divided farms. The main beneficiaries from this scheme were the Kikuyus, primarily because they had accumulated earlier than most of the other communities and could offer higher bids to the out-going settlers.

Even before the initial *majimbo* project was designed, the issue of migration into the Rift Valley was already a dominant theme in the politics of the ethnic coalition that constituted the project. The argument of the members of this coalition was that these immigrants should support their political cause if their continued stay in the Rift Valley was to be guaranteed. The question of political support was also perceived within the broad context of the dominant economic role played by the immigrant nationalities. Being wealthier than the locals due to their earlier involvement in agrarian sources of accumulation, the political initiatives which the immigrant nationalities supported tended to be better organised and funded. There was, therefore, some fear among the locals that they would also be dominated politically by the immigrant nationalities. This concern has proliferated the neo-*majimbo* project, although in a different way. We shall return to this in a while.

THE INITIAL *MAJIMBO* PROJECT

The initial *majimbo* project was developed in the last quarter of the 1950s. It brought together a coalition of ethno-regional leaders from among the KAMATUSA, the Luhya from western Kenya, the Taita, the Miji Kenda from the coastal region, and the European settlers. It developed as a counter-hegemonic project to the GEMA-Luo alliance and was motivated by numerous concerns. At the base of it was the fear of elite and ethnic exclusion and the fact that, unlike the GEMA and Luo communities, the groups in the "alliance for *majimbo*" had less Western education, only limited exposure beyond their com-

munities, and a thin experience in wage labour, trade, and cash crop agriculture. In forming a coalition in opposition to the GEMA-Luo alliance therefore,
they hoped to drive a better bargain for themselves and their supporters (Colin
Leys, 1975:212). They were to use the *majimbo* project as a bargaining chip.

Apart from the collective self-interest that bound them together, all the
communities in the alliance for *majimbo* also had their own individual reasons
for backing regionalism. The settlers feared that a GEMA-Luo government
would assume a radical stance and probably expropriate their property. Given
the manner in which this property was acquired, they wanted a system of government that would protect them from a possible backlash from the communities whose land they had alienated. As far back as July 1942, Sir Arthur Dawe
had drafted a memorandum known as *A Federal Solution to East Africa* in which
he proposed the creation of *jimbos* throughout East Africa for the protection of
white interests. Although this idea did not gain wide acclaim at the time, by the
second half of the 1950s it was beginning to make sense to several groups. But
since the creation of a settler *jimbo* in the post-colonial Kenya was politically
and geographically unviable, the settlers had to enter into an alliance with other
forces fearful of GEMA-Luo domination in a post-independence political
arrangement. Through this alliance, they would push for the creation of a
regional system of government by *majimbo*. And this is how the settlers and the
KAMATUSA formed a coalition to front for *majimboism* before independence.

To realise this agenda, the colonial government, in coalition with the leaders
of the "excluded" communities, founded KADU. Although the settlers did not
openly declare themselves to be members of KADU since they had founded
their own party, the New Kenya Party, they basically financed it and gave it
advisory support. Apart from the KAMATUSA and the settlers, the other
formidable force in KADU was the Luhya constituency. The Luhyas were
"created" as an ethnic group in 1948 from a myriad of related clans. But they
had (as yet) no strong stream of ethnic consciousness connecting them and a
good percentage of them had migrated as casual labourers to the Rift Valley
where they lived as small "clans" unaware that they had been conglomerated
into a "tribe". Hence, their weight as a community could not be felt in KANU
which was a coalition of fairly cohesive and large ethnic communities with high
levels of ethnic consciousness. Besides, the Luhya could not possibly penetrate
the GEMA-Luo fraternity, developed over the years.

To heighten their stakes therefore, the Luhyas joined the "small" ethnic
groups congregated in KADU with Masinde Muliro representing the Luhyas in
the Rift Valley and Martin Shikuku with Peter Okondo, among others, representing the Luhya in western Kenya. As for the coastal communities, apart from
being a minority community, they also had no place in KANU's exclusive political hierarchy. Although they had been subjected to much suffering under
colonial rule because of their Muslim faith, political expediency demanded that
they enter into coalition with the settlers and the other ethnic "minorities" in
KADU.

Prior to the Lancaster House Constitutional Conference, KADU announced that it would not accept a constitution without the *majimbo* provision. Martin Shikuku, one of its key proponents and KADU's General Secretary, even declared that " ... his party would do without independence for ten years if it did not get its way over regionalism" (Odinga, 1967:228). William Murgor, a representative from Eldoret, was even more forthright about the necessity for the adoption of *majimbo* by the independence constitution. He threatened to " ... sound a whistle to (his) people declaring civil war" if regionalism was not accepted (Odinga, 1967:227). There were even threats that non-KAMATUSA ethnic groups would be evicted from the Rift Valley should KANU disagree with the position written into the constitution regarding the place of minorities in post-independence Kenya (Goldsworthy, 1982).

There were, however, those who attempted to lend some rationale to *majimbo* without threatening the imposition of sanctions if their goals were not realised. Ronald Ngala, KADU's first president, for instance, argued that the only way the new state could avoid dictatorship was through the creation of numerous power centres. In his view, this goal could only be realised through regionalism (Odinga, 1967:227). In articulating the case for its viability, Peter Okondo saw the *majimbo* system spreading to neighbouring Tanzania, Uganda, Nyasaland, and Rhodesia. From this proliferation he " ... visualised a large state consisting of anything up to thirty or forty regions and to be known as the Federated States of Africa" (*The Times*, October 6, 1961).

The draft independence constitution was debated at Lancaster House for months on end before KANU leaders finally gave way to the *majimbo* constitution. KADU's success was attributed to the support the party received from the settlers, local Asian leaders, and the British government. Conceding defeat, KANU argued that " ... we might be forced to accept a constitution we (do) not want, but once we (have) the government, we would change (it) ... " (Goldsworthy, 1982:192). Under the new constitution, the country was to have a bi-cameral legislature and six regional assemblies with different rights but limited financial powers (Goldsworthy, 1982:192).

What followed the drawing of boundaries for the six regions revealed deep-seated differences between different groups. Given that most of these groups had been involuntarily absorbed into the country by the colonial administration, the boundary-drawing exercise provided an opportunity for some of them to seek to secede. While the Meru and Embu delegations, for instance, indicated a desire not to be put in the same region as the Kikuyu in the Central Province, the Somali delegates were unanimous in their desire to secede from Kenya and rejoin Somali land. Incidentally, during the first decade of independence, they pursued this desire through the Shifta Wars in the Northern Frontier.

After the 1963 elections, KADU was wooed into joining KANU with the aim of setting in motion a process of national integration. In those elections, KANU won 83 seats out of 124 with KADU dominating the remaining 61 opposition seats. Arguably, KADU was not negotiating a merger with KANU from a position of weakness. Yet, the speed with which some of its members agreed to this arrangement put to doubt the depth of their commitment to the *majimbo* project. It also revealed the desire among ethno-regional leaders to be situated next to state coffers in order both to create avenues of accumulation for themselves and tap resources that would enable them to deliver on the development promises which they had made to their constituents. Apparently, a pragmatic politics of "development" was taking precedence over the politics of regional autonomy. It is interesting to note that the first KADU member to defect to KANU was Daniel arap Moi, Kenya's incumbent president, at the time the president of the Rift Valley Region. Of all the KADU defectors, Moi was given the most powerful ministry—Home Affairs—and was to win the confidence of the late Jomo Kenyatta.

After all the opposition members of parliament had defected to KANU, the process of dismantling the *majimbo* constitution was put in place. Two key players in the government were charged with the task of revising the *majimbo* constitution to allow for a unitarist one. These were T.J Mboya, then Minister for Justice and Constitutional Affairs and Charles Njonjo, the Attorney General. The two began by "weeding" out the key European players in KADU who were also mainly the people behind the *majimbo* project. Mboya, for instance, slapped a ban on F.M. Bannett, a Conservative Member of Parliament in Britain, who had acted as a key advisor to the *majimboists*. His offence was that " ... he had played a large part in formulating KADU's *majimbo* policy..(and)..Mboya evidently decided to make an example of Bennett to dramatize his implacable opposition to the regionalist principle" (Goldsworthy, 1982:221).

The government also introduced rules concerning citizenship through which Asian and Boer *majimbo* activists were clamped down upon. Having done this, the second order of business was the actual revision of the constitution itself. At this point, the regime had sufficiently consolidated itself not only to return the country to a unitary state system , but also to begin the process of establishing the doctrine and practice of political monolithism. After all the *majimbo* clauses in the constitution had been expunged. Mboya was to declare that it would be inaccurate to describe the entire process as " ... a death blow to *majimbo*. It would be more accurate to describe it as a cutting of the wood in the present constitution which is already dead" (Goldsworthy, 1982:226).

What is empirically unexplored is whether the spirit of *majimboism* lived beyond the absorption of KADU by KANU. It is however possible to postulate that President Moi always saw a return to *majimbo* as a "trump card"—one which he could always play should his incumbency be threatened. It is however doubtful that he could ever put together a broad coalition like the one under KADU should he ever find the need to revive *majimbo*. The nature of such a new project would also differ substantially from what it was in its initial formulation. This is so because the initial project emerged out of a contest of numerous political interests and it therefore represented the lowest common denominator among the ethnic groups that constituted it. Given that this coalition has since disintegrated and the forces accounting for the initial formulation have now been subsumed under other broader concerns, a reconstituted *majimbo* project would only be a parochial project.

THE NEO-*MAJIMBO* PROJECT

This project has had two basic components, both of which also dominated the initial *majimbo* idea. The first is the constitutional reforms project which serves as the *rational face* to the entire project. The second is ethnic cleansing and it constitutes the lifeblood of the project.

The construction of the entire *majimbo* project has been systematic and well calculated. It started with the *majimbo* rallies of September 1991. These had however been preceded by growing opposition in civil society championed by the church and numerous professional associations. Some of the events associated with this growing opposition included the *Muoroto riots* of mid-1990 which were followed by the Sabasaba unrests of July 1990. In June of that same year, the government had appointed the KANU Review Committee (later known as the Saitoti Commission) charged with the responsibility of going around the country soliciting *wananchi's* views on plural politics and the repeal of section 2 (a) of the Kenya Constitution. After completing its work, the committee reported that "Kenyans were unanimous in their choice of a one-party State". It is at this point that the opposition notables, led by the late Jaramogi Oginga Odinga, founded the Forum for the Restoration of Democracy (FORD). In law, since this group comprised 6–7 members, it did not need registration. The other notables that could not be included in the Forum founded various groups, among which the Friends of FORD (FOF) was the most active.

The formation of these organisations was seen by the hitherto unchallenged Moi regime as synonymous to a declaration of war. Given its Kikuyu-Luo content, it was seen as a regrouping of the independence coalition that constituted the *ancien régime* in Kenya. This was therefore interpreted as not only an assault on the presidency of Moi but also on the "minority" ethnic groups which had lost out in the 1963 elections but whose turn had come through Moi's ascension to the presidency in October 1978. Hence, while FORD was founded in August 1991, the process of reconstituting the "abandoned" *majimbo* project began a month later in September 1991 with the *majimbo rallies*. It is noteworthy however that the new project was not the concern of the old KADU "alliance for *majimbo*". The Luhyas were in opposition and both their leading ex-*majimbo* exponents, Martin Shikuku and Masinde Muliro, were among the exclusive few who founded FORD. The coastal groups were represented by the Hon. Sheriff Nassir while some of the other chief ex-*majimbo* players from the coastal region chose to found their own party after the repeal of Section 2(a) of the constitution. The Federal Party of Kenya (FPK), probably founded to revive the late Ronald Ngala's agenda in KADU, was still-born. It is however significant that some of the coastal leaders were not willing to go the new *majimbo* way with the new players.

Apparently, the new project was a KAMATUSA concern. But even then, it was predominantly Kalenjin as some of the notable Masaai leaders, like John Keen, were not party to it. To the new *majimboists*, multi-party politics was little more than the project of a coalition of ethnic communities opposed to Moi's rule. With this perception in mind, they came to the conclusion that the proponents of multi-partyism had to be dealt with using maximum force and whatever other forms of coercion that were available to the KAMATUSA elite. The *majimbo* rallies were meant to prepare the KAMATUSA communities for "war" just in case the anti-KANU/Moi elements infiltrated the Rift Valley or the resident non-Kalenjin communities turned against the region's "only recognised party"—KANU. The *majimbo* activists therefore declared the Rift Valley a "KANU Zone" and braced their communities for battle.

POPULARISING THE PROJECT: THE *MAJIMBO* RALLIES

There were basically five of these rallies, two of which were especially crucial to the *majimbo* project. These were held at Kapsabet in Nandi and Kapkatet in Kericho Districts, both in the Rift Valley. Before these rallies were held, we must note that the non-KAMATUSA communities in the Rift Valley had been threatened with eviction should they join the growing opposition to KANU. The Minister for Local Government, William Ole Ntimama, had demanded that the non-Masais resident in his Narok district should "lie low as envelopes" if their future in the district was to be secured. He was to later warn that " ... the Title Deeds owned and cherished by such non-Masaais were mere papers that could be disregarded anytime ... " (Republic of Kenya [Kiliku Report], 1992:58). This set the mood of the rallies.

The messages delivered at the rallies were numerous. Foremost among them was the fact that the KAMATUSA communities were ready to protect the Moi presidency at all costs. This was said in the context of a possible return to competitive politics and the possibilities for multi-party elections in Kenya. At the Kapkatet rally held on 21 September 1991, Nicholas Biwott declared that " ... FORD members would be crushed and ... KANU youth wingers and *wananchi* were ready to fight to the last person to protect the government of President Moi". He added that " ... Kalenjins were not cowards and that they were ready to encounter attempts to relegate them from leadership" (*Daily Nation*, 22 September 1991).

The second message that came from the rallies was that since the "democratic reforms" were a camouflaged form of a Kikuyu-Luo ethnic agenda, they must be countered with their logical equivalent—even if it took force to do so. The proponents of this position reasoned that the most effective counter-force to the democratic reforms was the restoration of *majimbo*. This alone would silence the multi-party advocates who were against the government of President Moi (Kuria, 1994:8). Arguing that *majimboism* was the only way the Rift Valley could contain the pluralist wave, Hon. Joseph Misoi the KANU Member of Parliament for Eldoret South, asserted that " ... unless those clamouring for political pluralism stop, we must devise protective mechanisms by launching this movement" (*Africa Watch*, 1993:12). Both the Kapsabet and the Kapkatet rallies further instructed the Rift Valley communities to use all means at their disposal to fight pluralism and in particular FORD members. In the Kapkatet rally, Hon. Timothy Mibei " ... instructed *wananchi* in the Province to visit beer halls and crush any government critics and later make reports to the Police that they had finished them" (*Daily Nation*, 22 September 1991). Hon. Paul Chepkok further " ... urged *wananchi* to arm themselves with pangas, rungus, bows and arrows to destroy any FORD members on sight" (*Daily Nation*, 22 September 1991)

Thirdly and related to the two messages which we discussed above, these rallies called for the eviction of non-KAMATUSA communities from the Rift Valley. This is probably the only component in the neo-*majimbo* project that is borrowed from the *majimbo* campaigns of the 1960s. The theme of eviction had occurred as early as 1989 when Mark Too, then KANU chairman in Nandi district urged the Sabaots (a sub-group of the Kalenjin) to remove *madoadoa* (spots) from their midst if they expected any forms of development. This was later echoed by the Nandi District Commissioner, Mr Changole, when addressing the Sabaots in the Kalenjin language in Chemoge market in December 1991. He urged them to remove *madoadoa* and *chui* (leopards) from amidst their flock (Republic of Kenya [Kiliku Report], 1992:36). Speakers at the *majimbo* rallies were even more blatant in that they called the so-called *madoadoa* by name. Referring to the Kikuyu, Luhya, Abagusi and Luo residents of the Rift Valley, the rallies promised that once the *majimbo* constitution was in place, all outsiders would have to move back to their motherland and leave the Rift Valley for the KAMATUSA children.

These three themes notwithstanding, at the heart of the new *majimbo* project is the protection of elite interests. In particular, the incumbent elite hopes to forestall a probable prosecution, as has happened to Kamuzu Banda and his allies in Malawi, should the opposition come to power in Kenya. According to John Keen, the former Democratic Party Secretary General, the Rift Valley leaders are introducing *majimbo* "...because of the serious political and economic sins they have committed against Kenyans"(*Standard*, 5 May 1994). He further observes that "...a few people who feel insecure after looting the economy are now using ...majimbo... as a safety valve..." (*Daily Nation*, 5 December 1993). This hypothesis is supported by the manner in which the ethnic clashes that followed the rallies were conducted. Apart from fulfilling the agenda set by the rallies to the letter, the levels of violence and the sophistication of weapons employed suggested that the clashes were more than the handiwork of peasant farmers in the Rift Valley. The attacks were well-organised and were executed by well-trained and -motivated personnel who acted as the KAMATUSA elite desired. We shall demonstrate this in the next section.

THE ETHNIC CLASHES

The ethnic clashes began less than two months after the *majimbo* rallies. They took place in two distinct sites. They were most pronounced in the first site—the Rift Valley—and in particular in those areas where the Luhya, Kikuyu and Abagusii immigrants had settled. The second site was basically around the borders of the Rift Valley with Kisii, Kisumu, Kakamega and Bungoma districts. These districts house the Luo, the Abagusii, and the Luhya. These communities either fully or partially supported the opposition in the struggle against KANU's political monopoly and in the subsequent multi-party elections that took place. Apart from the Luo, KANU needed the support of the Luhya and the Abagusii to win the 1992 elections. Ethnic clashes directed against these communities were meant to warn them of the consequences that would befall them if they failed to support KANU in the election.

Basically, one can single out four belts within which the clashes took place. The first is the Nakuru belt. In this belt, most of the clashes took place in Molo and Olenguruone. Molo is one of the places where Moi was to facilitate the settlement of Kikuyu peasants as part of the arrangement built into his appointment to the vice-presidency by Kenyatta. Similarly, Olenguruone was, as we noted earlier, a settlement for Kikuyu squatters from as far back as the 1940s. It is also a place which is significant to the Kikuyu in the diaspora in that it was the site for the earliest forms of ethnic resistance to Kikuyu expulsion from the Rift Valley in the 1940s. Both areas recorded some of the most brutal forms of violence during the clashes as so-called Kalenjin warriors evicted Kikuyu settlers.

While the first belt saw the Kalenjin pitted against the Kikuyu, the second belt was the site for Kalenjin-Luhya rivalry. It combines Bungoma and Trans Nzoia which are predominantly Luhya with the Kalenjin-dominated West Pokot, Elgeyo Marakwet, Uasin Gishu and Nandi. Trans Nzoia is predominantly Luhya due to certain historical circumstances mentioned earlier in this chapter. According to the 1989 National Census results, 60 per cent of the district is Luhya. The Kalenjin however claim the district as one of their ancestral lands. The trouble in Trans Nzoia has to do with the rivalry between the Saboats, a Kalenjin sub-group and the Bukusu Luhya, dating back to the colonial period. The bone of contention is that the Saboats did not want to be placed in the same district as the Bukusu. They wanted their own district—Mt. Elgon—which the colonial commission drawing out the administrative borders refused to grant them. If this was a remote cause of the conflict, the *majimbo* rallies cashed in on it to incite the Saboats against the Bukusu. Added to this were disagreements between Bukusus from Mango Farm and Saboats from

Namutokholo society over the purchase of a farm owned by a certain Mr Mwangi (Republic of Kenya [Kiliku Report], 1992:26). This disagreement coupled with incitement from the Saboat Member of Parliament, Mr Kisiero, provided the occasion for the first ethnic clashes in the area to erupt in November 1991 (Republic of Kenya [Kiliku Report], 1992:32). According to the Kiliku Report (1992), the Bungoma clashes were also between the Bukusu and the Saboats, and the *majimbo* rallies account, in part, for the violence (Republic of Kenya [Kiliku Report], 1992:36). However, the neighbouring Kalenjin districts were also said to have aided the Saboats with some "warriors" and training facilities.

The third belt of conflict combines Kakamega and Kisumu, homes to the Luhya and Luo respectively, with the Rift Valley settlements of Kericho, Nandi and Uasin Gishu that border them. In this belt, most of the clashes took place in the Kalenjin areas as opposed to the borders. The presence of Luhyas, Luos, Kikuyus and Abagusii in these Kalenjin areas dates back to the colonial period as we mentioned earlier. Further to this, in the 1970s, " ... some of the Kalenjins who got land in the settlement schemes or society and company farms, started selling off some of it to members of these four communities" (Republic of Kenya [Kiliku Report], 1992:43). Following the *majimbo* rallies, the Kalenjin who had lately began seeing these communities as enemies, decided to expel them from the membership of an influential farm-buying company, the Meteitei Farmers Company in Nandi. Like the land-buying case of the Bukusu and the Saboats, the events that followed sparked off most of the clashes in the area. The role of Nandi KANU politicians was noticeably pronounced, according to the Kiliku Report.

The fourth belt covers Kisii and Nyamira on the one front and Narok and Bomet on the other. Evidence summoned by the Kiliku Report in this area reveals that clashes in the belt were also caused by the *majimbo* rallies. After the rallies, the "kwekwe" or non-Kalenjin were " ... constantly reminded by their Kalenjin neighbours who presumed all Abagusii and Luo were pro-multi-partism, that with (the coming of *majimbo*) ... their evacuation would start" (Republic of Kenya [Kiliku Report], 1992:59).Within Narok, the community to be evacuated was Kikuyu. Although they were spared immediately after the *majimbo* rallies, in the post-election period they were evacuated *en mass*. This is particularly so in Enoosupukia where William Ole Ntimama, the Local Government Minister, openly organised "Masai *morans*" to evict the Gikuyu from a settlement they had occupied since the 1970s. The argument was that it is a water catchment area and, according to Ntimama, settling people there " ... would be a matter of life and death to us and would be tantamount to an act of war" (*Standard*, 7 November 1994).

ANATOMY OF THE CLASHES

All the areas visited by the Kiliku parliamentary team linked the clashes that occurred to the *majimbo* rallies and the introduction of political pluralism in Kenya, among other things. Evidence summoned by the Kiliku report further reveals that the clashes were systematically organised and executed. It further implicates most of the speakers at the *majimbo* rallies, arguing that they were involved either in the financing, ferrying, and/or training of warriors, or the organisation of attacks. The NCCK report on the clashes—the *Cursed Arrow* (1992)—corroborates this information. As we have already observed, the cattle rustlers and peasant farmers in the Rift Valley were not capable of carrying out such sophisticated operations. The operations often began with leaflets, scattered in all the cosmopolitan parts of the Rift Valley and warning the *kwekwes* to leave the region by given dates or face the wrath of the Kalenjin "warriors", or Masaai *moran*. What followed were military operations completely untypical of "traditional" fighting methods. The attacking warriors were armed with bows, arrows, *pangas* (machetes), spears, axes, fire igniters, paraffin, petrol and guns. They were dressed in white or red T-shirts, black shorts, and a white sheet spread over with a knot on one of the shoulders.

Both the Kiliku and the NCCK reports argue that these "warriors" were transported to their areas of operation by cars owned by either politicians or the government (Republic of Kenya [Kiliku Report], 1992:51 and 75). It was also argued that the youths in the "warrior" groups were not recruited from the local populations where the attacks took place. This is so because most of them were not conversant with the geographical details of the areas of operation (Republic of Kenya [Kiliku Report], 1992:51). According to available evidence, the "warriors" had been trained over a long period of time. One of the witnesses to the Kiliku committee, Abdul Kadir arap Kigen, observed that the training of a special military group began in the second half of the 1980s but the actual agenda of this group only emerged in October 1991. Kigen, who was one of the "warriors", told *Finance Magazine* in a sworn affidavit that the warriors were trained in the Masai Mara and Olenguruone areas and had been told that " ... the Rift Valley must be cleared and people from other provinces in Kenya removed ... (and) that the private army in these camps ... would be called the Kalenjin Warriors, and if Moi was defeated in the election, the army would be called the Kalenjin Liberation Front ... " (*Finance Magazine*, 15 September 1992:20–26) Kirgen further admitted that while at the camps, they were trained by the General Service Unit of the Kenyan military and personnel from the anti-stock theft unit.

During their operations, the "warriors" also received military support as evidence available in both the Kiliku and Africa Watch reports indicates. Military helicopters were seen in most of the clash areas, and each time they landed, instead of disarming the "warriors", the fighting seemed to intensify on their departure. According to the Kiliku Report, the Rift Valley Provincial Commissioner, Yusuf Haji, admitted that apart from to himself, military helicopters were also made available to, among others, the Nakuru and Kericho District Commissioners (Republic of Kenya [Kiliku Report], 1992:73). The Kericho District Commissioner, one of those to whom a helicopter was made available, was also one of the politicians implicated in the clashes by the Kiliku Report (1992:69). Where the security forces did not give direct support to the "warriors", they chose not to take " ... tangible measures to restrain the warriors ... and when it seemed like they were taking action, it was to shoot in the air which never distracted the Kalenjin warriors from their mission" (Republic of Kenya [Kiliku Report], 1992:71). In some instances, they were even open about their support for the "warriors". At Owiro Farm in Tinderet for instance, the Administration Police openly declared that " ... they could not restrain the Kalenjin 'warriors' in their mission as the "warriors" were carrying out orders from above" (Republic of Kenya [Kiliku Report], 1992:72).

The provincial administration was also involved in facilitating the mission of the "warriors". As documented in the Kiliku Report for instance, in Belgut Division of Kericho District, the Kericho District Commissioner, Timothy Sirma, " ... maintained inaction as the "warriors" burned down houses in Koguta. Later, at a public baraza ... Mr Sirma directed the withdrawal of the beefed-up security from the area, and turning to the "warriors", he wonders aloud "why are houses still standing?". Immediately thereafter, the burning of houses commenced" (Republic of Kenya [Kiliku Report], 1992:69). Similar roles were played by the district officers, chiefs and their assistants.

The role of the *majimbo* activists in the clashes was also phenomenal. They basically financed the operations and facilitated the missions through the provincial administration. Evidence received by the Kiliku committee indicates that the "warriors" were hired and " ...were paid sums ranging from Ksh 500 for safe return from the clash front, Ksh 1,000 to 2,000 for killing one person or burning a grass thatched house and Ksh 10,000 per permanent house burnt. Several witnesses also alleged that some of the persons funding the wages of the "warriors" were K.N.K Biwott, Reuben Chesire, Ezekiel Bargentuny, and Wilson Leitich (all Members of Parliament and associated with the *majimbo* rallies" (Republic of Kenya [Kiliku Report], 1992:75). Further evidence reveals that these politicians provided transport to and from the "war zones".

THE RESETTLEMENT PROGRAMME

Over four years after the first ethnic clashes were reported, only one out of every four displaced persons has been resettled. Even then, this statistic, supplied by the United Nations Development Programme (UNDP), has been disputed by several organizations. According to the UNDP, out of the 250,000 displaced victims of the clashes, 75,000 people have been resettled. Of these, 30 per cent are already settled in their former farms, while 50 per cent are closer to where their farms were situated. (*Clashes Update*, September 1994:3). Several organizations working with the clash victims and refugees, including the NCCK, argue that this figure is a " ... calculated exaggeration that fell short of giving the actual picture on the ground" (*Clashes Update*, September 1994:1). They went further to challenge the UNDP to publish the names of those who had been resettled, the details of their ethnic background, where they were evicted from, where they have been resettled, and the ownership of the land they now occupy (*Clashes Update*, September 1994:1–2). The UNDP did not respond to this challenge, mainly because its resettlement programme is implemented through the provincial administration and the data it gave came from the implementing agencies. In the meantime, it should be recalled that the provincial administration was implicated in the clashes.

What emerges from the resettlement programmes is the government's unwillingness to resettle the victims, especially those from the opposition communities. This is consistent with the eviction agenda of the *majimbo* project as articulated at the *majimbo* rallies. The regime has used both legal and administrative measures to ensure that this eviction is total and final. In the Nakuru belt, the Molo and Burnt Forest areas were declared "security zones". These are the areas occupied by the Kikuyu. In these zones, only those cleared by the security agencies and the administration are allowed entry. Those who frequent the zones with minimal difficulties are personnel of relief NGOs and church ministers. With the two areas sealed off, proper evacuations with press blackouts can take place and land re-allocations be done incognito and without publicity. This is probably why, even as "security zones", with heavy security presence, instances of sporadic clashes keep erupting.

In the "non-security zones", cases of land re-allocation have been reported. According to the NCCK's Christian Outreach Rural Development and Services (CORDS) which has been giving relief services to the clash victims in the camps and monitoring their resettlement, land surveys and reallocations in favour of the Kalenjin are going on in Nandi District. This is land belonging to 200 families from non-Kalenjin communities evicted from Meteitei and Kitoroch farms in Tinderet Division of Nandi. The families had lived for over three years in trading centres at Kopere and Songhor. According to *Clashes Update*, a monthly publication of CORDS, " ... self-imposed land committees (have) been established to solicit money to organize demarcations aimed at benefiting members of the Kalenjin community" in the "cleared areas" (*Clashes Update*, 1994:4).

In the Mount Elgon area, the same publication argues that the secret recruitment of homeguards (meant to fight cattle rustlers) has been going on in several places. All of these homeguards are Saboats (a Kalenjin sub-group) and are " ... former policemen, army personnel and even GSU ... (a majority of whom) ... actively participated in the clashes, killing people and torching the houses of the non-Saboats" (*Clashes Update*, 1994:6). Given the role of the administration in the clashes, the idea of recruiting an ethnic homeguard is suspicious. This is all the more so as " ... the 1991 tribal clashes ... (in the area) ... were preceded by such illegal recruitment of bandits in the name of homeguards who then caused continued mayhem in the area" (*Clashes Update*, 1994:6).

In other areas like Uasin Gishu and Kericho, clash victims/ refugees have either been invaded in their camps, or turned away by the administration as they attempted to resettle, the argument being that their return would trigger off new waves of clashes (*Economic Review*, 16–22 January 1995:6). The provincial administration has also been known to evict the victims from their camps. This has been done with a view to returning the victims to their original homes. The Maela crisis which took place in December 1994 and January 1995, is one such case in point.

The Maela victims had moved into Maela Catholic Church after their eviction from Enoosupukia by Masaai *morans* at the instigation of the Minister for Local Government, Ole Ntimama. Maela camp was the only remaining such camp in Nakuru district and it was certainly destined for demolition, according to the Nakuru District Commissioner, Aden Noor Aden (*Weekly Review*, 13 January 1995:4). According to Mr. Aden, the grounds on which Maela camp stood belonged to a co-operative society called Ngati Farmers whose members had served the victims with two quit notices. At the expiry of these notices, the local administration moved into the camps and evicted all the families present. This was in spite of the Catholic Church's insistence that it was the *bona fide* owner of the land on which the camp stood and that it could produce a title deed. Depending on what was indicated as their homes of origin in their identity cards, the victims were repatriated to various trading centres in Central Kenya. The government argued that " ... it did not evict anyone from Maela. All it did was to enforce the eviction notice issued by the owners of the farm on which the families were living" (*Weekly Review*, 13 January 1995:8). It further argued that it was so kind as to even provide "transport" for the victims to return to their original homes in Kikuyu land. This was one "successful" case of the repatriation of non-KAMATUSAs from the Rift Valley back to their original homes as promised by the *majimbo* rallies.

POLITICS OF CONSTITUTION-MAKING AND THE *MAJIMBO* PROJECT

The second and third decades of independence in Kenya have been dominated more by *constitution-making from above* than by *constitution-making from below*. The Change the Constitution Movement (CCM), for instance, was a project of Kikuyu capital, and was pursued at an elite/sectarian level. Similarly, the neo-*majimbo* project and its proposals for constitutional reforms are a concern of the KAMATUSA elite with little built-in popular content. What is significant about all of the efforts that have been made at constitutional reform is the fact that the constitution itself has not, so far, been put through a process of popularisation with a view to generating public interest in it, a fact that has resulted in its de-legitimisation. Our argument here is that the legitimacy of a constitution " ... is concerned with how to make it command the loyalty, obedience and confidence of the people" (Nwabueze, 1973:24). This has to begin with people understanding it and having a stake in it as a common property of all. Without this sense of " ... identification, of attachment and involvement, a constitution ... (will) ... remain a remote, artificial object, with no more real existence than the paper on which it is written" (Nwabueze, 1973:25).

The current constitution-making process in Kenya has been dominated by two forces. On the one hand, we have the state forces who are basically controlled by the *majimbo* advocates. The debate on constitutional reforms began with the announcement by the members of this group that they had produced a *majimbo* constitution which they were ready to table in Parliament in due course. On the other hand, we have the civil society forces, mainly organized around the Law Society of Kenya (LSK), the Kenya Human Rights Commission (KHRC), and the International Commission of Jurists (ICJ) (Kenya Chapter). While the state forces basically represent the KAMATUSA coalition, the oppositional forces are sympathetic to the efforts from below to reform the constitution. The state, not surprisingly, views the "LSK group" as representing the ethnic groups that currently form the core of the opposition to the Moi regime. These groups—the Kikuyus and Luos in particular—are basically the ones that founded the original KANU with a view to constructing a post-colonial unitary state.

Prior to this new process of constitutional reforms, several other steps that bear on the constitution had been taken in Kenya. These include the committee on the National Code of Conduct established in 1983 under the chairmanship of Bethuel Gichaga, and whose mandate was to solicit views aimed at establishing a "normative dialogue" between the state and the citizens. The second was the KANU Electoral Review Committee set up in June 1990 under Vice-President George Saitoti. While the first one died a natural death, the Saitoti committee gave a thoroughly abridged version of what its findings were. This was despite people's optimism about the ability of the committee to convey to the government, their wishes about the system of government they wanted. Thus, although participation in constitution making processes is not a new experience for most Kenyans, their fatigue and disappointments with "democratic politics" and their experiences with the Saitoti Committee may hinder their full participation in efforts at constitutional reform.

Although the need for constitutional reforms had been widely discussed prior to the 1992 multi-party elections, serious debates on the matter did not begin to take place until after the *majimbo* activists openly declared that they already had a draft constitution. As the tempo in the *majimbo* debate rose, the Attorney General hinted that " ... the current public debate on *majimbo* might eventually go to parliament for debate as a basis for a constitutional amendment" (*Standard*, 9 December 1993). What followed this was a contest between the two forces mentioned above.

During the last half of 1994, the *majimbo* activists declared that their constitution was ready for discussion in parliament. The LSK, in a move designed to counter the *majimboists*, announced that it was, together with its supporters, also preparing a draft constitution for presentation in parliament. In October 1994, the LSK called on the government to hold a constitutional conference to discuss constitutional reforms. This conference, the society argued, " ... would give the *majimbo* advocates a chance to table their proposals which would face the real democratic test—the people" (*Standard*, 4 October 1994). This call was construed by KANU as being connected to the agenda of the ethnic coalition that dominates the opposition. The President responded in person by saying " ... if any constitution is to be drafted, care must be taken so that it is not done by one community but by all the 42 tribes in Kenya ... you cannot entrust one community to draft the constitution" (*Standard*, 6 October 1994). He promised to call a meeting of local and international experts where all Kenyans will give their views on constitutional reforms.

In November 1994, the LSK, ICJ and KHRC tabled their draft constitutional model at Ufungamano House in Nairobi. After dismissing this model as "tribal", Moi announced on 31 December 1994 that he would form a commission to look into constitutional reforms in Kenya. This commission would invite experts from numerous federal states world-wide. Following this announcement, the rival constituencies involved in the national constitutional debate restated their claims. The *majimbo* activists declared that the time had come for *majimbo* to be re-introduced constitutionally; it was a mistake to have abolished it in the first place. They warned Kenyans that *wapende wasipende* (whether they like it or not), a *majimbo* system of government would be introduced (*Standard*, 30 September 1994). According to Bishop Daniel Tanui, the Member of Parliament for Kipkelion, the parliamentary process to ratify the majimbo constitution would simply be a going-through-the-motions procedure.

The civil society forces, while welcoming the announcement by the President that a constitutional committee would be set up, declared that they would not let KANU seize the initiative from them. They were not prepared simply to present their model constitution to a committee set up by the KANU government. They founded the Citizens Coalition for Constitutional Change which the *majimbo* advocates described as " ... a pseudo-legal constituent assembly which has no room in an established democratic set-up" (*Weekly Review*, 13 January 1994).

In many ways, the processes connected to the renewed constitutional debates are reminiscent of the Lancaster House constitutional consultations of the 1960s. Thus, for example, as with the Lancaster House meetings, there are unitarists and federalists involved in the on-going constitutional reforms debate. But there are also many forces in Kenyan politics whose interests and concerns have changed substantially since the Lancaster House negotiations. Although the core of the ethnic coalitions on both sides is still basically the same, unlike at Lancaster House where, without the support of the colonial

state, the "alliance for *majimbo*" would have been toothless, in the current constitutional reform processes, the *majimbo* group, located as it is within the structures of state power, is in the driving seat and, therefore, sets the rules. What is
worrying is the fact that, as in the 1960s, in the face of insecurity, the group will
take nothing short of *majimbo*. This becomes more disconcerting given that
those who are running the *majimbo* coalition are also the ones running the state
machinery. As we have demonstrated with the ethnic clashes, this predominantly Kalenjin project might seek to reach its logical conclusion, if necessary by
the use of force. And at this point, what the *majimbo* advocates would be negotiating for is not regional autonomy but secession.

Civil society forces are pitted against the *majimbo* activists from a position of
weakness. Apart from having financial limitations, they also embody and reflect
some of the worst forms of polarisation in civil society itself. There are already
reports of intra-elite conflicts over the "ownership" of the process, an indication
that the elite is probably not ready to relinquish the process of constitution-
making to the political market forces. Apart from intra-elite contests, there is an
undeclared clamour for control over the process from large civil institutions and
the politicians. Such important institutions as the church have been relegated to
a secondary position, with selected clergymen "invited" to the "club's" sym-
posia. This tendency to exclude other institutions from both the emerging pro-
reform formations and the processes associated with them has the net effect of
creating apathy among the excluded. This, in turn, has tended to weaken civil
society initiatives for constitutional reform.

One other weakness in the struggle of civil society groups for reform has to
do with the model constitution which they produced and launched. It has been
argued that it is just a draft proposal meant to provoke debate. But meaningful
debates result from a meaningful and well articulated agenda. The contents of
the document are particularly lacking in real, substantive proposals for far-
reaching reforms. The draft reads like a "protest" document, with its sharpest
barbs directed towards the presidency. In identifying what is wrong with
Kenya, it zeros in on the presidency and rips off most of its powers without
doing much else. It is on this account that Ole Ntimama's critique of the model
is valid when he observes that it deals with the " ... excessive powers of the
President ... avoiding the most fundamental and pivotal issues like land"
(*Weekly Review*, 13 January 1995:15). In failing to deal with the sensitive issue of
land and other related problems that affect the daily lives of ordinary Kenyans,
the draft constitution presented by the civil society groups appears to have be
driven, too one-sidedly, by forces representing one section of the great national
divide.

REVISITING AN UNFINISHED AGENDA

Since the protest movements of the last quarter of 1800 and the peasant uprisings of the 1920s, the question of land has remained at the centre of Kenyan politics. It was a central issue in the fight for political independence, and continues to play a dominant role in the current efforts at re-thinking the unitary state in the country. According to H. Okoth-Ogendo, if we were to re-write history in Kenya, almost all the documentation on economic and political processes and formations would be written as footnotes to the issue of land (Okoth-Ogendo, 1991). But while the politicisation of this question in the first half of 1900 was sourced, predominantly, from peasant activism, during the second half of the century, it became increasingly hijacked by the various ethno-regional elites. As these elites constructed their political platforms, the question of land, already politicised through the process of expropriation, was at the top of their agenda. In the initial *majimbo* project land was, therefore, a fundamental issue. But also fundamental to this project was the question of power distribution among the emerging elite and the protection of the existing system of accumulation, dominated at the time by the forces of colonialism.

At independence, the *majimbo* constitution offered, for a while, some guarantees on land and power-sharing. The question of land was, however, not taken to its conclusive end as was desired by the *majimbo* activists. During the 1962 constitutional consultations at Lancaster House, all the communities concerned were made to renounce their claims to the land that had been expropriated by the colonial administration. It was agreed that the settlers should sell this land to the Africans on a "willing buyer/willing seller" basis. This is how all the communities that settled in the Rift valley highlands got their land. This includes the KAMATUSA.

But unlike the Kikuyu, the KAMATUSA had not accumulated sufficiently to buy substantial tracts of land in the Rift Valley. Apart from what they had accumulated, the Kikuyu also had access to the credit facilities which had been created under the Commodity Production Programme in the Swynerton Plan. This system of agricultural credit was further supported by the Kenyatta regime in favour of the Kikuyu. Hence, the Kikuyu land-buying companies would offer much higher bids to the settlers as opposed to those of the other communities, and especially the KAMATUSA (Leys, 1975). The result was that the Kikuyu migrated into the Rift Valley from a position of advantage. Apart from being favoured by certain policies, their interaction with settler capital as well as their expansionist disposition also accounted for their dominance in the Rift Valley, especially after the sale of the Scheduled Areas in the 1970s.

The KAMATUSA's disadvantaged position was partly because of their failure to interact productively with agrarian capital, but also because of the discriminatory agrarian reform programmes put in place by both the colonial and post-independence governments. The neo-*majimbo* project purports to want to redress this situation. It has put to question the 1962 agreement and the purchasing of land by several companies in the 1970s. While some of these issues could be pertinent, the underlying motive in pursuing them under *majimbo* is the furtherance of an elite agenda. The bottom line in this agenda is the protection of what the KAMATUSA have accumulated throughout the *Nyayo* (Moi) era against a possible onslaught from pluralist reformers. It can be argued that they also fear possible prosecution for their involvement in both economic and political scandals.

Hence, the neo-*majimbo* project is not about a federal system of government in the traditional Swiss sense envisaged by the initial project. It is even doubtful that the project is about the creation of ethnic regions for the small communities in Kenya, because not all the minorities are with the *majimbo* activists. Besides, such an arrangement can always be reversed the way the *majimbo* constitution was revised at independence. If this happens, the possibilities of prosecution of the *Nyayo* era KAMATUSA elite could arise, an eventuality that they are afraid of. Given the above therefore, some oppositionist forces have argued that in the event that Moi ceases to be the president of Kenya, they might push for a secession, founding a KAMATUSA state (*Finance*, 15 October 1994).

Although the possibility of a KAMATUSA secession may appear to be far-fetched, the elevation of Eldoret Town into a cosmopolitan city with almost all the necessary amenities of a large city may lend some credence to this thesis. Eldoret is the centre of Kalenjin private capital and is basically dominated by a coalition of Kalenjin, Indian and Boer/settler concerns. Since the last half of 1980s, the town has been supplied with numerous essential services. It now has a branch of the Central Bank, a university with a fully fledged medical department and a referral hospital built by the Chinese, the third biggest polytechnic in Kenya, next to the ones in Nairobi and Mombasa, and it is the main beneficiary of the western Kenya oil pipeline. Apart from this, the TransAfrica road now transverses the town instead of passing though Kisumu. This links it with all the major African urban centres. Plans are also underway to construct an international airport at a total cost of USD 85 million. This is to be financed through the national budget, a move that has provoked much uproar. The town also has a large military college, an external telecommunication facility, and a television booster. All these developments have been linked by some commentators to a grand project whose main phases have included the *majimbo* rallies, the ethnic clashes, and the constitutional reforms project (*Economic Review*, 23–29 January 1995:6). It remains to be seen if the new *majimbo* project will ultimately translate into a direct challenge to the very foundations of the current, beleaguered unitary state.

BIBLIOGRAPHY

Ferudi, Frank, 1976, "The Kikuyu Squatters in the Rift Valley: 1918–29", in B.A. Ogot (ed.), *Economic and Social History in East Africa*, Kenya Literature Bureau, Nairobi.

Gibbon, P , 1993, "Civil Society in the Post-Developmentalist State in Africa", (mimeo), Copenhagen.

Goldsworthy, D., 1982, *Tom Mboya: The Man Kenya Wanted to Forget*, Heinemann, London.

Harbeson, John, 1973, *Nation-Building in Kenya*, Northwestern University Press, Evanston, Ill.

Karimi, J. and P. Ochieng, 1979, *The Kenyatta Succession*, Longman, Nairobi.

Kuria, G.K., 1994, *Majimboism, Ethnic Cleansing and Constitutionalism in Kenya*, Kenya Human Rights Commission, Nairobi.

Leakey, L.S.B., 1977, *The Southern Kikuyu before 1903*, Academic Press, London.

Leo, C., 1984, *Land and Class in Kenya*, University of Toronto Press, London.

Leys, C., 1975, *Underdevelopment in Kenya*, Heinemann, London.

Munene, J.C., 1993, *Constitutionalism as a Normative Value*, (mimeo).

Nwabueze, B.O., 1973, *Constitutionalism in Emergent States*, C. Hurst & Co., London.

Ogot, B.A., 1972, *Politics and Nationalism in Colonial Kenya*, East African Publishers, Nairobi.

Ogot, B.A., (ed.), 1976, *Economic and Social History in East Africa*, Kenya Literature Bureau, Nairobi.

Okoth-Ogendo, H.W.O., 1991, *Tenants of the Crown*, ACTS, Nairobi.

Odinga, O., 1967, *Not Yet Uhuru*, Morrison and Gibb Ltd., London.

Republic of Kenya, 1992, *Report of the Parliamentary Select Committee to Investigate Ethnic Clashes in Western and Other Parts of Kenya*, (The Kiliku Report), Government Printers, Nairobi.

Roseberg, C.G. and J. Nottingham, 1966, *The Mau Mau Myth: Nationalism in Kenya*, TransAfrica Press, Nairobi.

Sorrenson, M.P.K., 1967, *Land Reform in Kikuyu Country*, Oxford University Press, London.

Swainson, N., 1980, *The Development of Corporate Capitalism in Kenya: 1918–77*, University of California Press, Los Angeles.

Wooley, Thomas and E. Keller, 1994, "Majority Rules and Minority Rights: American Federalism and African Experience", in *Journal of Modern African Studies*, Vol. 32, No. 3.

Zwanenberg, R.M.A., 1975, *Colonial Capitalism and Labour in Kenya 1919–1939*, East African Literature Bureau, Nairobi.

NEWSPAPERS AND JOURNALS

Africa Confidential.
Africa Watch (Report on Ethnic Clashes, 1993).
Clashes Update.
The Economic Review (Nairobi).
Finance.
Finance Magazine.
Standard.
The Times.
The Weekly Review (Nairobi).

CONTRIBUTORS

Osita Agbu, PhD, University of Nigeria, Nsukka; Research Fellow, Nigerian Institute of International Affairs, Lagos, Nigeria.

Emmanuel Akwetey, PhD, Stockholm; Lecturer, Department of Political Science, University of Stockholm, Sweden.

Jibrin Ibrahim, PhD, Bordeaux; Senior Lecturer, Department of Political Science, Ahmadu Bello University, Zaria, Nigeria.

Liisa Laakso, Lic. Soc. Sc., Helsinki; Research Fellow, Institute of Development Studies, University of Helsinki, Finland.

Nestor Luanda, PhD, Cambridge; Senior Lecturer/Head, Department of History, University of Dar es Salaam, Tanzania.

Mutahi Ngunyi, MSc, Nairobi; Lecturer, Department of Government, University of Nairobi, Nairobi, Kenya.

Adebayo Olukoshi, PhD, Leeds; Associate Research Professor, Nigerian Institute of International Affairs, Lagos, Nigeria; Co-ordinator, Nordiska Afrikainstitutet research programme on "The Political and Social Context of Structural Adjustment in Sub-Saharan Africa".

Lloyd Sachikonye, PhD, Leeds; Senior Research Fellow/Head of Department, Institute of Development Studies, University of Zimbabwe, Harare, Zimbabwe.

Ernest Wamba-dia-Wamba, MA; Associate Professor of History, University of Dar es Salaam, Tanzania; former President, Council for the Development of Social Science Research in Africa.